The *Odyssey* of Homer

Elizabeth Vandiver, Ph.D.

THE
GREAT
COURSES·

PUBLISHED BY:

THE GREAT COURSES
Corporate Headquarters
4840 Westfields Boulevard, Suite 500
Chantilly, Virginia 20151-2299
Phone: 1-800-832-2412
Fax: 703-378-3819
www.thegreatcourses.com

Elizabeth Vandiver, Ph.D.

Visiting Assistant Professor of Classics, University of Maryland

Elizabeth Vandiver did her undergraduate work at Shimer College, Mt. Carroll, Illinois, where she matriculated in 1972 as a 16-year-old "early entrant." After receiving her B.A. in 1975, she spent several years working as a librarian before deciding to pursue graduate work in Classics at the University of Texas at Austin. She received her M.A. in 1984 and her Ph.D. in 1990.

In addition to her current position at the University of Maryland (flagship campus at College Park), Professor Vandiver has held visiting professorships at Northwestern University, the University of Georgia, The Intercollegiate Center for Classical Studies (Rome, Italy), Loyola University (New Orleans) and Utah State University.

In 1998 Dr. Vandiver received the American Philological Association's Excellence in Teaching Award, the most prestigious teaching award available to American classicists. Other awards include the Northwestern University Department of Classics Excellence in Teaching award for 1998 and the University of Georgia's Outstanding Honors Professor award in 1993 and 1994.

Dr. Vandiver has published a book, *Heroes in Herodotus: The Interaction of Myth and History*, and several articles, as well as delivering numerous papers at national and international conferences. She is currently working on a second book, examining the influence of the classical tradition on the British poets of World War I.

Dr. Vandiver is married to Franklin J. Hildy, Ph.D., Professor and Chair, Department of Theatre, at the University of Maryland.

This course is dedicated to the memory of Gareth Morgan, teacher of Greek, lover of Homer.

Table of Contents
The *Odyssey* of Homer

The *Odyssey* of Homer

Scope:

Just as knowledge of the Trojan War legend is necessary for understanding the *Iliad*, so too the *Odyssey* assumes that its audience knows how the war ended and what happened next. Lecture One of this course sketches out the events that took place between the two epics, and then considers two primary types of epic, *kleos* and *nostos* (or "return") epic. The lecture also looks at the opening lines of the *Odyssey* and discusses the effect of its complicated chronology and narrative structure. Lecture Two introduces another key cultural concept, *xenia* (the "guest-host relationship") and explains its importance both for the *Odyssey* as a whole and for the first four books, which focus on Odysseus' son Telemachos, in particular. In Lecture Three, we get our first view of Odysseus himself, and are introduced to key elements in his character, particularly his caution, his great rhetorical skill, and his longing for his own homecoming (*nostos*). Lecture Four analyzes Odysseus' interactions with the Phaiakians, the people who will help him on his journey home. This lecture also covers the opening of Odysseus' great first-person narrative of his travels since leaving Troy, a narrative which continues for four full books of the *Odyssey*.

Lectures Five and Six continue our examination of that narrative, identifying and analyzing Odysseus' motivations in telling the story and its effect on his audiences both inside and outside the epic. In Lecture Seven, we look closely at Odysseus' long-delayed return to Ithaka and his meeting there with the goddess Athena. His reunion with his son Telemachos and its implications are the main focus of Lecture Eight, which also covers Odysseus' return to his palace in disguise as an old beggar. Lecture Nine provides a close analysis of Odysseus' conversation with his wife Penelope, and considers the crucial critical question of whether Penelope recognizes this "beggar" as her husband. This lecture also explores the narrative significance of the scene in which Odysseus' old nurse, Eurykleia, recognizes him from a scar on his thigh. In Lecture Ten we consider the scene of vengeance in which Odysseus kills the suitors who have been plaguing his wife Penelope, and in Lecture Eleven we discuss the final reunion of Odysseus and Penelope and the end of the *Odyssey*.

Lecture Twelve provides an epilogue to this course and its companion, *The Iliad*, by addressing the issue of the historicity of the Trojan War. This final lecture surveys the recent archaeological evidence for an actual conflict, and discusses the possible relationship between that event in the 12th century B.C. and the legendary war as described in the 8th century B.C. epics.

Lecture One
Heroes' Homecomings

Scope: In this lecture, we turn from the *Iliad* to the *Odyssey*. The lecture begins with an overview of those events in the traditional Trojan War story which took place after the *Iliad*. Just as the *Iliad* constantly refers outside itself to other episodes in the Trojan War story, so the *Odyssey* too assumes in its audience complete familiarity with the story (including the events of the *Iliad*). After this overview of the background story, we examine the difference between *kleos* epic, with its primary focus on glory, and *nostos* epic, which focuses instead on homecoming. We then turn to an examination of the structure of the *Odyssey* itself, and discuss its very complicated chronological arrangement. The lecture concludes by considering the overall narrative effect of Odysseus' delayed entry into the epic.

Outline

I. Just as a knowledge of Achilles' inevitable death and the destruction of Troy are essential for understanding the *Iliad*, so the events of the end of the War and its aftermath are essential for appreciating the *Odyssey*.

II. The events following the *Iliad* were told in a series of epics, no longer extant, called the Epic Cycle. These included events that are directly referred to in the *Odyssey*.

    A. The *Aethiopis* (five books) picked up the action immediately after the funeral of Hektor. This epic told of Achilles' death.

    B. The *Little Iliad* (four books) told of the after-effects of Achilles' death and of the Sack of Troy.

        1. Aias the Greater killed himself after the Greeks voted to award Achilles' armor to Odysseus.

        2. The Greeks built the Trojan Horse and used it to gain entry to Troy. This was Odysseus' idea.

    C. The *Ilioupersis* (two books) overlapped somewhat with the *Little Iliad* in telling the story of the Sack of Troy. It described several outrages committed by the Greeks during the Sack. These influenced subsequent events, including those in the *Odyssey*.

1. Achilles' son Neoptolemos killed Priam at his household altar.
2. Astyanax (son of Hektor and Andromache) was thrown from the walls of Troy.
3. Aias the Lesser raped Priam's daughter Kassandra in the temple of the goddess Athena, a major sacrilege.

D. The *Nostoi* or *Returns* (five books) told the story of the Greek warriors' voyages homeward.
   1. Agamemnon was killed by his wife Klytaimestra and her lover Aigisthos when he reached home.
   2. Menelaos and Helen were driven off course and spent several years in Egypt, finally reaching Greece only in the eighth year after the Sack.
   3. Aias the Lesser was drowned at sea for his sacrilege in the temple of Athena.

III. *Nostos* (i.e., "homecoming" or "return") is the obvious theme of the *Odyssey*, just as *kleos* is of the *Iliad*.

   A. Epic can be divided into *kleos* epic and *nostos* epic.

   B. An equally valid distinction might be between war epic and peace epic. *Kleos* is still very important in the *Odyssey*, but no longer depends on death in battle.

IV. Like the *Iliad*, the *Odyssey* begins *in medias res*. But the fact that this is a *nostos* epic is stressed from the very beginning.

   A. In the proem, the bard runs through a brief resume of Odysseus' adventures after the fall of Troy.
      1. Although Odysseus is not named until line 21, he is identified in the very first line by the epithet *polutropos*. This sets his "character note" for the epic, as well as establishing that this epic is about one man's struggles to get home, not about warfare.
      2. The first 13 lines contain the word *nostos* in some form three times.

   B. After identifying Odysseus by summarizing his adventures, the bard asks the Muse to start the story "from some point."

   C. The bard then implies that the Odyssey will start in the tenth year after the Trojan War, when Zeus (at Athena's insistence) sends the messenger god Hermes to tell the nymph Kalypso that she must let Odysseus go.

D. After sketching out Odysseus' history and placing him on Kalypso's island, the bard changes direction and takes us on a side-journey to Ithaka. Odysseus does not actually appear in the *Odyssey* until Book V.

V. The narrative structure of the *Odyssey* is complicated and anything but straightforward.

   A. The first four books are concerned primarily with Odysseus' son Telemachos.

   1. Books I and II show Telemachos at home on Ithaka.

   2. Books III and IV show Telemachos traveling to visit Nestor and Menelaos.

   B. Books V–VIII take up Odysseus' story as he leaves Kalypso's island and journeys to Scheria, land of the Phaiakians, a people who will help him home to Ithaka.

   C. Books IX–XII are a flashback to Odysseus' adventures from the time he left Troy until he arrived at Kalypso's island. This section of the *Odyssey* is narrated in the first person by Odysseus himself.

   D. With Odysseus' arrival on Ithaka in Book XIII, the structure returns to straightforward chronology.

   E. Thus, a purely chronological arrangement of the *Odyssey* would put Books IX–XII first, followed by V–VIII, followed by XIII–XXIV. Telemachos' adventures in Books I–IV happen at the same time as Books V–VIII.

VI. By delaying Odysseus' entrance for four full books, the bard lets us see how badly Odysseus is needed on his home island of Ithaka, both by his family and his society.

   A. Odysseus' absence causes great problems for his family.

   1. Odysseus' wife Penelope is left not knowing whether she is wife or widow.

   2. Odysseus' son Telemachos is left not knowing if he should guard the kingdom for his father or assert his own right to be king.

   3. Thus, both Penelope and Telemachos are left in a kind of limbo in which their proper courses of action are unclear.

B. Odysseus' absence causes great problems for his society, which like all the societies shown in the *Odyssey* is unquestioningly monarchical.

    1. The *Odyssey* takes for granted that a country must have a king.

    2. Ithaka has been without its king for 20 years, and has suffered great disarray as a consequence.

C. The suitors of Penelope are the focal point for these troubles in both family and society.

    1. As suitors, they are destroying Odysseus' household and threatening his marriage.

    2. Implicit in their suit is the idea that whichever one of them marries Penelope will become ruler of Ithaka. They are thus threatening Telemachos' rights as well.

    3. Their wanton disregard of the proprieties can be seen as a result of the disordered state of Ithaka.

VII. Homer starts the *Odyssey* at the precise moment when the situation on Ithaka is coming to a head and something must give.

A. Telemachos is grown, and so should assert himself as master of his household.

B. While Telemachos was a child, Penelope could concentrate on rearing him and waiting for Odysseus. But now, she should allow her son to act as a grown man.

C. Penelope had held the suitors at bay for three years with a trick, weaving a shroud during the day and unweaving it at night. But they have found her out, so this trick will work no longer.

D. Thus, the situation has become desperate; Odysseus is needed back on Ithaka *now*.

Essential Reading:

Odyssey, Book I.

Supplementary Reading:

Clay, *Wrath of Athena*, Chapter 1, pp. 25–53.

Nagy, *Best of the Achaeans*, Chapter 2, pp. 26–41 (on *kleos* and *nostos*).

Questions to Consider:

1. What is the impact of the *Odyssey*'s complicated chronological structure, with its doubling back on itself and extended flashback? Would the impact of the story be different if the *Odyssey*, like the *Iliad*, were told in straight chronological order?

2. Compare the proems of the *Iliad* and the *Odyssey*. What differences of tone and approach, if any, do you find in them?

Lecture One—Transcript
Heroes' Homecomings

Hello, and welcome to "Homeric Epic, The *Odyssey*." My name is Elizabeth Vandiver; I teach classics at Northwestern University in Evanston, Illinois, and I will be talking to you for the next several hours about Homer's great epic, the *Odyssey*. In this first lecture we'll begin with an overview of the events in the traditional Trojan War story that took place after the end of the *Iliad* but before the opening of the *Odyssey*, since the *Odyssey* assumes that its audience is completely familiar not only with the *Iliad* but also with the intervening events that happened between the end of the *Iliad* and the beginning of the *Odyssey*. After this overview of the background story, we'll move on to a discussion of the difference between epics which focus on glory and warfare, such as the *Iliad*, and epics that focus on homecoming, *nostos*, with the *Odyssey* is our main example. We'll then turn to an examination of the structure of the *Odyssey* itself, and discuss its very complicated chronological arrangement. The lecture will conclude by considering the overall effect of the delay in Odysseus' appearance in the *Odyssey*, since he dos not appear until Book Five of the epic.

Now, just as the knowledge of the death of Achilles and the destruction of Troy are essential for a full understanding of the *Iliad*, even though those events are not narrated in the *Iliad* itself, so, a knowledge of the subsequent events—the fall of Troy, the events that happen during the fall of Troy, the adventures of other heroes other than Odysseus on their way home—those episodes are essential for an understanding and appreciation of the *Odyssey*. The events that took place between the end of the *Iliad* and the opening of the *Odyssey* were recounted in several epics that are no longer extant, several shorter works than the *Iliad* and the *Odyssey* that have not survived from antiquity up until the present day. We do have summaries of those now-lost epics, and so we know what they said and what events they narrated. Now, I should say that these no longer existing epics were not by any means as great or as long as the *Iliad* and the *Odyssey*. Already in antiquity, it was recognized that these intermediate epics, the ones that narrated the intermediate events, were of much lower quality and much less impressive than the *Iliad* and the *Odyssey*. Still, it is a shame that they have disappeared—it would be nice to still have them, but we don't. We do know their titles, how long each one was, and what they talked about.

The first epic in this so-called Epic Cycle picked up right after the events of the *Iliad*. It was called the *Aethiopis*; it was five books long. That is, it took five average-size papyrus scrolls to write out the *Aethiopis*, as opposed to the twenty-four scrolls required for the *Iliad* or the *Odyssey*. So you can see how much shorter this secondary epic was. It picked up the action immediately after the funeral of Hektor, and it told of Achilles' death. Achilles died when he was shot in the heel by Paris—Paris, the Trojan prince who had abducted Helen and thereby started the Trojan War. The next epic in the epic cycle was called the *Little Iliad*; it was four books long and it narrated the aftereffects of Achilles' death and the Sack of Troy itself. The two main episodes that are important for understanding the *Odyssey* which appeared in the *Little Iliad* were the story of how Aias the Greater— the second greatest warrior, second only to Achilles himself among the Greeks—committed suicide after the Greeks had voted to award the armor of Achilles not to Aias but to Odysseus. There was a question, after Achilles' death, of who should be given his magnificent armor, which had been made for him by the god Hephaistos himself. The Greeks voted on this question of who should get the armor; and by awarding the armor to Odysseus, in effect they said they prized cunning, intelligence, craftiness, all of Odysseus' qualities, above sheer prowess in battle, which was Aias' main strength. And Aias, in shame and outrage over this affront, as he saw it, to his honor, committed suicide. The *Little Iliad* also narrated the story of how the Greeks finally built the great wooden horse, which allowed them to infiltrate the walls of Troy and sack Troy by night. And of course the wooden horse was the idea of none other than Odysseus himself. He invented it; he thought it up.

So, the *Little Iliad* told of the suicide of Aias and the building of the wooden horse. The next epic in the Epic Cycle, called the *Ilioupersis*, which simply means the Sack of Ilium or the Sack of Troy, was only two books long. It overlapped a bit with the *Little Iliad* in telling the story of the Sack of Troy. Most importantly, for our purposes in understanding the *Odyssey,* the *Ilioupersis* narrated several outrages, several acts of excessive violence that the Greeks committed during the Sack of Troy; three in particular are worth mentioning. The Greeks threw Hektor's baby son Astyanax from the walls of Troy and killed him. Achilles' son Neoptolemos killed King Priam, the old king of Troy, at Priam's household altar where Priam had gone for refuge. By going to the altar in his house and putting his hands on it, Priam was in some sense under the protection of the gods, and so to kill him there was a kind of sacrilege against the gods; but Achilles' son Neoptolemos committed this sacrilege and killed Priam at his own household altar.

Finally, Aias the Lesser—there are two heroes named Aias, Aias the Greater committed suicide—Aias the Lesser was guilty of perhaps the worst sacrilege of all in the Sack of Troy. He raped Priam's daughter, Kassandra, who had taken refuge in the temple of the virgin goddess Athena. Aias dragged her away her away from Athena's statue and raped her in the temple, which is a violation and a sacrilege in all sorts of ways. The fact that he did this in a temple, the fact that Kassandra had taken refuge at the statue of a virgin goddess, all of these add to the sacrilege of the act.

Now, in the fourth epic that fills the gap between the *Iliad* and the *Odyssey*, the so-called *Nostoi* or "Returns" homecomings or returns, which was an epic five books long, the story was told of the homecomings of the Greek warriors other than Odysseus. And because of the acts of sacrilege that the Greeks had committed during the Sack of Troy, most of them either did not make it home or had trouble on their way home. Most importantly, for our purposes, Agamemnon, the leader of the Greek expedition, made it home from Troy but was killed when he arrived home by his wife, Klytaimestra and her lover, Aigisthos. Menelaos and Helen—Helen and her original husband, Menelaos—wandered for seven years, spent several of those years in Egypt, only made it home from Troy in the eighth year after the Sack of Troy. Aias the Lesser, by the way, was killed at sea because of his sacrilege in raping Kassandra. So the outrages that the Greeks committed during the Sack of Troy in some degree motivated the troubles they had on their way home.

Now, as I said, this last intermediate epic was called *Nostoi*, which means homecomings or returns, and the singular of that in Greek is *nostos*. *Nostos*, homecoming, is obviously the main theme of the *Odyssey*, just as the concept of imperishable glory, *kleos* in Greek, was one of the main themes of the *Iliad*. In fact, some scholars say that ancient epic can be divided into *kleos* epic and *nostos* epic, into epic about glory and warfare and epic about adventures and troubles during homecoming; that these were the two main sub-genres, if you will, of ancient epic in the bardic tradition. I think perhaps an equally valid distinction would be to say that we can divide epic into war epic and peace epic; because *kleos*—glory, what people say about you, your reputation—is still very important in the *Odyssey*, as we will see in some key scenes. Odysseus and other characters are still concerned with their *kleos*, with what people say about them, with whether their exploits are known or not. The difference is that while in the *Iliad kleos* is seen as the only kind of meaningful immortality a warrior can seek—what people will say about him after his death, in the *Odyssey* there is less of a focus on *kleos* as immortality after death, and more of a focus on maintaining your reputation, keeping your *kleos* alive while you are yourself alive. The focus is simply different, because in the *Odyssey* we are not thinking about war and the very likely death in battle of any given hero; rather, we are looking at the aftermath of war and Odysseus attempt to return home. So, as I said, I think that perhaps a distinction between war epic and peace epic is as valid as a distinction between *kleos* epic and *nostos* epic—or perhaps that is just another way of saying the same thing.

Like the *Iliad*, the *Odyssey* begins in *medias res*, in the middle of its subject matter. Because we are dealing with an epic here that was composed in an oral tradition, by a bard working in an oral tradition, the bard is able to start the story anywhere he likes. The first thing he does is run through a little introduction, *proem* as it is usually called, in which he sets the scene. He announces to the audience who it is that he is going to sing about, or what it is that he is going to sing about; he very rapidly gives a little summary of what's happened leading up to the point where he'll begin his story; and he focuses in on exactly where he wants his story to begin. The first ten lines of the *Odyssey*, then, are in English as follows:

> Tell me, Muse, of the man of many ways, who was driven
> far journeys, after he had sacked Troy's sacred citadel.
> Many were they whose cities he saw, whose minds he learned of,
> many the pains he suffered in his spirit on the wide sea,
> struggling for his own life and the homecoming of his companions.
> Even so, he could not save his companions, hard though
> he strove to; they were destroyed by their own wild recklessness,
> fools, who devoured the oxen of Helios, the Sun God,
> and he took away the day of their homecoming. From some point
> here, goddess, daughter of Zeus, speak, and begin our story.

Now there are several points I want to bring out about that proem, about that opening. First of all, the bard runs through a brief resume of Odysseus' adventures in those opening lines. He gives Odysseus credit for sacking Troy; that has got to be a reference to the Trojan Horse, Odysseus' cleverness, his cunning, his thinking of the stratagem of the Trojan Horse that allowed Troy to be sacked. So we are talking about the man who sacked Troy; who then was driven far journeys; who saw many different people; who suffered a great deal—and notice the stress on homecoming. He was trying to bring about the homecoming not just of himself, but also of his companions.

Now, right away, in these opening lines of the *Odyssey* there is an attempt on the bard's part—and we'll see this again on Odysseus' own part—to get around an inherent problem in the story of the *Odyssey*. The *Odyssey* is Odysseus' story; for it to have full narrative power we need to see him absolutely alone, coming home absolutely alone, having lost all his companions; and yet Odysseus is a leader. He took these men of Ithaka, his home island, off to Troy with him; he is the only one who makes it back alive. This is not exactly indicative of good leadership, or of what you would expect from a fine clever warrior and leader. There has got to be some way to explain how Odysseus could have lost all his men without making Odysseus seem blameworthy; and right in these very opening lines, the bard addresses that. Odysseus was striving for his companions' homecoming but they, fools that they were, were destroyed by their own recklessness. This is a theme that will be returned to many times in the *Odyssey*, the fact that Odysseus tried to bring his companions home but they were destroyed by their mistakes, their own foolishness.

Secondly, you may notice that Odysseus is not named in the proem of the *Odyssey*. Unlike the first line of the *Iliad*, where the bard says, "Muse, goddess, sing the wrath of Peleus' son Achilles," the name Odysseus does not occur until line 21 of the *Odyssey*. And yet Odysseus is established as the subject of the *Odyssey*, not just in the first few lines of the proem where we are told that this was the man who sacked Troy, but actually in the very first line; because Odysseus is described, in the first line of the *Odyssey*, by the epithet, the essential adjective, *polutropos*. This is not his most common epithet in the *Odyssey*, but it is one of his most important epithets. The word *polutropos* is utterly untranslatable into one English word. I can tell you what it means; I can't come up with a good one-word translation for it. It means, literally, "many turns." *Polu* means "many," as in words like polygon; any other word that has *poly* or *polu* in it, that means "many" in Greek. *Tropos* means "turns," "turn," or "turning." So the *polutropos* man is the man of many turnings.

Now, what does that mean for Odysseus? I think there are two levels of meaning in this word. First off, he is literally a man of many turnings; he is blown back and forth on the sea, trying to get home to Ithaka. He keeps being turned off course, he keeps being blown back in the direction he has already come from. So literally, this word refers to his many wanderings. But it also refers to his cleverness; he is *polutropos* in his mind. He is able to think his way out of any situation, to think on his feet, to reason his way out of troubles, to come up with stratagems, clever ploys, to get himself out of any difficulty; and the word *polutropos* picks up on both of those aspects of Odysseus' story, his wandering and his cleverness. It is a very difficult challenge for a translator; right there, in the center of the first line of the *Odyssey*, is this word that is thematically of the utmost importance for the *Odyssey*, and can't be translated into one good English word or even one good English phrase. Our translator here gives "the man of many ways," which is nicely ambiguous, but maybe a little too ambiguous; it doesn't quite get the punch of *polutropos* across.

The very first word of the *Odyssey* is *andra*, which means the man. So the first line of the *Odyssey* begins with the word man, just as the first line of the *Iliad* begins with the word wrath or anger. The first word of each of these poems sets its tone; from the instant you hear the opening word of the *Iliad* you know that you are going to hear about anger, wrath, and a great quarrel. From the instant you hear the opening word of the *Odyssey* you know that you are going to hear about one man, one individual and his adventures. And of course, the *Odyssey* is first and foremost about Odysseus' struggles to get home. The first thirteen lines—I read you the first ten—the first thirteen lines include the word *nostos*, homecoming or return or a derivative of it, no less than three times in just thirteen lines. In line 5, already he is longing for or striving for the *nostos* of his companions. In line 9, we are told that the Son God takes away his companions' *nostimon êmar*, the day of their homecoming, the day of their *nostos*. In line 13, which I did not read to you, but perhaps most importantly of all, we are told that Odysseus is longing for his *nostos* and for his wife—the two things that he wants, the two things that he is striving to regain in the *Odyssey*, his homecoming and his wife, Penelope. So very clearly, from the opening of the *Odyssey*, the idea that this is the story of Odysseus' struggle for his *nostos* is set up right from the very beginning.

After identifying Odysseus by summarizing his adventures, the bard asks the Muse to start the story "from some point." As I already said, a bard working in the oral tradition can pick up the story anywhere he wants to. We have been told we are going to talk about Odysseus; we are going to hear a story of Odysseus' return home. But where is that story going to start? It could start anywhere. It could start right after the Sack of Troy; it could start the day before Odysseus arrives back on Ithaka; anywhere in that whole ten-year time period that he spent trying to get from Troy to Ithaka the story could start. Our bard says to the goddess, to the Muse of poetry, the Muse who inspires him with the story, "pick it up at some point; from some point begin the story."

The bard then implies that the *Odyssey* will start in the tenth year after the Trojan War. He very quickly runs through a little resumé of what has happened to everybody else, and to Odysseus. He tells us that the other heroes have all either made it home or died; everyone who didn't die at Troy or get shipwrecked at sea is now home again. Only Odysseus is still missing, and the bard tells us that Odysseus is being held prisoner by a nymph, or a goddess, named Kalypso, on her island in the middle of the sea. As the *Odyssey* opens—we are still within the first thirty lines here; Athena the virgin goddess, as we'll see in the *Odyssey*, is Odysseus' primary patron deity—Athena beseeches the great god Zeus, the king of the gods, to send the messenger god Hermes to tell Kalypso that she must let go Odysseus go.

So it seems as though we are going to start right at the point where Odysseus is freed from his seven years' captivity on Kalypso's island and is allowed to go home to Ithaka; Athena says to Zeus, "Send Hermes to tell Kalypso she must let Odysseus go." But then, after giving us this false lead, in effect, this belief that we are going to immediately go to Kalypso's island and see Odysseus there and move on to Ithaka, the bard suddenly changes direction and goes off on a side-story. Athena says that while Zeus is sending Hermes to tell Kalypso it is time to let Odysseus go, she, Athena, will go to Odysseus' home island of Ithaka and visit his son there. And so we suddenly take this detour; we go off to Ithaka, and spend the first four books of the *Odyssey*— and that would be about four hours of performance time—not with Odysseus at all, but rather following the adventures of his son, Telemachos. Odysseus only shows up in person in the *Odyssey* in Book Five.

So the narrative structure of the *Odyssey*, already from this beginning point, is extremely complicated and anything but straightforward. As I just said, the first four books of the *Odyssey* are concerned primarily with, not with Odysseus at all, but with his son, Telemachos. In Books One and Two of the *Odyssey* we see Telemachos at home on his island of Ithaka. In Books Three and Four of the *Odyssey* we see Telemachos traveling to visit Nestor and Menelaos, two of Odysseus' old comrades-in-arms, two characters from the *Iliad*. So, the first four books are taken up with Telemachos. Books Five through Eight introduce us to Odysseus himself, and take up his story as he leaves Kalypso's island and journeys to the land of a people called the Phaiakians, who will show him great hospitality and help him on his homeward journey. So you would expect then, after Book Eight, if the Phaiakians are going to help Odysseus home, Book Nine should take him to Ithaka, right? Well, it doesn't. Books Nine through Twelve—the heart of the *Odyssey*, the most famous section of the *Odyssey*—are actually a flashback section, in which Odysseus narrates in the first person his adventures from leaving Troy up to arriving at Kalypso's island. Then finally, in Book Thirteen, the bard changes to a straightforward chronological sequence; and Books Thirteen through Twenty-Four show us Odysseus' homecoming to Ithaka, all the way through his killing of the suitors of his wife, Penelope, and regaining of his status and power in Ithaka.

So, a purely chronological arrangement of the *Odyssey* would have to put Books Nine through Twelve first, followed by Books Five through Eight, followed by Books Thirteen through Twenty-Four. And the first four books, the adventures of Telemachos, really don't fit at all; they take place in the same time frame as Books Five through Eight, when Odysseus is traveling from Kalypso's island to the land of the Phaiakians.

Now, this extremely complex structure has struck some critics, over the centuries, as a blemish on the *Odyssey*, or even as an indication that the *Odyssey* is a not-very-skillfully assembled collection of shorter poems, that somebody put together rather carelessly without really thinking about much about what he was doing when he put it together. Other scholars—including me—think that the complex structure is quite the opposite, is one of great beauties and glories of the *Odyssey*, that it adds immeasurably to the *Odyssey*'s power. One reason I think that—there are many; but one reason I think that is specifically because of the effect that is gained by delaying Odysseus' entry until Book Five of the *Odyssey*. Let's think about that a little bit. We do not see Odysseus for four full books; instead, we go to Ithaka and see Odysseus' family and country in his absence. Odysseus has been gone for nearly twenty years at this point, and this has caused immeasurable problems both for his wife and son and for his society.

Let's start with his family. Of course, in any culture, one of the most heartwrenchingly tragic things that can happen to a family is to have a member of that family be missing in action, to have someone go off to war, never return, and you don't know what happened to them. That is unutterably terrible for any family, in any culture; but for Odysseus' family, in the culture portrayed by the *Odyssey*, it is even more terrible than perhaps would immediately be obvious to a modern audience. Penelope, Odysseus' wife, is caught between two absolutely conflicting duties, with no way of knowing which one she should follow. If she is still a wife, it is her absolute unquestioned duty to remain loyal to her husband. If Odysseus is still alive, Penelope must protect his household, must not remarry, and must keep his goods, his family, and his home intact for him until he returns. This is a society in which there is no possibility of divorce *in absentia*, no way to have someone declared dead after a certain number years have passed—not that those are easy things to do, emotionally speaking, but they do at least allow someone in Penelope's situation to finish that episode of her life and figure what to do next. Penelope has no such possibility. Also this is a culture, the culture of the *Odyssey*, that has no place for an unmarried woman. Penelope needs to be married; there is no role in this society for an independent, unmarried woman. So, if Odysseus is still alive, Penelope's absolute unquestionable duty is to remain loyal to him. On the other hand, if he is dead—since this is not a society that accepts unmarried women as contributing members of society—if Odysseus is dead, she has no less absolute a duty to remarry; to turn Odysseus' household over to her son, Telemachos, and to go off with a new husband and make a new life elsewhere.

So Penelope is caught in an agonizing dilemma; she has no way of knowing what her status is—is she a wife or she is a widow? Her duty is absolutely clear, either way; but those duties are absolutely conflicting, and she has no way of knowing which applies to her. Telemachos is in a similar situation, not knowing his status; is he guarding the kingdom for his father, or is this his own kingdom and his own household that he should claim as a grown man for himself? And so Penelope and Telemachos are both left in a kind of limbo, in which their proper course of action is unclear and in which they have no way to figure out what their proper course of action is. Odysseus' absence also causes great problems for his society. Like all the societies reflected in the Homeric epics, Ithaka is a monarchy. It seems never to have occurred to anyone on Ithaka that you can have any form of society except a monarchy. Ithaka, therefore, is a monarchy whose monarch has been missing for twenty years, and the disorder this causes in society is vast. There is no proper working of Ithakan society while its king is gone.

The focal point for these troubles, in both family and society, are the suitors of Penelope, young men of Ithaka who are trying to marry Penelope and by so doing to take over Odysseus' household and take over the rule of Ithaka. These suitors assume that by marrying Penelope they would be able, in fact, to take over the kingdom; that is, they assume that Telemachos is still so immature that he would not be able to stop them. And Telemachos, as the *Odyssey* opens, *is* very immature. He must be about twenty years old; he can't be any younger than that, and yet he has never yet asserted himself as an adult, he has never yet tried to put himself forward as a grown man in a position of authority. We'll talk more about Telemachos' maturity—or lack of maturity—in the next lecture. So the suitors are threatening Odysseus' marriage; we know that, because we know that Odysseus is still alive. They are threatening Telemachos' inheritance; in their wanton disregard of the proprieties, they force themselves into Telemachos' house; they destroy his goods and his livelihood; they bother Penelope, who doesn't want them around—they are very clearly not acting as suitors ought to act. Their wanton disregard of the proprieties can been seen as a result of the disordered state on Ithaka, or almost as paradigm of the disordered state on Ithaka.

So, Homer starts the *Odyssey* not at some random moment, and the focusing on Telemachos for the first four books is not an unmotivated digression. Rather, Homer starts the *Odyssey* at the precise moment when the situation on Ithaka is coming to a head, and something must give; Telemachos is now grown and should assert himself as master of his own household. While Telemachos was still a child, Penelope could put off any kind of decision about whether Odysseus was alive or dead by focusing on bringing Telemachos up; she was maintaining the household, if not for her husband, at least for her son. But now that Telemachos is grown, she should hand the household over to him; and if she is in fact a widow, she should remarry. Also, Penelope had managed to hold the suitors at bay for three years by telling them that before she could choose which one of them to marry, she needed to fulfill her final duty to her first marriage by weaving a burial shroud for her father-in-law, Laertes. Laertes is not yet dead; but Odysseus was an only son, there are no other daughters-in-law, Odysseus mother is dead, so Penelope, in effect, said, "Let me discharge this final duty to my first marriage, so that when Laertes dies he can be properly buried." And of course, in her very famous weaving trick, she wove the shroud every day, unwove it at night, so it never got finished. This worked for three years but then a maid of Penelope's told the suitors what she was doing, the suitors caught Penelope at the trick—that trick will not hold the suitors off any longer.

Thus, we enter the scene, we start the *Odyssey*, at the exact moment when the situation has become desperate. The suitors have seen through Penelope's trick; Telemachos is grown and should assert himself; Odysseus is needed back on Ithaka right now. In our next lecture, we'll look in more detail at the first four books of the *Odyssey* and at the treatment of Telemachos in those books.

Lecture Two
Guests and Hosts

Scope: This lecture defines and examines *xenia*, a concept which is of key importance for understanding the *Odyssey*. Often translated as "the guest-host relationship," *xenia* is a major theme throughout Odysseus' wanderings. This lecture concentrates on the way in which *xenia* permeates the first four books of the *Odyssey* and the effect this has on the audience's understanding of the characters of Telemachos and the suitors. Finally, the lecture examines how the conventions of *xenia* allow the bard to integrate Nestor and Menelaos into his narrative, by sending Telemachos to visit them and establish a bond of *xenia* with them. In addition to examining *xenia*, the lecture also highlights two other important narrative elements that are established in the *Telemachy*: the use of Agamemnon's story as a parallel for Odysseus' own, and Telemachos' need to assert his maturity.

Outline

I. The first four books of the *Odyssey* highlight one of its key themes, the concept of *xenia*.

    A. *Xenia* is usually translated "guest-host relationship." It is a reciprocal relationship between two *xenoi*—a word which means guest, host, stranger, friend, and foreigner.

        1. It is not based on friendship, but rather on obligation.

        2. It works only if each side does not violate the terms of *xenia*. To do so is to offend Zeus himself.

    B. Throughout the *Odyssey*, Odysseus' homecoming and regaining of his family and kingdom are either helped or hindered by the kind of *xenia* he meets on his journeys.

    C. The primary importance of *xenia* is established throughout the first four books of the *Odyssey*, where Telemachos experiences it from every possible angle.

II. Telemachos is the most important character in these first four books; in fact, they are often called the *Telemachy*. *Xenia* is a crucial element in the bard's characterization of Telemachos.

A. In Books I and II, we see Telemachos dealing with issues of *xenia* from the host's perspective, at home on Ithaka.

B. In Books III and IV, we see Telemachos experiencing *xenia* from the guest's perspective, in the courts of Nestor and Menelaos.

III. *Xenia* is also crucial for our understanding of the suitors. Their wrongdoing is couched almost entirely in terms of a violation of *xenia*.

A. Telemachos himself stresses this in Book II, when he calls an assembly of the men of Ithaka.

B. The suitors ignore the essentially reciprocal nature of *xenia*.

IV. The first two books, set on Ithaka, use the concept of *xenia* to highlight the conflict between Telemachos and the suitors.

A. Our first view of Telemachos shows him receiving the disguised Athena as a guest. He shows her proper *xenia*, in the first of the *Odyssey*'s many "host-greeting-guest" scenes.
1. Telemachos greets his guest at the door, and takes her spear away from her.
2. He bids her welcome, and tells her that her needs will be seen to.
3. He offers her food, a bath, and a bed for the night.
4. Only after her immediate physical needs have been attended to does he ask her who she is.

B. Telemachos has two main concerns: his grief over his absent father and his anger at the suitors' behavior. Athena advises Telemachos to go visit Nestor and Menelaos to seek news of his father. She also tells him to call a council of all the men of Ithaka, and to assert himself to the suitors.

C. In the council, Telemachos directly accuses the suitors of violating *xenia*. He is backed up by the prophet Halitherses, who predicts misfortune for the suitors if they do not mend their ways.

D. The spokesman of the suitors, Eurymachos, makes it very clear that the suitors do not care about *xenia* or any other mores of their society.

E. The contrast between Telemachos and the suitors is enhanced by the fact that most of the suitors, too, are sons of absent fathers. The disorder in Ithakan society is represented by the disorder in *xenia*.

V. Books III and IV present a view of *xenia* working properly, with Telemachos in the role of guest.

    A. In Book III, Telemachos visits Nestor at Pylos.

        1. Nestor receives Telemachos properly, as a good host should.

        2. Nestor suggests that Telemachos should visit Menelaos, recently returned home to Sparta. He provides Telemachos with horses and a chariot so that he can make the journey.

        3. Nestor's son Peisistratos joins Telemachos as a traveling companion.

    B. In Book IV, Telemachos and Peisistratos visit Menelaos and Helen, recently returned to Sparta after seven years' wandering.

        1. Again, they are greeted and entertained properly.

        2. They are given gifts when they leave.

VI. Books III and IV also provide crucial background information and set up narrative elements that will be important throughout the rest of the epic.

    A. At Telemachos' request, Nestor recounts events after the fall of Troy.

        1. He tells about the homecoming of several Greeks, but does not know what has happened to Odysseus.

        2. He describes Agamemnon's murder at the hands of his treacherous wife Klytaimestra and her lover Aigisthos, and how Agamemnon was avenged by his son Orestes. This story appears over and over in the *Odyssey* as a comparandum for Odysseus, Penelope, and Telemachos' situation.

    B. In Sparta, the conversation turns to Troy, and Telemachos weeps when Menelaos praises Odysseus.

        1. Helen recognizes Telemachos. She gives the three men an Egyptian drug, *nepenthe*, so that they will stop grieving.

        2. Helen tells a story about how she helped Odysseus once during the Trojan War. Menelaos counters with a story about how only Odysseus' cunning kept Helen from betraying all the Greek soldiers when they were inside the Trojan Horse.

        3. Finally, Menelaos recounts his conversation with the sea-god Proteus, who told him about the deaths of Aias the Lesser and Agamemnon, and about Odysseus' captivity on Kalypso's island.

C. Thus, Telemachos now knows his father was alive as recently as two years ago, and he has renewed reason to hope for his return.

D. Telemachos has also had the chance to assert himself as an adult in his own right before his father's return.

VII. The *Telemachy* ends with a brief look back at Ithaka.

   A. The suitors scheme to murder Telemachos when he returns.

   B. Penelope weeps for Odysseus.

   C. The situation on Ithaka is set firmly enough in our minds that the bard can now put it "on hold" for the next several books, and turn to Odysseus' own story.

Essential Reading:

Odyssey, Books II–IV.

Supplementary Reading:

Norman Austin, *Helen of Troy*, Chapter 3.

S. Douglas Olson, *Blood and Iron*, Chapter 2.

Richard Seaford, *Reciprocity and Ritual*, Chapter 1.

Questions to Consider:

1. Telemachos is often described as being unrealistically immature; on any reckoning, he must be 20 years old by the time the *Odyssey* opens. Does the charge of immaturity seem valid, or is Telemachos a realistic portrait of a young man in his situation?

2. Why does Athena send Telemachos off to visit Nestor and Menelaos, instead of simply telling him that his father is almost home?

Lecture Two—Transcript
Guests and Hosts

Hello, and welcome to Lecture Two. In our previous lecture we discussed the structure of the *Odyssey* and looked especially at the way the opening scenes in Ithaka stress the need for Odysseus' return. In this lecture we are going to continue our examination of the first four books of the *Odyssey*, and give special attention to how these books set up and define a key theme of the *Odyssey*, the concept of *xenia*.

Now, *xenia* is one of the most important themes in the *Odyssey*, and it is yet another Greek term that lacks an adequate English definition. The term *xenia* is often translated as the "guest-host relationship," and that rather cumbersome, rather awkward, formulation tells you right away that we have neither exactly an equivalent word nor exactly an equivalent concept in English for the Greek concept of *xenia*. "Hospitality" is also sometimes used as a translation, but that is much too weak a word, because it does not include with it the sense of divine sanction, of absolute responsibility, of hospitality as a duty, not as something that one chooses to do or not to do. *Xenia* is a reciprocal relationship in the *Odyssey*—and in the *Iliad* as well for that matter. *Xenia* is a reciprocal relationship between two *xenoi*—that is the plural; the singular is *xenos*. We can get a little bit closer to understanding what *xenia* is, perhaps, by looking at what the word *xenos* means. *Xenos* can be translated, depending on context, as guest, host, stranger, foreigner, and friend. Now, if I can get you to understand how one word can mean five things that, in our way of thinking, seem so very different—guest, host, stranger, foreigner, and friend—then I can bring you to an understanding of what *xenia*, the abstract relationship between one *xenos* and another, actually is.

Xenos means these five different things, because it is a word that refers to a particular kind of friendship; not affection or fondness, but the relationship that two people enter into once they have been in the guest-host relationship with one another. Let's look at it from the guest's point of view first off. Let's imagine that in the *Odyssey*, or in any other epic from this timeframe, someone is traveling away from his own community. At nightfall, what does he do?—and I say "he" here, because with the exception of disguised goddesses such as Athena, it always is a "he" who partakes in *xenia*. When night falls, what does the traveler do, what does this person do? He can't go to a hotel; there is no such thing. He needs somewhere to stay, he needs shelter, he needs a meal, he needs a bath, a change of clothing, all of those things—what can he do? What he does is, he presents himself at the door of a house that looks as though it is about his same social status. If he is a very poor man, a beggar, he would go to the hut of another poor man. If he is a king's son, he would go to the palace in the town that he has come to. Once he gets there, he knocks on the door and basically says, "Here I am; put me up for the night."

So, he is a *xenos* in the sense of being a guest, because the person onto whose house he has come will take him in, and put him up for the night. But he is also clearly a *xenos* in the sense of being a foreigner. "Foreigner," here, is defined very, very narrowly; basically someone who's from another town counts as a foreigner. (And of course, by the way, it's that sense of *xenos* that gives us our word xenophobia, "fear of foreigners.") So this person who appears and knocks on the door, as soon as he crosses the threshold, he will be a guest; he is also a foreigner; he is also a stranger—the householder has never seen him before. Once he has been taken in, given a meal, allowed to sleep overnight, and so forth, he becomes a friend; but again only this stylized sense of friend. This has nothing to do, again, with fondness or affection, but simply with the recognition that a bond has been established between these two people that remains—and carries on hereditarily, by the way. Their children, if they ever meet, will have obligations to one another. The householder, obviously, is a *xenos* in the sense of host in this set up; and so the word *xenos* means all of these things—guest, host, stranger, foreigner, friend—and the relationship between one *xenos* and another is the concept that we describe by the term, *xenia*.

Now, obviously such a concept, such a situation, can only work if both participants in it are very strongly motivated not to abuse the relationship of *xenia*. The guest must not rob, murder, or otherwise mistreat his host; similarly, the host must not in any way mistreat the guest. I always say to my students, when I am teaching the *Odyssey* in college, not to try this at home; do not, when you are traveling in a strange city, go and knock on someone's door and say, "Hello, I need somewhere to stay for the night; and by the way, I would like a really good meal while you are at it." It is not going to work. For it to work in any society, obviously, there has to be a very strong sense of obligation and a sense of sanctions against you if you violate *xenia*. And this is where, as so often in the *Iliad* and the *Odyssey* both, the gods come into play. *Xenia* is validated by, is protected by, and is overseen by no less a god than Zeus himself. One of Zeus' titles is Zeus *Xenios*, Zeus the god of *xenia*. So, a guest who mistreats his host, a host who mistreats or turns away a guest, has directly offended the god Zeus, and will undoubtedly suffer for it.

And now you are in a position to think back on the episode, or the cause, of the Trojan War, when Paris abducted Helen. Along with everything else he was violating by doing that, he was violating *xenia*. Paris had gone to stay with Helen and Menelaos, he was Menalaos' *xenos*, and he ran away with Menalaos' wife; that is about as bad a violation of *xenia* as one can well imagine. That is something a guest is absolutely not supposed to do; you are not supposed to run away with your host's wife. So the Trojan War, among all its other aspects, is fought over a violation of *xenia*, so this is an extremely important concept, particularly for the *Odyssey*, but also for the *Iliad* as well.

Throughout the *Odyssey*, Odysseus' homecoming and regaining of his family and kingdom are either helped or hindered by the kind of *xenia* he meets on his journeys. Since he is away from home and traveling, obviously he is dependent on this guest-host relationship to help him on his way or to hinder it. So *xenia* becomes one of the central themes of the *Odyssey*, purely because Odysseus has to depend on it so much. Its primary importance as a conceptual framework, almost, for the *Odyssey* is set up throughout the first four books of the *Odyssey*, which I now want to turn back to. In the first four books of the *Odyssey* we see Telemachos experiencing *xenia* from just about every possible angle. Along with everything else that these books are doing thematically, they are setting up, describing, painting a picture, of *xenia* and how it ought to work—and how it ought not to work.

Telemachos is, without question, the most important character in the first four books of the *Odyssey*. In fact, the first four books are often called the *Telemachy*. If the *Odyssey* is a book about Odysseus, the *Telemachy* is a book about Telemachos, and the first four books of the *Odyssey* are conventionally referred to as the *Telemachy*, simply to stress how crucially important Telemachos is in these books. And *xenia* is one very important element in the bard's characterization of Telemachos. In Books One and Two, we see Telemachos dealing with *xenia* from the host's perspective, while he is at home on Ithaka. In Books Three and Four, we see him traveling to visit his father's old comrades-in-arms, Nestor and Menelaos; there he experiences *xenia* from the guest's point of view, when Nestor and Menelaos both take him into their houses and treat him as hosts should treat a guest.

Xenia is also crucial for understanding of the suitors, those suitors who are trying to marry Penelope and take over Telemachos' household.

Interestingly enough, their wrongdoing is couched almost entirely in terms of a violation of *xenia*. Telemachos himself stresses this in Book Two of the *Odyssey*, when he calls an assembly of the men of Ithaka and talks publicly about what the suitors have done wrong; the terms in which he puts it are terms that make sense in *xenia*. He says that the suitors have done wrong not just by courting Penelope when she doesn't want them to court her, but by hanging out in Telemachos' house, sacrificing and eating his flocks of animals, drinking his wine. He actually says that they are wasting away his substance, they are destroying his possessions. And one crucial aspect of *xenia* that I have not yet mentioned is that it is supposed to be an absolutely reciprocal relationship. If a guest can, he is supposed to give a gift to his host; if he can't give a gift to his host, he is at least supposed to leave before he's worn out his welcome. He is not supposed to hang out for years, eating his host's food, wearing his host's clothes and so forth.

The reciprocity of *xenia* normally plays itself not between two individual guests and hosts, but rather in the broad idea that if I am a guest this year, next year I will be a host, perhaps not to the same man who hosted me this year, but to someone; so that it balances out in the long run, and a host is supposed to feel a sense of obligation because of the times in the past when he had been a guest, and vice versa. The suitors are ignoring the essentially reciprocal nature of *xenia* by giving nothing in return to Telemachos, and this is how Telemachos states what they have done wrong in the assembly in Book Two of the *Odyssey*. He says that they give nothing in return. They eat his animals; they drink his wine; they give nothing in return.

So, *xenia* helps us understand Telemachos; it also is very important in characterizing the suitors. When we first see Telemachos in Ithaka, we also see the concept of *xenia* used to highlight the conflict between Telemachos and the suitors. Our very first view of Telemachos shows him receiving a *xenos*, a guest; this guest happens to be Athena in disguise. She is disguised as a human man, which always give me a little bit of a problem at this point in discussing the *Odyssey*. I don't know whether to refer to Athena as "her" or as "him" at this point. Telemachos sees a man come to the door; we know it is Athena, the bard tends to use "her," so I guess I will stick with the female pronouns here. But remember that Telemachos thinks he is hosting a human man; he doesn't know he is hosting the disguised goddess Athena.

When Athena comes to the door of the palace—and this is the very first time we actually see Telemachos—the first things we see Telemachos do are greet his guest, in the first of many of the *Odyssey*'s host-greeting-guest scenes. Telemachos goes to the door; greets Athena; takes her by the hand;

says, "Welcome, *xenos*" to her—and that is another challenging translation problem for any one dealing with this scene in the *Odyssey*. Telemachos says, "Welcome, *xenos*"; how do you translate *xenos* there? Welcome, friend; welcome, guest; welcome, stranger; and welcome, foreigner—in English, you have to pick one. The word Telemachos says means all of them. He takes her hand; bids her welcome; takes her spear away from her—now that is an interesting little point. Obviously, from the guest's point of view, the host is supposed to take any burdens you are carrying, take whatever luggage you have, anything you are carrying with you. From the host's point of view, it makes very good sense to disarm your guest. If the guest happens to be carrying a spear or any other weapon, you very politely take that and set it aside, just until you are sure that this guest does recognize the protocols of *xenia* and will abide by them.

Telemachos then takes his guest into the palace; offers her food, a bath and a bed for the night; and here comes an absolutely crucial element of *xenia*. It is only after the guest's immediate, physical needs have been met—usually the most immediate need is for a meal—it is only after the immediate physical needs have been attended to that the host may ask the guest, "Who are you?" Telemachos waits until after Athena has eaten before he asks her who she is. I think the point of that little detail—the reason that it is seen as a violation of *xenia* to ask your guest, "Who are you?" the instant you go to the door and meet the guest—is because the relationship of *xenia*, the practice of *xenia*, is not supposed to depend on whether the host likes the guest or doesn't; knows the guest or doesn't; in any way has any feelings about the guest or not. It is supposed to be purely a matter of this person is here, and needs help, and the host must help him. If the host begins by saying, "Who are you?" there is, implicit in that, the idea that if the host doesn't like the answer—if it turns out that this person is the grandson of your old arch enemy or some such—that the host can say, "Go away; I am not going to help you." So one of the protocols of *xenia*—I try to avoid the word "rules," because there wasn't a rule book; this wasn't ever set out anywhere formally—but one of the protocols of *xenia* was that the host may only ask the guest, "Who are you?" after the guest's most immediate needs have been attended to.

So when we first meet Telemachos, so to speak, in the *Odyssey* we see that he knows how to act as a proper host in his greeting of his guest Athena; and while they are eating, and after their meal, they have a conversation in which Telemachos' two main concerns, the two things that are troubling him, are brought out. He unburdens himself; he opens his heart to Athena, tells her his troubles, and his troubles are two-fold—his grief over his absent father and his anger at the suitors' behavior. Now Athena, of course, is here specifically to advise Telemachos, and to help Telemachos; we as the audience know that. Athena said to Zeus, at the beginning of Book One, that while Zeus was sending Hermes off to tell Kalypso to let Odysseus go, she, Athena, would go down to Ithaka and see Telemachos; she says, specifically, to put some heart into him, to stir him up a little bit, to give him that last little push to launch him into maturity. Up until this point, Telemachos has not asserted himself; he strikes many readers as rather surprisingly immature for a young man who must after all be about twenty years old by this time. He acts much younger than that in many ways. Athena's motivation, in going to Ithaka to see him, is not just to allow him to find out that his father is still alive—he will find that out from Menelaos—but more than that, to encourage him to assert himself as an adult, to take action.

And Athena encourages Telemachos to do this in two ways. She tells him to call the counsel of all the men of Ithaka—in Book Two, he does this—and to openly and publicly denounce the suitors for how they are acting, how they are destroying his substance, for their violations of *xenia*. She also tells him to travel and visit Nestor and Menalaos, and see if he can get any news of his father. Now, Athena of course knows that Odysseus will be home any day now; she has just told Zeus to send Hermes to tell Kalypso to let Odysseus go. She could just tell Telemachos, "I am Athena; Odysseus will be home any day now." But she doesn't do that, because, again, she wants Telemachos to assert himself, to go off on his own, to have a chance to act as an adult in his own right before his father does, in fact, return home.

So Telemachos takes the advice of this guest—who, of course, he does not know is Athena—and in the counsel that he calls in Book Two of the *Odyssey*, he directly accuses the suitors of violating *xenia*. Now, neither he nor Athena ever used the term "violating *xenia*," but that is clearly what they are talking about, in effect, though they don't put it in exactly that terminology. Telemachos, as I already mentioned, denounces the suitors for destroying his goods without ever giving anything in return, and he is backed in this denunciation of the suitors by a prophet, an old man, a seer, a reader of omens, Halitherses, who predicts misfortune for the suitors if they do not mend their ways. Halitherses sees an omen, a flight of birds in the sky; and, as very frequently in the *Iliad* and the *Odyssey* both, birds flying by are omens that specially trained or specially gifted seers and prophets can interpret. In this omen, Halitherses sees two eagles fly by that Zeus sends; they fly by overhead and tear at one another with their talons. Halitherses interprets this omen to mean that Odysseus is going to return home soon, and that there will be terrible repercussions for the suitors if they do not change their behavior before Odysseus comes home.

Now, the response of the suitors to Halitherses' prophecy is, I think, absolutely essential for our understanding both of the suitors' character and of how we are supposed to view these suitors in the *Odyssey*. One of the suitors, their spokesman Eurymachos, responds to Halitherses, after Halitherses has said that Odysseus is about to come home and the suitors must change their ways or suffer the consequences. Eurymachos, answering Halitherses, says:

> Old man [*sic* sir], better go home and prophesy to your children,
> for fear they may suffer some evil to come. In these things
> I can give a much better interpretation than you can.
> Many are the birds who wander under the sun's rays wander
> the sky; not all of them mean anything; Odysseus
> is dead, far away, and how I wish you had died with him
> also. Then you would not be announcing all these predictions
> nor would you so stir up Telemachos, who is now angry.

Eurymachos continues his speech—it is a fairly long speech—by saying, "If you keep doing this, Halitherses, if you keep stirring up Telemachos, we'll lay a penalty on you that will make you very sorry and that Telemachos must tell Penelope choose a husband and marry now, we are not going to go away until she does" because, he concludes:

> … in any case we fear no one,
> and surely not Telemachos, for all he is so eloquent.
> Nor do we care for any prophecy, which you, old sir,
> may tell us, which will not happen, and will make you even
>   more hated
> and his [that is, Telemachos'] possessions will wretchedly be eaten
>   away, there will not
> be compensation, ever, while she [Penelope] makes the Achaians
>   put off
> marriage with her.

Now, what Eurymachos has done in this speech is really rather stunning. In one fell swoop he has shown disrespect, disregard, and contempt for just about every important element of the mores of his society. He has shown disrespect to an old man, to begin with, and this is a society in which the old are definitely respected. He has shown disrespect to a prophet, which by implication means disrespecting the god whom that prophet serves—in this case, Zeus. He has said "Odysseus is dead," and made it quite clear that he is glad Odysseus is dead. This is showing disrespect to his rightful king; and if Odysseus is dead, in that case, who is Eurymachos' rightful king? Well, Telemachos—and what does Eurymachos say about Telemachos? Nothing good, I am afraid. He goes on to say we don't care about prophecies, which in effect means we don't care about the gods; we are going to force Penelope, whether she likes it or not. Everything that ought to be respected in this society—the old; prophecy; gods; king; the rights of the king; the rights of the king's son—all of those, in one speech, Eurymachos simply spits on.

And I think this is very important, as I said, for understanding not just Eurymachos' character but the character of all the suitors. Odysseus, before the end of the *Odyssey*, is going to kill all of these suitors; there are 108 of them, by the way. He is going to kill all of them, and it seems to me— although not all scholars would agree with this—it seems to me that we are supposed to approve of that; that we are supposed to see the suitors as so beyond the pale of decent society, as having so set themselves outside the mores of their society, that they have to be dealt with harshly. There is nothing else to be done with them.

The contrast between Telemachos and the suitors is enhanced by the fact, underlined by the fact, that most of these suitors, like Telemachos, are sons of absent fathers. When Odysseus went off to war, he didn't go alone; he took all the men of Ithaka who were of fighting age with him. Now, some of the suitors have fathers still present on Ithaka; some of them have fathers who were too old to go to war twenty years previously, and now are very old indeed. But most of their fathers are gone with Odysseus, and so the disorder in Ithakan society can be seen as, in one way, reflecting what happens to a society when all the fathers are gone. And I think, in that regard, the character of Telemachos, on the one hand, and the character of the suitors, on the other hand, are an almost frighteningly realistic portrait of what can happen to young men who grow up with no fathers. Telemachos is immature, unable to assert himself—until Athena encourages him but up till this point he has unable to assert himself—, and to use a term I normally don't much like, a "mama's boy." The suitors, on the other hand, are completely out of control; completely disregarding all the mores of their society; completely reckless. Those seem to me to be really the two extremes of what does happen, what would happen, in a society where all the fathers were missing and the sons grew up without any fathers to guide them and to teach them how to behave. So the disorder in Ithakan society runs much deeper than disorder in *xenia*, but it is represented by, indicated by, this disorder in *xenia* that plays itself out in Telemachos' or Odysseus' household.

Moving on to Books Three and Four; in these books we see a view of *xenia* working properly, with Telemachos, this time, as guest rather than as host. In Book Three, Telemachos visits Nestor, the oldest and wisest of the Greeks, at Pylos. He is guided there by Athena, disguised this time as a human being named Mentor, an old friend of Odysseus; and this is of course where we get the term "mentor" for an older person who guides a younger person. Mentor, a.k.a. Athena, guides Telemachos to Pylos, where Telemachos meets and interacts with Nestor. Nestor receives Telemachos absolutely properly, as a good host should. He gives him a meal; provides a bed; he provides a bath the next morning; he doesn't ask Telemachos who he is until after Telemachos has eaten. All the elements of proper *xenia* are there. Nestor also suggests that Telemachos should visit Menalaos in Sparta, because Menalaos has just recently returned home from his own wanderings, and he provides Telemachos with horses and a chariot so that Telemachos can make the journey, in the hope that Menalaos, recently returned home as he is, may have heard something about Odysseus.

Nestor also gives his son Peisistratos to Telemachos as a traveling companion on his journey to Sparta, and in Book Four Telemachos and Peisistratos visit Menalaos and Helen at Sparta. Once again they are greeted and entertained properly, and feasted, given beds and baths, and so forth. And one other element of *xenia* that I haven't mentioned yet; they are given guest-gifts when they leave, gifts that are provided for guests. Now we don't actually see Telemachos leave Sparta in Book Four—in fact, Telemachos doesn't actually leave Sparta until Book Fifteen—but Menalaos talks about the wonderful gifts that he will give to Telemachos when Telemachos actually leaves.

Books Three and Four, along with stressing *xenia*, also provide some crucial background narrative material, crucial both for Telemachos and for us. At Telemachos' request, Nestor recounts events that took place after the fall of Troy. He talks about the homecomings of several Greeks, although he doesn't know what happened to Odysseus, but also, more importantly, Nestor tells Telemachos the story of how Agamemnon was murdered by his wife Klytaimestra and her lover Aigisthos, when Agamemnon returned home from Troy. Now this story—Agamemnon's homecoming to be murdered by a treacherous wife and her new lover—this is repeated over and over again, throughout the *Odyssey*, as a kind of alternative version of what could happen to Odysseus if Penelope were not faithful. Agamemnon and Klytaimestra keep coming up in the *Odyssey*; people keep talking about them. We'll even see the ghost of Agamemnon himself in Book Eleven of the *Odyssey*. Nestor stresses the aspect of the story in which Agamemnon's son Orestes avenged his father's murder, and Nestor seems to be saying pretty clearly to Telemachos, "Go thou and do likewise; go and get rid of the suitors, defend your father's honor." It is a little bit rough on Telemachos—there are 108 suitors, after all—a little bit much to expect him to get rid of all of them by himself; but Nestor is pretty clearly citing this story as a paradigm for Telemachos to try to follow.

In Telemachos' visit to Menalaos and Helen in Sparta, the conversation turns to Troy, and Telemachos weeps when Menalaos mentions Odysseus. This is a very interesting little episode, this visit to Menalaos and Helen. Helen recognizes Telemachos; she says he looks so much like Odysseus that he must be Odysseus' son, and when Telemachos is weeping over his lost father, and Menalaos is weeping over all the men who were lost at the war, and Peisistratos, Nestor's son, is weeping over his elder brother who died in the war, Helen drugs the three men. She gives them an Egyptian drug called *nepenthe*, which means "no pain" or "no grief," so that they will stop grieving. And while they are under the influence of nepenthe—which we are told is so powerful that someone who had drunk it could feel no grief at all, even if his family was slaughtered before his face that very day, he could feel no grief—while the men are under the influence of this drug, Helen tells the story, supposedly to show how clever Odysseus was, about how Odysseus once came into Troy in disguise and she recognized him and helped him. Menalaos counters with the story about how, when the Greeks were hiding in the Trojan Horse, Helen walked around mimicking their wives' voices, trying to lure them out, and Odysseus was the only one who recognized what was going on and kept the others from crying out. So Menalaos, in effect, says, "Yes, Helen, you are right; Odysseus was indeed a very clever man. Why, I remember that time when you tried to murder all of us, and he was the one who kept you from doing it."

This episode between Helen and Menalaos, as I said, is an extremely problematic one; there is a lot of scholarship that has been written on this episode. One thing it does, at least, is to show us that Helen is still being ambiguous, just as she was in the *Iliad*. Even here in the *Odyssey*, she still is ambiguous. Did she want to be at Troy? Did she not want to be at Troy? She seems to imply no; Menalaos seems to imply yes.

Most importantly for Telemachos, Menalaos recounts his conversation that he had, while in Egypt, with a minor sea god named Proteus, who told Menalaos about Agamemnon's death, about the death of Aias the Lesser at sea in recompense for raping Kassandra, and—this is a crucial point— Proteus told Menalaos that Odysseus was being kept captive by the nymph Kalypso. Now this means that Telemachos knows his father was still alive as recently as a couple of years ago, when Menalaos spoke to Proteus. It is not entirely good news—Odysseus is a prisoner of a goddess—but it gives Telemachos reason to hope that Odysseus will in fact return, and Telemachos, as we have seen, has also had the chance to assert himself as an adult in his own right before his father's return.

The *Telemachy* ends, Book Four of the *Odyssey* ends, with a brief look back at Ithaka. We see the suitors plotting to murder Telemachos when he returns. Now that he is acting like an adult, now that he has asserted himself and taken some authority, they decide the only way to deal with him is to kill him, and they plot to murder him when he returns. We see Penelope weeping for Odysseus one more time before Book Four of the *Odyssey* ends; and so the situation on Ithaka is now set firmly enough in our minds that the bard can put it on hold for the next several books of the *Odyssey*. We won't see Telemachos again until Book Fifteen; we won't see Penelope until Book Sixteen. The bard has established how desperately Odysseus is needed; he has set the scene on Ithaka; the suitors are waiting in ambush to kill Telemachos; now the bard can turn to Odysseus himself, as we will do in the next lecture.

Lecture Three
A Goddess and a Princess

Scope: In this lecture, we turn to Odysseus himself as a character in the *Odyssey*. We examine Odysseus' first appearance in Book V and his interaction with Kalypso, as well as his encounter with the Phaiakian princess Nausikaa in Book VI. The lecture concentrates on the aspects of Odysseus' character that are foregrounded in these two books. In Book V, we see his desire to return home as a desire to reestablish his own identity; in both books, we see him as a superbly skilled rhetorician, who is able to craft his speech to appeal to whomever he is addressing. Finally, we discuss the ongoing thematic importance of *xenia* in Nausikaa's welcome of Odysseus in Book VI.

Outline

I. Book V opens with a restatement of the gods' plans for Odysseus.

   A. Athena again reminds Zeus of Odysseus' plight, and also mentions the suitors' plan to murder Telemachos.

   B. Zeus sends Hermes to Kalypso's island to tell her that she must let Odysseus go.

II. Our first view of Odysseus himself comes when Kalypso goes to take him Hermes' message. He is sitting by the seashore, looking out over the water and weeping.

   A. In Book I, Athena had said that Odysseus was longing to see even the smoke rising from his own country, and that he wanted to die.

   B. Here in our first view of him, this sense of profound longing and helplessness is reiterated. On Kalypso's island, Odysseus is largely passive, and thus unlike his true self.

III. Odysseus' first interaction with another character, his conversation with Kalypso, sets up several crucial points about his character and about themes of the *Odyssey*.

   A. He is cautious. He makes Kalypso swear by the River Styx that she is not plotting some trick against him before he trusts her.

    B. He understands what it means to be human. Kalypso has offered him immortality, but he rejects it.

        1. Greek mythology is filled with stories of humans who try for immortality; these attempts almost always end disastrously. By rejecting Kalypso's offer, Odysseus indicates that he accepts and desires the human condition.

        2. Odysseus' desire to return home is a desire to return to his full humanity and self-hood. He cannot truly be Odysseus away from Ithaka, Penelope, and Telemachos.

    C. One of the most important aspects of Odysseus' character is his skill in rhetoric and persuasion. His speech to Kalypso in which he explains why he wants to return to Penelope is a masterpiece of tact.

IV. With Kalypso's help, Odysseus builds a raft and leaves her island. However, Poseidon wrecks his raft at sea. Odysseus washes up on the shores of the island Scheria, naked, battered, starved, and more dead than alive. He falls asleep in a pile of leaves by the bank of a river as Book V ends.

V. The people of Scheria are called the Phaiakians. They are dedicated to *xenia*, and particularly to providing ships for stranded travelers. They will help Odysseus on his way homeward, though he does not know this himself.

    A. Athena appears in a dream to the Phaiakian princess Nausikaa, and inspires her to go do the family's laundry by the river where Odysseus is sleeping.

    B. After Nausikaa and her serving maidens do the laundry, they pass the time by playing ball. They wake Odysseus.

    C. Upon waking, Odysseus first wonders where he is, then analyzes and reacts to his situation.

        1. Odysseus wonders where he is and if the people there know *xenia*.

        2. He then ponders how best to approach Nausikaa without terrifying her.

        3. There is an implicit threat of rape underlying this scene, which Odysseus recognizes and has to work against.

4. He plucks a branch to cover his genitals and then comes out of the bushes. The other girls run, but Nausikaa stands still to talk to him.

VI. Odysseus' interaction with Nausikaa once again demonstrates his skill in rhetoric and his ability to fit his words to his audience. She responds in kind.

   A. He carefully constructs his speech to reassure her that he will not assault her (alluding to the virgin goddess Artemis), while never directly mentioning that possibility.

   B. Nausikaa responds properly, promising him clothing and gifts and whatever he needs. She also calls her attendants to help him bathe.

   C. Odysseus' refusal of the attendants' help while he bathes reiterates his recognition of the abnormal nature of this encounter.

   D. Athena beautifies Odysseus after he bathes, and Nausikaa comments to her maidens that she would be happy to marry him if he would stay on Scheria.

   E. Nausikaa gives Odysseus instructions about going to the city, in a speech which demonstrates that she, too, is skilled in rhetoric.

VII. The interaction with Nausikaa assures both Odysseus and the audience that he has arrived in a highly civilized country where he can expect proper *xenia*.

Essential Reading:
Odyssey, Books V and VI.

Supplementary Reading:
H. A. Shapiro, "Coming of Age."

Jean-Pierre Vernant, "The Refusal of Odysseus."

Questions to Consider:
1. What is the point of including Nausikaa's story in the epic? Is she purely incidental to the narrative, or does her encounter with Odysseus serve some thematic function?

2. Consider the implications of Odysseus' refusal to accept Kalypso's offer of immortality. What does this refusal imply about Odysseus' view of what it means to be human, as compared to Achilles in the *Iliad*?

Lecture Three—Transcript
A Goddess and a Princess

Hello, and welcome to Lecture Three. In our previous lecture we discussed *xenia* and its importance both in the *Telemachy* and for the *Odyssey* as a whole. In this lecture we are going to turn to Odysseus himself as a character in the *Odyssey*. We'll examine Odysseus' first appearance in Book Five, and his interaction with the goddess Kalypso, and then move on to talking about his encounter in Book Six with the Phaiakian princess, Nausikaa. The lecture will concentrate on the aspects of Odysseus' character that are foregrounded these two books; specifically, his desire to return home as a desire to reestablish his own identity, and his superb skill at rhetoric and at a persuasive speech. Finally, we'll discuss the ongoing thematic importance of *xenia* in Nausikaa's welcome of Odysseus in Book Six.

Now, Book Five opens with a restatement of the gods' plans for Odysseus. At this point it makes very good sense for the bard to restate exactly what Odysseus' situation is. This has been established in Book One and we have seen Athena tell Zeus it is time to send Hermes to make Kalypso let Odysseus go. But of course that bit of Book One was four hours ago in performance time, if you imagine the bard reciting the *Odyssey* steadily over the intervening four books that we have discussed in the last lecture. So at this point, at the opening of Book Five, the bard recaps for us where Odysseus is, what his situation is, and we get another scene in which Athena once again reminds Zeus, "Send Hermes to Kalypso's island and tell Kalypso to let Odysseus go." And at this point we get that scene of Hermes going to visit Kalypso which we have expected from the opening of Book One, but which was then put on hold for the four books of the *Telemachy*.

Zeus sends Hermes to Kalypso's island and tells Kalypso, through the agency of Hermes, that she must let Odysseus go. Our first view of Odysseus himself comes when Kalypso goes to take him Hermes' message. Now remember, at this point Odysseus has been held captive on Kalypso's island for seven long years. All of his companions, all the men who went to Troy with him, are long lost; we'll follow the story of how he came to lose all of his companions when we talk about Books Nine through Twelve. At this point, Odysseus has been held as a solitary prisoner for seven years; in our first view of him, he is sitting by the seashore looking out over the water and weeping. We are told he does this every day, that he spends all his days gazing out over the ocean, longing for a sight of Ithaka and crying.

In Book One, when Athena first mentioned Odysseus to Zeus, she said that Odysseus was longing to see even the smoke rising from his own country—to catch even a glimpse of smoke rising from Ithaka—and that he wanted to die. This is how we see him, in our first view of him in Book Five.

And this sense of profound longing and helplessness on Odysseus' part, in a way, is an indication that Odysseus is, as long as he is on Kalypso's island, very unlike himself—in a sense, not Odysseus at all. On Kalypso's island, Odysseus is largely passive. There is nothing he can do; he cannot get away from her. There is no-one to help him; his wits will not help him here; he can't contrive a scheme, come up with a plan to get away. He is enforcedly passive, and a passive Odysseus is scarcely Odysseus at all. He is completely unlike his true self, as long as he is on Kalypso's island. It's probably not coincidental that Kalypso's name literally means, "I shall hide" or "I shall conceal." Kalypso is the goddess who conceals Odysseus from the world, but in a sense conceals the real Odysseus even from Odysseus himself. He is, as long as he is on her island, unable to act, unable to plan, thus in a kind of limbo, in a kind of state between real existence and death. As soon as Kalypso tells Odysseus that he may go, that she has decided to let him go, we see him start to exhibit character traits that will be his hallmark throughout the rest of the *Odyssey*. Once he is told, "There is an action that you can take," he reasserts his essential self, and starts to become Odysseus again.

In this first interaction with another character that we see in the *Odyssey*, in this conversation with Kalypso, the bard sets up several crucial points about Odysseus' character and, as so often, about underlying themes of the *Odyssey*. First off, one of the hallmarks of Odysseus' character throughout the *Odyssey* is his caution. When Kalypso comes to him, as he is sitting on the seashore weeping for his lost homeland, and says, "I have decided to let you go home," Odysseus does not immediately jump up, say, "Great, lead me to a ship or a raft or something; let's go, let's get started on arranging for my homecoming." Instead, he is cautious; he makes Kalypso swear that she is not plotting some trick against him. He makes her swear a great oath by the River Styx—which is the inviolable oath of the gods; when a god promises by the River Styx, the god is bound by that promise. Odysseus makes Kalypso swear by the River Styx that she is not tricking him, not planning to hurt him, not scheming something to harm him. So his caution is foregrounded here in his very first interaction with another character in the *Odyssey*.

Another very important point that comes out in his interactions with Kalypso, here in Book Five, is that Odysseus understands and even welcomes the human condition. Kalypso offers Odysseus immortality; she tells him that he may stay with her on her island and that she will make him an immortal; she will make him a god, in effect. Now, Greek mythology is absolutely permeated with stories of human beings who try to gain immortality. These attempts almost inevitably end in utter disaster. Perhaps the most frightening story of a human who becomes an immortal and has a disastrous ending for him, is the story of Tithonos, who was made immortal by his lover, the dawn goddess. But she forgot to ask for agelessness, so that Tithonos was and is immortal, can never die, will live forever; but grows forever older and older and older and older. That, I think, is a paradigmatic story, to indicate that immorality is inappropriate for human beings; it does not work for human beings. The crucial dividing line between humans and gods, between those two types of entities, is that humans must die while gods cannot die. So, despite the fact that Greek myth is filled with stories of humans who want immortality, immortality almost never works for humans.

Odysseus seems to understand this; when Kalypso offers him what so many humans think they want beyond all else, a chance at eternal life, he rejects it. He wants humanity; he wants to be Odysseus; he wants to return home. By rejecting Kalypso's offer of immortality, Odysseus is implicitly accepting and, as I said, even welcoming the human condition, even though that implies age and death, even though he has now missed twenty years out of his life, Penelope's life, Telemachos' life—still he prefers to return home, as a human, than to become an immortal, but no longer truly be Odysseus. His desire to return home is in fact, I think, precisely that—a desire to return to his full humanity and his true selfhood. In a very real sense, Odysseus is not Odysseus, away from Penelope, Telemachos, and his father Laertes, Ithaka. An individual in isolation, in the culture that we are shown in the Homeric epics, is scarcely a human individual at all. Just as Achilles' self-imposed isolation in the *Iliad* cuts him off, in a very real sense, from being human, and he is only reintegrated into his humanity at the end of the *Iliad*, when he reaccepts the human condition including death, so here, Odysseus separated from community, separated from family, separated from home, is not truly Odysseus. His choice to return home rather than staying with Kalypso is a choice to return to being himself, to being Odysseus.

Now one of the most important aspects of Odysseus' character is his skill in rhetoric and persuasion. We'll see him, over and over again throughout the

Odyssey, crafting his speech to appeal to his audience; moving what he says into a pattern in which the people he is talking to will be most receptive to it; thinking of whom he is talking to before he says whatever he has to say. Our first example of this has to do especially with what I have just been talking about, Kalypso's offer of immortality and Odysseus' rejection of it. After she has told him—after Kalypso has told him that she is going to send him home, and he has made her swear that she is not trying to trick him, they eat a meal together; and we are given the detail that he eats regular human food, while she eats nectar and ambrosia. She is, in fact, a goddess. And then Kalypso reminds him that she has in fact offered him immortality. She says, "If you knew all the troubles you'd go through before you make it home, I think you would rather stay with me. I can make you immortal, and besides—what is so great about Penelope anyway? Do you really like her better than me? is she really better looking? I am a goddess, and she is just a human being."

Now Odysseus is in a very touchy situation here. It is not wise to offend, annoy, or anger a god or a goddess; they can do very unpleasant things to human beings. Kalypso has just said to him, "Why do you prefer Penelope to me? Do you really think your wife is better looking than I am?" And she puts it in terms of physical appearance—"Is Penelope more beautiful than I am?" Odysseus has to craft his answer to that very, very carefully. He has got to think of some way to say to Kalypso, "I want to go home," without insulting her, without her annoying her. Listen to what he actually says:

> Goddess and queen, do not be angry with me. I myself know
> that all you say is true and that circumspect Penelope
> can never match the impression you make for beauty and stature.
> She is mortal after all, and you are immortal and ageless.
> But even so, what I want and all my days I pine for
> is to go back to my house and see my day of homecoming.

Notice what he does not say. He does not say, "But Kalypso, I love Penelope and I don't love you"; he doesn't say, "But she is my wife and you are not." He doesn't even say, "But she is a human being and so am I, and I want a human being, not a goddess." He says, "I want my home"; he puts it in terms that Kalypso can hear without an affront to her sense of dignity, without annoying her, without angering her. This is just the first, very brief, example of Odysseus' skill at rhetoric that I will come back to over and over again, both in this lecture and in later lectures.

So, with Kalypso's help, Odysseus builds a raft; she gives him provisions—wine, water, food—and he leaves her island. He sails on his raft for eighteen days and is very near to the island where he will in fact make landfall, the island of Scheria where he will be met with excellent *xenia* and helped on his way home. However, on the eighteenth day of Odysseus' journey, Poseidon sees him on his raft, and Poseidon wrecks the raft. Now, Poseidon hates Odysseus for reasons that will become abundantly obvious in a later lecture. And it is an interesting little detail about the Homeric picture of the gods that Athena had seized an opportunity when Poseidon was, so to speak, out of town to motivate Zeus to help Odysseus in the first place. Poseidon has been off in Ethiopia, getting sacrifices from the Ethiopians. When the *Odyssey* opens, we are told that is why Athena speaks to Zeus right then—Poseidon is away. It gives Athena a chance to do something behind Poseidon's back. In other words, these gods, though they know a great deal, are not omniscient. Poseidon doesn't know what is going on when he is off in Ethiopia.

Now, we are told that Poseidon is coming back from Ethiopia; he is striding across the sea; and he looks down and sees Odysseus on a raft. And Poseidon realizes that Odysseus is fated to return home. Gods cannot, or at least do not, intervene with fate to the extent of changing it, but Poseidon says to himself, "Well, I can't keep Odysseus from reaching Scheria and then going home, but I can make some more trouble for him," and that is what Poseidon does. He wrecks Odysseus' raft, Odysseus is left swimming for his life, literally, and after two nights and two days swimming alone on the open sea, Odysseus finally washes up on the shores of the island Scheria. When he arrives there he is naked, battered, starved, basically more dead than alive. He has been smashed against the cliffs around the island, he's battered and bruised and torn and bloody and covered with salt from the sea, and just generally in really terrible shape. When he washes up finally onto a river on the island of Scheria, he prays to the god of the river to help him, and it does; it pulls him up on the island. Odysseus crawls out of the river, and as Book Five of the *Odyssey* ends, he falls asleep more dead than alive in a pile of leaves. Homer uses a simile, saying that Odysseus buries himself in pile of leaves like a man will bury a burning log in a pile of ashes to preserve the fire overnight—a very vivid image of how the little spark of life left in Odysseus at this point.

Odysseus doesn't know it, but he is on an island where he will get the best possible *xenia* any one could hope for. The people of this island, the people of Scheria, are called the Phaiakians. I know it seems like they should be called the Scherians but it is not that simple; they lived in a place called Phaiakia before it they immigrated to Scheria and they kept their name, the Phaiakians. They are particularly dedicated to *xenia* and to helping people homeward, particularly to providing ships for stranded travelers. So, Odysseus is actually in very good shape. However, Odysseus is sleeping in a pile of leaves by a river; the Phaiakians are off in their city. Somehow, Odysseus has to be found by the Phaiakians before they can help him, and he is in such terrible shape that he is not just going to be able to spring up the next morning and go off looking for help himself. Athena comes to his rescue, as she has done already in the *Odyssey* and will do again. She is his particular patron deity, and here she engineers a very clever way for Odysseus to be found and helped. Athena appears in a dream to the young Phaiakian princess, Nausikaa, and inspires the young girl to go and do the family's laundry by the river where Odysseus is sleeping.

Now, Nausikaa is, I think, in most readers' estimations, one of the most vividly memorable and just basically appealing characters in the *Odyssey*. She appears only in this one section, and she is really given much attention only in Book Six, and yet she is drawn so vividly that she stays in readers' minds even when some of the more major characters in the *Odyssey* perhaps have faded. She is about fourteen years old, which in this culture is about the age to get married. And she is clearly anticipating getting married; no fiancé has been picked for her yet, but that doesn't matter because in a society where marriages are arranged the important fact is that she is of an age to get married, and she is thinking about her marriage. In fact, when she tells her father, the king of the Phaiakians, Alkinoos, that she needs to use the wagon to go take the laundry down to the river and wash it, her father recognizes that what she is thinking about—though she doesn't come right out and say it—is washing clothes for her upcoming marriage. So, Nausikaa is about to be married, but no lucky bridegroom has actually been picked yet.

Nausikaa takes several slave-women with her, girls about her own age. They do the laundry, and then spread the clothes out on the ground to dry. While they are waiting for the clothes to dry, they pass the time by playing a game of catch, tossing a ball back and forth. One of them misses the ball; it falls into the river, and the splash of the ball in the water awakes Odysseus. Now, upon waking, Odysseus first wonders where he is, then analyses and reacts to his situation. When he first wakes up, he says to himself some lines that he will repeat in two other crucially important situations in the *Odyssey*. He wakes up and says to himself—wondering where he is and if the people there know *xenia*, he says to himself:

> What are the people whose land I have come to this time,
> and are they violent and savage, and without justice
> or hospitable to strangers, with a godly mind?

Notice what he is doing there; he is naming *xenia* as the defining characteristic of civilization. Are these people violent and savage and without justice, on the one hand, or are they hospitable to strangers? *Xenia* here stands for all of civilization.

First he says these lines to himself; then he starts to ponder what exactly he should do. He is, to put it mildly, in an awkward situation. As I have already established, he is stark naked, his clothes have been torn off of him, he is bruised and battered, his hair is matted, he is covered with dry seaweed and salt and so on; and he hears the voices of the maidens, and peeking out from the shrubbery, he sees there are a bunch of young girls out here. Now, how is he to approach them without terrifying them? How can a naked, battered, bruised, wild-looking man come bursting out of the bushes and get these girls to stand still and listen to him long enough to persuade them that he is not going to hurt them? It is a very tricky situation, to put it mildly. It is a scene with a lot of humor in it, I think, particularly when we are told Odysseus ponders whether he should run up to Nausikaa, who is clearly the leader of these girls, and throw himself at her feet and grab her knees—or whether that might possibly anger or annoy her. I think that has got to be meant humorously; that he would even entertain the idea of bursting out of the bushes, running up to her and grabbing her—no, this is not the proper approach to take under this situation. And as he thinks it over, he decides it would be better to stand back and supplicate her with words, rather than with the usual standard gestures of supplication where you do kneel in front of someone and grab their knees with your arm.

The scene is humorous, and yet there is a serious underside to it. There is an implicit threat of rape in this scene; there is an implicit secondary story that could be a rape story here. In Greek literature and Greek mythology, the seashore is a particularly dangerous area for young girls. There are many stories of young girls being raped when they were at the seashore, when they were near the coast. Young girls, in this society, almost never would be out without male protectors of some sort or another. Perhaps that is one reason for the association of the seacoast with rape or abduction; that going to do the laundry near the mouth of a river is one of the few times women would be by themselves, so it is one of the few times they would be vulnerable. Also, piracy was a problem in the ancient world; obviously, a woman on a seacoast would be vulnerable to being abducted by pirates for sexual purposes, or to be sold into slavery. More generally than that, just the idea of a young girl off by herself—as far as male protection is concerned; Nausikaa has her maids with her, of course—and a naked man bursting out of the bushes and running towards her; clearly there is the possibility that this could be misread as a rape scene by Nausikaa, or that if these characters were not who they are, it could turn into exactly that sort of a situation.

So, Odysseus has got to find some way to persuade Nausikaa that he won't hurt her, without offending her, without frightening her by saying, specifically, that he won't hurt her. He plucks a branch to cover his genitals and walks out of the bushes. The other girls scatter; they run away. Athena puts courage into Nausikaa's heart, and she stands and waits for Odysseus to speak to her. His interaction with Nausikaa, once again, demonstrates his superb skill in rhetoric and his ability to fit his words to his audience. In fact, Odysseus' speech to Nausikaa here, where he is trying to gain her favor and get her to help him, is, I think, one of the finest pieces of rhetoric in the *Odyssey*, and actually one of my favorite bits from the entire *Odyssey*. He approaches her, stands off from her, doesn't come too close to her— remember he is holding a branch in front of himself—and he says to her:

> I am at your knees, O queen. But are you mortal or goddess?
> If indeed you are one of the gods who hold wide heaven,
> then I must find in you the nearest likeness to Artemis
> the daughter of great Zeus, for beauty, figure and stature.
> But if you are one among those mortals who live in this country,
> three times blessed are your father and the lady, your mother,

And he goes on to say that he has never seen anything so beautiful as Nausikaa before in his life.

He starts out by saying, "I think you must be a goddess"; his mention of the specific goddess, Artemis, is very carefully chosen. Artemis is one of three goddesses who remain forever virgin. The other two are Athena, the goddess of wisdom and war, and Hestia, the goddess of the hearth. But Artemis is a far more militant virgin than the other two. There are many stories about the goddess Artemis inflicting terrible punishments on men who in any way seemed to trespass upon her chastity. One story of man who saw Artemis naked, inadvertently, he didn't mean to, but he saw Artemis naked—his punishment was to be turned into a stag and torn apart by his own hunting hounds, while his mind remained human and he knew what was happening to him. In other words, if ever there was a goddess that no man in his right mind would think about approaching sexually, that goddess is Artemis.

So think of what Odysseus has just done. He has said to Nausikaa, "Do not worry, I am not planning to assault you." He has said, "I think you must be Artemis," which carries with it entire subtext of "and since I think you must be Artemis, I am in no way going to assault you, I am in no way going to hurt you, I am going to keep my distance; you are in power here." But by putting it that way, by saying "I think you must be Artemis," he has avoided actually having to say, "I am not going to rape you"—because of course if he says that, he indicates that at least the thought was in his mind, in some sense, in a negative way. So, he has reassured Nausikaa. He has also put in some pretty good flattery here. "You look like Artemis; if you are human your parents are incredible blessed; I have never seen anything so beautiful in my life."

He goes on to say, "Well, actually, I did see one thing so beautiful once before; a palm tree growing by the temple of Apollo on the island of Delos." This establishes that he is a civilized man, that he knows about Apollo, he knows about Apollo's sacred island of Delos; he is well-traveled. Then, moving along, he says, "Have pity, O queen." He tells her about his adventures and how he was shipwrecked:

> Have pity, O queen. You are the first I have come to
> after much suffering, there is no one else that I know of here …
> Show me the way to the town and give me so rag to wrap me
> in, if you had any kind of piece of cloth when you came here.

The laundry is spread out drying on the ground, remember—"give me some rag to wrap me in."

> and then may the gods give you everything that your heart longs for;
> may they grant you a husband and a house and sweet agreement
> in all things.

At the end of the speech, you see, he makes it very clear that he knows precisely what she is. She is not a goddess; she is a young girl who is the right age to be married. When he gets to the end of his speech, after he has called her a goddess, then he has called her a queen, then finally he says, "May the gods give you what you want—and of course what you want is a husband, a house of your own, and a really good marriage." So he has established his credentials, he has made it clear that he is superbly civilized, that he knows exactly how to act, and he has done it all in an extremely carefully-crafted speech that appeals to her and in no ways threatens her.

She responds in kind. She knows *xenia*; she knows how to help him. She gives him clothing, she gives him food, and she calls her attendants to help Odysseus bathe. Now, in the culture of the Homeric poems, women bathe men. Men sit in a tub, and women come in and bathe them. In Book Three of the *Odyssey*, Telemachos is bathed by Nestor's youngest daughter, so there is nothing at all odd about Nausikaa offering her maids as help for Odysseus to take a bath in the river. And yet Odysseus says no; he says, "I will bathe myself; I would be ashamed to appear naked in front of these young girls." I think that, again, is an indication of just how delicate he is being here, in this situation with no men around; better not to have any contact with these young girls at all.

Athena beautifies Odysseus after he bathes, and Nausikaa comments to her maidens that she would be happy to marry him, if only he would stay on Scheria. As he walks out of the river, Athena has made him look younger and more beautiful, and Nausikaa looks at him and says, "Well, he looks much better than he did a few minutes ago." As Book Six ends, Nausikaa gives Odysseus instructions about going to the palace in Scheria to approach her parents and ask for help. And in her speech she indicates that she is no less skilled in rhetoric than Odysseus is. She tells him, "Start out following me into the city; walk along with my wagon, but when we get to the city gates," she says, "hold back; don't come into the city with me. Wait till I have gone in, then you come in by yourself and ask someone directions." Because otherwise, she says, someone who saw us together might say:

> 'Who is this large and handsome stranger who Nausikaa
> has with her and where did she find him? Surely, he is
> to be her husband' ...

And then she goes on quoting this fictitious somebody, who might say, "Well, maybe this is a god who has come down to marry her, or maybe she found him herself somewhere else; and that is actually a good thing, because:

> 'she pays no heed to her own Phaiakian
> neighbors, although many of these and the best ones court her.'
> So, they will speak, [she says,] and that would be scandal against me,
> and I myself would disapprove of a girl who acted
> so, that is without the good will of her dear father
> and mother making friends with a man, before formally married

This she says to the man she has just made friends with, without her parents knowing it.

Think of what she has done here. She has told him her name; she has told him that she is being courted by all sorts of really noble men but doesn't like any of them; she has told him that she is very willing to marry him if he is willing to marry her; and she has wrapped that all up in saying, "I would disapprove of any one who said this to a man." It is a wonderful little speech. She has put her proposal of marriage to him in a way that leaves him able to refuse her without having to refuse her; he doesn't have to say to her, "I don't want to marry you," or "I am already married," or anything else, because she has never proposed marriage at all. She has said exactly what she would *not* do.

So as Book Six ends, Nausikaa has made her interest in Odysseus clear. She has also helped him; she has provided *xenia* for him, she has told him to go to her parents' palace to get more complete *xenia*, and as we move on into the next lecture, we will examine how the people of Scheria, particularly Nausikaa's parents, entertain Odysseus royally and do in fact find finally send him on his way. We will also see Odysseus begin his own first-person narrative of his wanderings from Troy to Kalypso's island.

Lecture Four
Odysseus among the Phaiakians

Scope: This lecture continues to follow Odysseus' interactions with the Phaiakians, and moves on into the beginnings of his own great narrative of his past adventures. The lecture addresses several key themes, including the continued importance of *xenia* as offered by the Phaiakians and how the conception of *kleos* in the *Odyssey* differs from that of the *Iliad*. We discuss the role of the bard Demodokos in Book VIII, and how his appearance at this point of the narrative may reflect the original three-day performance structure of the *Odyssey*. Moving on into Book IX and Odysseus' first-person narrative, we see how the encounter with the Cyclops Polyphemos both shows Odysseus at his most clever and quick-thinking and causes all his subsequent troubles.

· Outline

I. With Athena's assistance, Odysseus reaches the palace of Alkinoos and Arete, and asks for their assistance.

   A. Disguised as a young girl, Athena leads Odysseus, concealed in a mist, through the city to the palace.

   B. Athena stresses the importance of Arete, the queen, in Phaiakian society. As we will see, Odysseus takes this into account in his later interactions with the royal couple.

II. The Phaiakians make a point of providing *xenia* and transportation to any shipwrecked travelers who land upon their island. Odysseus is thus entertained royally, with athletic games and with a bard's songs.

   A. The athletic games show us Odysseus in his past aspect of warrior, as he was in the *Iliad*.

   1. Athletic games are, in effect, practice for battle.

   2. When the young Euryalos says that Odysseus does not look like an athlete, therefore, he is in effect saying "you're no warrior."

   3. This insult so angers Odysseus that he reveals who he is—if anyone is listening carefully.

B. The songs of the bard Demodokos reiterate some of the crucial themes of the Trojan war story.

    1. Demodokos' first song tells of a quarrel between Odysseus and Achilles, which in essence honors Odysseus.

    2. Demodokos' second song recounts the love affair of Ares and Aphrodite.

    3. Demodokos' third song, at Odysseus' explicit request, tells the story of the Trojan Horse.

III. As Demodokos sings of the Trojan Horse, Odysseus weeps.

    A. The bard uses one of the most memorable similes of the *Odyssey* to describe his weeping.

    B. This song, which proves to Odysseus that his deeds have not been forgotten, that he has earned *kleos* (as though dead), also leads to his revelation of his identity to the Phaiakians after Alkinoos asks why he is weeping.

IV. Performance time is worth considering again. If the *Odyssey* was originally performed over three days, the end of Book VIII would coincide with the end of the first day's performance.

    A. In this context, Odysseus' compliment to the bard Demodokos is noteworthy.

    B. The end of Book VIII would make an excellent stopping point; the audience would certainly come back the next day!

V. As Book IX begins, Odysseus again praises Demodokos, then introduces himself to the Phaiakians and begins his story.

    A. Odysseus' words, "I am Odysseus, son of Laertes…and my *kleos* reaches the sky," stress the difference in *kleos* as it is conceived of in the *Iliad* and in the *Odyssey*. In *nostos* poetry, the hero's *kleos* does not depend upon his death.

    B. Odysseus' introduction begins a four-book section of first-person narrative, often called "The Great Wanderings." This is the section of the *Odyssey* in which Odysseus' memorable adventures with monsters, sorceresses, and so on are recounted.

VI. Odysseus begins his narrative with the Greeks' departure from Troy. The first adventures he narrates are straightforward, every-day acts of warfare. But very soon, he leaves the realm of the every day and moves into the realm of marvels, where every adventure presents danger to him and his companions.

    A. The lotus-eaters offered forgetfulness and pleasure.

    B. The Cyclops Polyphemos kills six of Odysseus' men and threatens to kill the rest.

VII. Odysseus' encounter with Polyphemos is perhaps the most famous of all his adventures. Certainly it is one of the most important; it highlights *xenia*, shows Odysseus at his most quick-thinking, and motivates all his further troubles.

    A. The episode's importance is marked out at its beginning by Odysseus' repetition of the formulaic lines he spoke at his arrival on Scheria, identifying *xenia* as the hallmark of civilization.

        1. On Scheria Odysseus receives the best imaginable *xenia*, but from Polyphemos he receives its exact opposite.

        2. Polyphemos obeys none of the protocols of proper behavior, and in fact eats six of Odysseus' men.

    B. This adventure shows Odysseus at his quick-thinking, clever best.

        1. He devises a successful plan to blind the Cyclops. He gets Polyphemos drunk, and then blinds him while he is asleep.

        2. He tells the monster that his name is "Outis," or "Nobody." Thus, when the Cyclops calls out for help to his friends, they all think that "nobody" is hurting him.

        3. Once the Cyclops is blinded, Odysseus and his companions escape from the cave by clinging to the bellies of Polyphemos' sheep.

    C. But this adventure also causes all the rest of Odysseus' troubles, because as he sails away he calls out his true name to Polyphemos. This allows the Cyclops to curse him. There are two possible explanations for why Odysseus reveals his name.

        1. He does so through excessive pride.

        2. He does so through a desire to perpetuate his own *kleos*.

Essential Reading:

Odyssey, Books VII–IX.

Supplementary Reading:

Jenny Strauss Clay, *Wrath of Athena*, Chapter 2, "Odysseus and Achilles," pp. 96–112; "Odysseus and Polyphemus," pp. 112–125.

Steven Lowenstam, *Scepter and Spear*, Chapter 3, Section 1, pp. 149–173.

Questions to Consider:

1. Is Demodokos' second song, the story of the love affair between Ares and Aphrodite, merely entertainment, or is it connected thematically with the rest of the *Odyssey*?

2. Do you think Odysseus' telling Polyphemos his name is an instance of reckless pride, or is he justified in doing so?

Lecture Four—Transcript
Odysseus among the Phaiakians

Hello, and welcome to Lecture Four. In the previous lecture, we discussed Odysseus' departure from Kalypso's island and his arrival at Scheria, where he met and was helped by the Phaiakian princess, Nausikaa. We saw how crucial aspects of Odysseus' character, his caution and his skill in rhetoric, in particular, were foregrounded from his very first appearance in the *Odyssey*. In this lecture, we will continue to examine Odysseus' interaction with the Phaiakians and we will see him begin his own first-person narrative of his adventures from Troy to Kalypso's island.

As we move into Book Seven of the *Odyssey*, with Athena's assistance Odysseus reaches the palace of Nausikaa's parents, Alkinoos and Arete, and asks for their help. Athena hides Odysseus by concealing him in a mist so that as he moves through the city of the Phaiakians no one sees him or knows that he is there. Athena herself is disguised as a young girl when she meets Odysseus and leads him to the palace of the Phaiakian queen and king. Athena, in her discussion of Phaiakian society with Odysseus, stresses the importance of Queen Arete. She tells him to beseech the queen, rather than the king, for aid when he arrives at the palace. This reiterates the instructions that Nausikaa had given him at the end of Book Six, when she tells him, "Speak first to my mother and ask her for help." Athena points out that in the society of the Phaiakians, Arete, the queen, is held in reverence almost equal to that of a god, and Athena says that Arete settles disputes even among men. So she is an unusually powerful woman. As we'll see later on Odysseus remembers this advice and takes it into account in his dealings with the royal couple, Arete and Alkinoos.

So Odysseus arrives at the palace of the Phaiakian king and queen; he goes inside; and Athena lifts the mist away from him and disappears herself, so that Odysseus is suddenly visible to Queen Arete and King Alkinoos. Following the advice of both Athena and Nausikaa, Odysseus does indeed go first to Arete, clasp her knees, and ask her for assistance. She greets him cordially, promises him any thing he needs—again, such as a meal, a place to sleep, all of those hallmarks of *xenia*—and also promises to give him a ship that will send him home to Ithaka. So Odysseus now has arrived among a people who will help him to reach Ithaka, and who will in fact give him a ship and an escort to get him there. Not only are they going to help him home—the Phaiakians pride themselves on providing *xenia* to any ship-wrecked wanderer and to helping any traveler who needs their help home to his own land—Odysseus will be entertained royally during his stay on the island of Scheria, and Book Eight, in fact, of the *Odyssey* is devoted to the entertainment that is provided for Odysseus by King Alkinoos and Queen Arete.

This entertainment takes two main forms. Odysseus is treated to a display of athletic games, in the first place, and secondly, he is entertained by listening to the songs of the bard, Demodokos, who in Book Eight sings three different songs to Odysseus and to the assembled Phaiakians. I want to talk about both of these forms of entertainment—first, the athletic games, and second, the songs of the bard, Demodokos. They are actually interleaved with one another in Book Eight. Demodokos sings a song, and then there are some athletic games, then Demodokos sings another song, and so on. But I want to separate them for purposes of discussing them.

The athletic games that are performed for Odysseus show us Odysseus in his past aspect of warrior, as he was in the *Iliad*. That may not seem immediately obvious; what do athletic games have to do with Odysseus being a warrior? But the answer to that question is in the context of Homeric epics, athletic games have everything to do with Odysseus, or anyone else, being a warrior. Athletics in the *Iliad* and the *Odyssey* are, in effect, practice for warfare. These are not athletics engaged in for the purpose of sport as we might think of sport; they are not something there purely for entertainment or for physical exercise. They are specifically practice for battle. Readers of the *Iliad* will remember in Book Twenty-Three, Achilles' dead friend Patroklos is honored by "funeral games," as they are usually described, athletic games held in his honor. There again, those games are practice of the kinds of maneuvers that Patroklos' fellow soldiers would have to perform in the battlefield. Chariot-racing; contests in throwing the spear; contest in throwing the discus; running races, jumping contests—all of those things are activities that would be useful on the battlefield and are therefore a stylized kind of practice for battle.

So the point of this for Odysseus, in Book Eight of the *Odyssey*, is that at one point in the games a young Phaiakian man named Euryalos says to Odysseus—first invites him to take part in the contests, and when Odysseus refuses, Euryalos says to Odysseus that he does not look like an athlete. He says, "I am not surprised that you don't want to take part in these contests, because you do not resemble an athlete." This comment makes Odysseus absolutely furious; the reason, of course, is that to say to him "You don't resemble an athlete" equals saying to him "You don't resemble a warrior;

you don't look like a fighting man; you don't look like a soldier," and those are words that Odysseus cannot tolerate. In fact, this is so grievous an insult, and makes Odysseus so angry, that he actually, if any one is listening carefully, reveals who he is. And that is a very important moment of Odysseus slipping, and giving way to his emotion, in a way that normally he does not in the *Odyssey*. He has not, up until this point, told the Phaiakians who he is. Arete had asked him; after he had had a meal, after his needs had been attended to, she asked who he was. Odysseus did not answer at that point. He told the story of his captivity on Kalypso's island, but he did not say who he, himself, was.

At this point in Book Eight, however, when Euryalos says, "You don't look like an athlete," Odysseus reacts in two ways. First, he seizes the discus, and manages to throw it further than anyone else who has competed so far has thrown it, of course; and secondly, he says to Euryalos and anyone who is listening, "I was excellent at all forms of warfare," he starts out by saying; but then he focuses in on archery. He says, When we Achaians were fighting at Troy, I was second-best with the bow; only Philoktetes was better than I was at using the bow and arrow." Now, if anyone is listening carefully—anyone of the Phaiakians—and knows about the Trojan War, they would recognize that this must be Odysseus. He has just given away— elliptically, yes, but he has just given away his identity. This is one of the few times, as I said, in the *Odyssey* when we see Odysseus giving way to an emotion, and letting a clue that he had wanted to hold back slip, as he does in this scene. The athletic games, therefore, are not an unqualified success as entertainment for Odysseus, because he ends up being insulted and feeling aggrieved by Euryalos saying that he doesn't look like a warrior or like an athlete.

The songs of the bard Demodokos, the other form of entertainment that we're shown in Book Eight, are both more successful as entertainment for Odysseus—or least, apparently more successful as entertainment for Odysseus—and also are, again, extremely important thematically for our transition from the earlier part of the *Odyssey* to Odysseus' own narrative of his wanderings after the fall of Troy. Demodokos sings three different songs, and among the three of them they reiterate some of the crucial themes of the Trojan War story. So they too, in a way, look back to Odysseus in his role as warrior, Odysseus from the *Iliad* rather than Odysseus who is now on his way home to Ithaka.

Demodokos' first song tells of a quarrel between Odysseus and Achilles while the Greeks were at Troy. Now, this is the only reference in extant ancient Greek literature to a quarrel between Odysseus and Achilles at Troy; no other author mentions this. It is worth taking a moment to consider what that might mean. There are two possibilities of what that might mean; first, that Homer, the composer of the *Odyssey*, whoever he was, invented this episode, simply made it up, decided that Demodokos would sing about a quarrel between Odysseus and Achilles, for whatever reason that the bard wanted to make that up. That is one possibility. Another possibility, of course, is that this quarrel was mentioned elsewhere in other ancient literature, but that other ancient literature has not survived to the present day. This is a problem we confront very frequently in dealing with classical literature; when something is mentioned only once in the literature we have, does that mean it was really mentioned only onc,e or does that mean, by the vicissitudes of what has survived and what hasn't, we happen to have only one mention of it?

Whichever is true in this case, Demodokos sings about a quarrel between Odysseus and Achilles, and says that Agamemnon rejoiced to see these two, the best of the Achaians, quarrelling with one another, because Agamemnon remembered a prophecy that said Troy would fall soon after the best of the Achaians quarreled. This reiterates Odysseus' status—in terms of what this song is doing in the *Odyssey*, it reiterates Odysseus' status as second only to Achilles. Achilles was the greatest warrior; Odysseus was the most clever among the Greeks. Aias the Greater, as I have already mentioned, was the second greatest warrior, in terms of physical prowess, to Achilles, but if Agamemnon looks at Achilles and Odysseus quarrelling and thinks of a prophecy about when "the best of the Achaians" quarrel, that reiterates the status of Odysseus as one of the two best of the Achaians. It also of course lets Odysseus know, and lets us the audience know, that the Phaiakians are cognizant of the Trojan War story, know about the Trojan War, and know the name Odysseus.

Demodokos' second song recounts the love affair between the god Ares, the god of war, and Aphrodite, the goddess of sexual passion. Now, at first glance, this may not seem to have a great deal to do with the themes either of the *Odyssey* or, for that matter, of the Trojan War itself, but I think on closer inspection in fact it is very closely connected to the *Odyssey* and to the Trojan War. Ares and Aphrodite, after all, are having an adulterous love affair. They are not married to one another. Aphrodite, according to the *Odyssey*, is the wife of Hephaistos; Ares is not married. So on one level, the love affair between Ares and Aphrodite picks up on that subplot, or secondary plot, of the *Odyssey* that I have talked about already in earlier lectures—the idea of a wife being unfaithful to her husband in his absence, the fear that Odysseus has that Penelope may not wait for him. On another level, of course, it recalls the cause of the Trojan War in the first place, when Paris and Helen engaged in a similar adulterous love affair at Aphrodite's prompting and thereby caused the Trojan War. One more interesting point about Demodokos' second song is that it is sung after the episode when Euryalos tells Odysseus he doesn't look like an athlete; that is, it is sung out on the playing field, in the area where the Phaiakian men are engaging in athletic games. There are no women present. The other two songs of Demodokos are both sung in the palace when women—at least Arete and perhaps others—are listening. It is possible that this by Homeric standards slightly risqué story, of Ares and Aphrodite being caught in bed together by the other gods, was seen as appropriate for a male audience, but not as appropriate for a female audience. We don't know, of course, what Homer's actual audience would have been, whether male or female, mixed or what; we simply don't know.

Demodokos' third song, which is sung near the end of Book Eight, is sung at Odysseus' specific request. The day is ending; the athletic games are over, the Phaiakians and Odysseus with them are eating their evening meal, and Odysseus sends a choice piece of meat to the bard, Demodokos—cuts it and sends it across the room to the bard as a gift, and asks the bard to sing a specific song for him. He asks Demodokos to sing about the Trojan Horse, "the horse," he says, "that great Odysseus made, contrived," and he tells Demodokos, "if you could sing of it properly, then I will tell everyone that you are one of the greatest bards that ever lived." Demodokos does sing the story of the Trojan Horse; he sings it in exquisite detail, and as he sings, Odysseus weeps, listening to Demodokos sing the song of the Trojan Horse. Now, Odysseus' weeping at Demodokos' third song is described by the bard with one of the most memorable similes in the *Odyssey*. Demodokos is singing of the Trojan Horse, how Odysseus thought up this ruse that led to the Sack of Troy, and as Demodokos sings, Homer tells us Odysseus "melted, and from under his eyes the tears ran down, drenching / his cheeks." Now here comes the simile:

> As a woman weeps, lying over the body
> of her dear husband, who fell fighting for her city and people
> as he tried to beat off the pitiless day from city and children;
> she sees him dying and gasping for breath, and winding her body
> about him she cries high and shrill, while the men behind her,
> hitting her with their spear butts on the back and the shoulders,

force her up and lead her away into slavery, to have
hard work and sorrow, and her cheeks are racked with pitiful weeping.
Such were the pitiful tears Odysseus shed ...

The reason I say this is a remarkable simile is because of what, in context, it would inevitably bring into the audience's mind. Demodokos has just sung about the Trojan Horse, which accomplishes the Sack of Troy; Homer then compares Odysseus' weeping to a woman weeping when her city is being sacked. There is no other sack we could think of here, other than the Sack of Troy. So Odysseus' weeping at hearing Demodokos' song is compared to the weeping of Odysseus' victims, the victims of the Trojan Horse, when Troy falls. It is an amazing technique, on the bard's part, to remind us of both sides of the story. The Trojan Horse, from Odysseus' point of view, from the Greeks' point of view, was a magnificent stroke of genius that won the war. But from the Trojans' point of view, it was catastrophe, it was disaster. In this simile the bard shows us both sides at once, and reminds us—as the characters of Hektor and Andromache and Priam remind us in the *Iliad*, the bard reminds us here of the war's cost, of what the Greeks' victory meant to the Trojans.

An obvious question, of course, is why is Odysseus crying. Certainly, I don't think he is crying over any kind of grief for the Trojans; he must be crying for some other reason. I think, there, he is crying mainly through relief, through a kind of recognition that his name, his deeds, his exploits are remembered, that they have survived him. They have survived his absence. He has been, to all intents and purposes, dead from the world for all these years since the end of the Trojan War, while Kalypso was holding him captive. If he had said to Demodokos, "Sing about the Trojan Horse," and Demodokos said, "Sing about what?" Or he had said, "Sing about the Horse that Odysseus thought up," and Demodokos said, "Odysseus? No, someone else thought up the Trojan Horse," then Odysseus would know that his *kleos*, his reputation, his fame, had not survived his absence. Demodokos' song lets Odysseus know that his *kleos* is intact, that people do know about his most memorable exploit.

One more point before I move on from Demodokos' third song. It is worth considering performance time here. If, as many scholars believe, the *Iliad* and the *Odyssey* were designed to be performed over three-day periods, we are just now at about the end of the first day of performance time for the *Odyssey*; and this is a marvelous place to stop the first day's performance in many ways. One thing, one detail that I always like to bring out at this point, is how much emphasis is put on the bard here in Book Eight. This the fullest picture we get of a bard in either Homeric epic, and I like the idea that this beautifully detailed, loving, and admiring portrait of a bard comes right at the end of the first day's performance. I particularly like the idea that Odysseus sends Demodokos a tip; he sends him the best cut of meat from the roast pig that they are eating as recompense for Demodokos' skill in singing. This is almost, it seems to me, like Homer getting ready to pass the hat at the end of his own first day of singing, reminding the audience what a really marvelous thing a really good bard is. Another way in which this is very fitting to end the first day of performance is, things are coming to such an obvious point of tension in the story right now. Odysseus is about to reveal who he is; he is about to tell the Phaiakians his story; and he is about to be sent home to Ithaka. This is a point where you could be quite sure that the audience would come back for the second day of performance; nobody is going to want to leave it here, at this point.

As Book Nine begins, then, as we move on into Book Nine of the *Odyssey*, Odysseus again praises Demodokos, and then introduces himself at last to the Phaiakians and starts to tell his story. He responds to Alkinoos' asking him "Who are you?" Alkinoos sees Odysseus weeping—as we have talked about with this marvelous simile—Alkinoos sees Odysseus weeping and asks him, "Why do you weep when you hear about Troy?" By this time, Odysseus has been given ample proof that the Phaiakians are trustworthy, that they are helpful, that they will indeed give him gifts and send him on his way. What he needs to do, now, is charm them, impress them, so overwhelm them with his story—both its content and its style—that they will give him the best imaginable guest-gifts and send him on his way as helpfully as he could possibly hope for. So, he starts in on his own first-person narrative of his adventures. He tells them what by this time some, at least, if not most of them must have guessed; he says, "I am Odysseus, son of Laertes, and my *kleos* reaches the sky." Up until this moment, up until he heard Demodokos' third song, he would not have been able to say "my *kleos* reaches the sky"; now he can. These words stress, once again, the difference in *kleos* as it is conceived of in the *Iliad*, where the main point of *kleos*, of imperishable fame, is that it lives on after the warrior is dead; and *kleos* as it is conceived of in the *Odyssey*, where the living Odysseus is still very much concerned about his reputation, his fame, what is said about him. *Kleos* is still important in the *Odyssey*; it is simply the focus is changed, from *kleos* as immortality after one is dead to *kleos* as what people think about one while one is still alive.

Odysseus' introduction of himself begins a four-book section of first person narrative often called "The Great Wanderings." From Book Nine through Book Twelve, we are going to listen to Odysseus narrating his own adventures, in his own voice, his adventures from the time he left Troy until he arrived on Kalypso's island, where he was held prisoner for seven years. This is the section of the *Odyssey* in which the most memorable adventures Odysseus has—encounters with mermaids, monsters, sorceresses and so on—are recounted. And it is also a *tour de force* on the bard's part. A narration in a character's own voice that lasts for four hours is no small accomplishment, and it is particularly noteworthy that the bard keeps perfect control, through these four hours of performance time, of what Odysseus could know and what he could not know. The bard never slips; Odysseus never tells us something that requires the narrator's viewpoint. He never tells us something that the narrator, Homer, could know, we assume, but that the character, Odysseus, could not. Throughout these four books of the *Odyssey*, Odysseus recounts his adventures in the way that Odysseus would have seen them and could know about them.

He begins his narrative with the Greeks' departure from Troy. The first adventures he narrates are straightforward, everyday acts of warfare; sacking one last city that was an ally of the Trojans, getting a little bit more booty before he and his men head home for Ithaka. But very, very quickly, Zeus sends a storm that blows Odysseus and his men off course, and then the story leaves the realm of the everyday and moves into the realm of marvels, and every adventure Odysseus and his men meet presents danger to him and his companions. The first strange adventure they have, the first truly unusual adventure, is their encounter with the group of people called the Lotus-Eaters. Now the Lotus-Eaters, unlike most of the adventures Odysseus has, seem benign. They are friendly; they are peaceful; all they do is offer Odysseus and his men flowers of the lotus plant, and when you eat these flowers, you are overwhelmed with forgetfulness, pleasure, sleepiness—you want to do nothing but lie down under a tree and dream all day long. This is a pleasant danger, but it is a danger nevertheless, because many of Odysseus' men don't want to leave the land of the Lotus-Eaters. They want to stay there, eat lotus forever, and never return home to Ithaka. Odysseus has to drag some of them away, literally. The next adventure he recounts, however, is anything but benign. Perhaps the most famous of his adventures in the *Odyssey*, this next one is Odysseus' encounter with the Cyclops Polyphemos, the one-eyed giant who kills and eats six of Odysseus' men and threatens to kill the rest.

As I said, the encounter with Polyphemos is perhaps the most famous of all Odysseus' adventures; certainly, it is one of the most important. It highlights *xenia*, showing Odysseus at his most quickthinking and motivating all of his further troubles through an examination of negative *xenia*, as I like to call it, or *xenia* as it ought not to work, *xenia* being violated and ignored. The importance of the episode of the Cyclops Polyphemos is marked out at its very beginning by Odysseus' repetition of the same lines, the same formulaic lines that he said when he arrived on Scheria. When he is about to go explore the Cyclops' island he leaves eleven of his twelve ships moored on a nearby island; he takes his own ships and the companions from that ship, sails to Polyphemos' island, and goes to examine it, to find out who lives there, see what things are like there. And he says that he wants the rest of his crew to wait behind while he and his companions:

> go and find out about these people and learn what they are,
> whether they are savage and violent, and without justice,
> or hospitable to strangers and with minds that are godly.

Exactly the same words he had said when he landed on Scheria and woke up, when Nausikaa and her girls threw the ball into the river and that awoke him. Here he is wondering, again, are these people civilized—and *xenia* is equated with civilization—or are they savage; and he is going to find out, to his sorrow, this time they are savage. On Scheria, the first time we hear him say those lines, he receives the best imaginable *xenia*. On Polyphemos' island, he receives its exact opposite; Polyphemos obeys none of the protocols of *xenia*, none of the rules of proper behavior, in fact he violates *xenia* about as directly as one could possibly imagine it being violated. Rather than giving his guests a meal, he has his guests for his meal. He starts out by killing and eating two of Odysseus' men, and says he'll eat another two for breakfast, another two for supper the next day, and so on, until they are all gone.

Now Odysseus, in his encounter with the Cyclops Polyphemos, is at his quick-thinking, clever best. He has to come up with a scheme to get away from Polyphemos, and he has to come up with a scheme that gets him away from Polyphemos without killing the Cyclops. Why? Because Odysseus and his men are in a cave; the Cyclops is a giant; and he has rolled a boulder against the mouth of the cave. If Odysseus simply kills the giant Polyphemos, then he and his men will never escape; they will starve to death in the cave. So what he needs to do is think of some way to disable the Cyclops but not kill him, so that when the Cyclops next removes the stone for the door, Odysseus and his men can get out without the Cyclops knowing it. The obvious way to do this is to blind the Cyclops, and this is what Odysseus does. He gets Polyphemos drunk, and then blinds him while the Cyclops is sleeping off his drunkenness.

Before getting him drunk, Odysseus tells Polyphemos that his name is Outis a Greek name that sounds very much like the Greek word for nobody. This is a crucial part of the scheme, because when Polyphemos wakes up with his eye poked out, when he wakes up blinded and screaming in pain, he calls out to his neighbors, the other Cyclopes, for help—that is the plural, by the way; one Cyclops, several Cyclopes—Polyphemos calls out to the other Cyclopes for help and they call back, "Who is hurting you?" Polyphemos says, "Outis is hurting me; 'Nobody' is hurting me," and his fellow Cyclopes say, "Well, if nobody is hurting you, this must be some disease sent by the gods and you better pray to your father Poseidon to help you." (Polyphemos is a son of the sea god Poseidon.) So, the trick has two prongs to it; blind the Cyclops, tell him your name is Nobody; then, when he calls for help, his neighbors will not understand what he is saying and will not come to see if they can help him. Once Polyphemos is blinded, Odysseus and his companions escape from the cave by clinging to the bellies of Polyphemos' sheep. Polyphemos rolls the stone away from the door of the cave to let his flock of sheep out to graze; Odysseus and his men cling to their bellies; the blind Cyclops, feeling the backs of the sheep, doesn't know they are escaping.

Now, Odysseus ought, at this point, to be free and clear, and yet it is this episode of blinding the Cyclops that leads to all his further troubles, because Odysseus cannot resist—either because he wants to insure the survival of his own *kleos* or because at this instant he gives way to excessive pride; both interpretations are possible—Odysseus cannot resist calling back to the Cyclops, from on board ship, and telling the Cyclops his name. He calls back and says:

> Cyclops, if any mortal man ever asks you who it was
> that inflicted upon your eye this shameful blinding,
> tell him that you were blinded by Odysseus, sacker of cities.
> Laertes is his father, and he makes his home in Ithaka.

This statement of who it was who did this to Polyphemos allows Polyphemos to curse Odysseus by name; Polyphemos calls out to his father Poseidon and says:

> grant that Odysseus, sacker of cities, son of Laertes,

who makes his home in Ithaka, may never reach that home;
but if it is decided that he shall see his own people,
and come home to his strong-founded house and to his own country,
let him come late, in bad case, with the loss of all his companions,
in someone else's ship, and find troubles in his household

… which of course is exactly what will happen to Odysseus. So by telling Polyphemos, his name Odysseus has given Polyphemos the means to curse him, and it is this curse of the Cyclops that motivates all of Odysseus' future wanderings, all of his troubles from this point on out. In our next lecture we'll continue Odysseus' description of his journey for Troy, and we'll see how Polyphemos' curse takes effect almost immediately.

Lecture Five
Odysseus Tells His Own Story

Scope: We continue following Odysseus' own narrative of the Great
Wanderings in this lecture. We see how quickly Polyphemos'
curse takes effect, and how Odysseus is tormented by sailing
within sight of Ithaka, but then being driven away from it again.
The lecture examines Odysseus' encounter with Circe, and
discusses some of the implications of the sexual double standard
reflected in it and in the rest of the *Odyssey*. Finally, the lecture
looks at the first half of the pivotal episode in the Great
Wanderings, Odysseus' narrative of his trip to Hades. We examine
Odysseus' conversations there, especially those with the prophet
Teiresias and with his own mother Antikleia, and note how for the
first time in the *Odyssey* Odysseus himself is warned about the
suitors. The lecture ends with a discussion of the abrupt break in
the narrative where the poem returns briefly to the third-person
narrative, and examines the reasons for and effects of that break.

Outline

I. The Cyclops' curse takes effect almost immediately.

    A. Odysseus' next stop is at the island of Aiolos, king of the winds.
        Aiolos gives him all the winds in a bag, but unfortunately
        Odysseus' comrades open the bag just before they reach Ithaka.

    B. The released stormwinds blow them back to Aiolos, who refuses to
        help them a second time.

    C. The next place Odysseus lands is the country of the Laistrygones,
        where he loses all his ships but one.

II. The next adventure is another very famous one, Odysseus' encounter
    with the goddess Circe, an enchantress who turns half his men into
    pigs.

    A. One-half of the men go to Circe's palace under the command of
        Eurylochos, Odysseus' second-in-command.

    B. The encounter with Circe stresses one sub-theme of the *Odyssey*,
        Odysseus' ongoing danger from seductive females. Circe,
        Kalypso, and even Nausikaa all present a threat to his

homecoming, since each of them offers Odysseus the possibility of staying on with her.

C. Circe is in many ways a doublet of the other goddess, Kalypso. However, the two are opposites in their interactions with Odysseus.

    1. Circe is threatening at first, but becomes helpful after Odysseus proves invulnerable to her magic. She tells him what he needs to do to leave, and does not try to detain him longer than he wants to stay.

    2. Kalypso is helpful at first, but becomes a jailer of an unwilling prisoner. She detains Odysseus for much longer than he wants to stay and only lets him go at Zeus' direct command.

D. Both of these encounters reflect a sexual double standard. Penelope must remain faithful to Odysseus, but Odysseus is not expected to remain sexually faithful to Penelope during his travels. This double standard can be explained in at least two ways.

    1. The Homeric epics assume a masculine viewpoint throughout, and this may simply be an example of narrative wish-fulfillment for a male audience.

    2. In a traditional patriarchal society, female infidelity threatens the family structure in a way that male infidelity simply does not.

III. After one year, Odysseus decides to resume his journey. Circe tells him that he must first undertake another journey, to the Land of the Dead. There he must consult the soul of Teiresias the Theban, a great seer, to find out what he must do to reach home safely.

A. A journey to the land of the dead seems to be one element that the greatest heroes have in common; Theseus, Herakles, and Orpheus all undertook such journeys.

B. On a more psychological reading of the myth, Odysseus' journey (often called "The *Nekuia*") can be seen as marking the "death" of the warrior Odysseus and the "rebirth" of the Ithakan Odysseus.

IV. Within the context of the *Odyssey*, the *Nekuia* serves several purposes.

A. It allows Odysseus to gain knowledge of the state of affairs on Ithaka.

B. It allows the audience to see some of the main characters of the Trojan War, and thus provides a fitting pivotal point for the epic's turn from Odysseus' past to his future.

C. Within the narrative itself, it enchants and astounds Odysseus' Phaiakian audience.

V. Circe tells Odysseus to sail on the "streams of Ocean" to Persephone's land. Once there, he must sacrifice two sheep and pour their blood into a pit.

   A. The "streams of Ocean" refers to the belief that the disk of the world was surrounded by an ever- flowing river.

   B. "Persephone's land" is located only very vaguely, but provides an entrance to the Underworld.

VI. After following Circe's instructions, Odysseus meets and speaks with several ghosts during the *Nekuia*. The first main group includes Elpenor, Teiresias, Odysseus' mother Antikleia, and a whole list of great heroines.

   A. The ghost of Odysseus' young companion Elpenor speaks to him first.

   B. Teiresias gives Odysseus explicit instructions about what he must do to return home safely. He also warns Odysseus about the suitors.

   C. Next, Odysseus speaks to the ghost of his mother.
   1. This lets him have news of Penelope, Telemachos, and Laertes.
   2. His mother tells him that longing for him caused her death.
   3. Odysseus tries to embrace her, but cannot.

   D. Odysseus describes a long list of heroines who appeared to him, then abruptly breaks off his narrative.
   1. The break allows the bard to remind the audience of where Odysseus is and whom he is addressing.
   2. The break shows Arete responding very favorably to Odysseus' words; once again, Odysseus the clever rhetorician has considered his audience in crafting his speech.
   3. Alkinoos begs Odysseus to continue, and asks if he saw any of his comrades from Troy.

Essential Reading:

Odyssey, Books X and XI, lines 1–375.

Supplementary Reading:

Jenny Strauss Clay, *Wrath of Athena*, Chapter 2, "Cyclopes and Phaeacians," pp. 125–132.

Questions to Consider:

1. Odysseus stays a year with Circe, and apparently is not particularly eager to leave her. Contrast this with the image we get of him in Books I and V, where he longs desperately to return to Ithaka; is the mere passage enough to explain the difference, or is his character simply inconsistent in this regard?

2. Does Teiresias' prophecy about Thrinakia and Helios' cattle in effect offer Odysseus and his men a choice of two fates, similar to the two fates Achilles chose between in the *Iliad*? In a wider sense, is the overall picture of *moira* consistent between the two epics?

Lecture Five—Transcript
Odysseus Tells His Own Story

Hello, and welcome to Lecture Five. In Lecture Four, we saw Odysseus' entertainment by the Phaiakians, discussed the bard Demodokos at work, and began our examination of Odysseus' own first-person narrative of his adventures after the fall of Troy. This lecture will continue following Odysseus' narrative of his Great Wanderings. We'll see how quickly Polyphemos' curse takes effect, and how Odysseus is tormented by sailing within sight of Ithaka but not actually reaching it. We'll then examine Odysseus' encounter with the sorceress Circe, and discuss some of the implications of the sexual double standard reflected in this encounter and in the rest of the *Odyssey*. Finally, we'll end the lecture by looking at the first half of the pivotal episode in the Great Wanderings, Odysseus' narrative of his trip to Hades, the Underworld, where he speaks to the souls of the dead.

So, to start out with, the Cyclops' curse, which we saw at the end of the last lecture, takes effect on Odysseus almost immediately. The next place that Odysseus and his companions journey to, after leaving the Cyclops' island, is the island of Aiolos, king of the winds. Aiolos receives Odysseus with excellent *xenia*, shows him great hospitality, and as a parting gift, as a guest-gift, Aiolos gives Odysseus all the winds of the world tied up in a bag, except for the one wind necessary to blow Odysseus' fleet back home to Ithaka. This should be foolproof; the king of the winds himself has given Odysseus all the contrary winds shut up in a bag. Odysseus should be home free and clear, and indeed it is about to work; Odysseus says, in his narrative to the Phaiakians, that they had gotten so close to Ithaka that they could see people tending fires, they could see fires on their home island. When Odysseus, who had been piloting his ship, fell asleep, his comrades, thinking that the bag that Aiolos had given Odysseus must contain gold or jewels or some sort of other precious loot, opened the bag. All the winds blew out; Odysseus and his men are blown right back to Aiolos' island.

I wanted to call your attention to the little detail of "we could see people tending fires on Ithaka," as Odysseus says. Remember in Book One, when Athena says to Zeus that Odysseus is looking out over the water from Kalypso's island, longing to see even the smoke rising from the his own country? At this point, he has gotten that close; it is the same imagery. He has gotten close enough to see fires on the shores of Ithaka, and then he is driven back to Aiolos' island. When he returns to Aiolos' island, Aiolos refuses to help a second time. He says to Odysseus, "The gods must really hate you; no-one could be this unlucky. The gods have to really hate you, and I am not going to help someone whom the gods hate." He refuses to let Odysseus land again, and sends Odysseus on his way.

The next place Odysseus encounters is the land of the Laistrygones, and this is where he loses all of his ships but one. Up until this point, Odysseus has had a fleet of twelve ships. In his encounter with the Laistrygones, a cannibalistic race of giants—sort of parallel to the Cyclopes, although these do not have only one eye each—when he encounters the Laistrygones, Odysseus loses eleven of twelve ships, so he is stripped down now to just one ship with only a few remaining companions in it. He has gone from being the commander of a fleet, of a few hundred men at least, to being a commander of one ship with only a handful of companions left to him. So, as I said, the curse of Polyphemos the Cyclops has taken effect immediately, and horrifically. They were almost home, were driven back off course all the way to Aiolos' island, then immediately thereafter, Odysseus loses eleven of his twelve ships.

The next adventure that Odysseus and his few remaining companions have is probably, next to the adventure with Polyphemos the Cyclops, the second most famous of Odysseus' encounters. This is his encounter with the goddess Circe, who is a sorceress, a witch, and an enchantress—whatever you want to call it—with a particular tendency to turn men into animals. When Odysseus and his ship land on Circe's island, they don't know where they are. They don't know where they have landed; they have even lost their sense of direction, they are so confused from having been whirled about by the storm winds released from Aiolos' bag. They have no idea where they are; they decide to divide into two groups. Half of them will go and explore the island, see if they can figure out who lives there—there is a palace, smoke rising from the palace, some one lives there. The other half will stay with the ship and wait for the first group to report back. They draw lots as to who will go and investigate and who will stay behind. Odysseus' lot comes up that he will stay behind in the ship, and so the adventuresome group, the exploring group, goes out under the command of Odysseus' second-in-command, a man named Eurylochos.

Eurylochos and his half of Odysseus' comrades go to Circe's palace—it s Circe's palace—and when they arrive there, Eurylochos hides outside and watches, and thus is able to report back to Odysseus. Circe turns Odysseus' men into pigs; one of my students once asked me if these were the original male chauvinist pigs, and I think the answer probably has to be yes. At any rate, Eurylochos reposts back to Odysseus and tells him what has happened, and then Odysseus goes to see if there is anything he can do to overpower Circe, to rectify the situation, whatever. On his way to Circe's palace, Odysseus meet the god Hermes, who presents him with a magic plant, a little plant called moly, that will protect him from Circe so that she cannot enchant him. When Odysseus arrives at Circe's palace she tries to turn him into an animal as well, but when she finds that she can't because he is holding this magic plant, moly, she suggests they should go to bed together.

Now, at this point, there are a couple of things I want to discuss in this encounter with Circe. First of all, Odysseus' relationship with Circe stresses one sub-theme of the *Odyssey*, namely the ongoing danger that Odysseus faces from seductive females: Circe; Kalypso, who keeps him captive for seven years; even in her own very different and very innocent way, Nausikaa all present dangers, threats to Odysseus' homecoming, because each one of them offers Odysseus the possibility of staying on permanently with her. You will remember Kalypso wanted to turn him into an immortal and keep him as her husband. Nausikaa wanted him to stay on Scheria, marry her, and be her husband. Circe now offers him the opportunity to stay with her. So, each of one of these women, in a sense, is a threat to Odysseus' homecoming, to his reunion with his legitimate wife, Penelope.

Now, Circe and Kalypso are in many ways doublets of one another, repetitions of the same theme; each of them is a goddess, each of them is very powerful, and each of them is interested in Odysseus sexually and initiates a sexual relationship with him. However, Circe and Kalypso are opposites in a couple of very important ways. Circe starts out being threatening; she tries to enchant Odysseus she does enchant his men, and she only becomes helpful after she has begun by being threatening. After she discovers she can't work her magic on him, then she becomes, in fact, very helpful. She doesn't try to keep Odysseus longer than he wants to stay; she tells him what he needs to do to leave her; and she gives him provisions to send him on his way of her own free will, rather than because of a command from a god as is the case with Kalypso. Kalypso, on the other hand, is helpful at first. When Odysseus arrives on her island—as we'll see at the end of Book Twelve, when we discuss Book Twelve—when Odysseus arrives on Kalypso's island, he is utterly helpless, shipwrecked, all alone; she takes him in, feeds him, basically saves his life. But then she becomes threatening, because she won't let him go; she wants to keep him with her. So, Circe and Kalypso in some ways mirror one another, in some ways are the opposite of one another. Both of them, however, present a threat to Odysseus' actual homecoming. In fact, with Circe, Odysseus stays quite happily with her for an entire year and his companions have to remind him that it is time to get going again, that it is time to set sail for Ithaka once again.

These two encounters with Circe and Kalypso also, obviously, reflect a sexual double standard that is at play throughout the *Odyssey* and for that matter throughout the *Iliad* as well. One of the absolutely essential themes of the *Odyssey*, one of the essential questions of the *Odyssey*, is Penelope's fidelity. It is absolutely required that Penelope must remain faithful to Odysseus, and that is a crucial question that troubles Odysseus, that troubles the audience to some extent, I think, throughout the *Odyssey*. On the other hand, it is equally clear that Odysseus is in no way expected to remain sexually faithful to Penelope during his travels, or for that matter during the Trojan War. Readers of the *Iliad* will remember how, in the *Iliad*, the Greek soldiers at Troy have concubines; Achilles has a concubine Briseis, Agamemnon has a concubine Chryseis. It is their quarrel over these concubines that starts the action of the *Iliad*. It never seems to even cross anyone's mind that a Greek warrior away at Troy might remain sexually faithful to his wife at home. So, what is going on with this double standard?

I think it can be explained in at least a couple of ways—probably more than that, but I have a couple of explanations to offer for it. The first one, and one that my students often suggest on their own, is that the Homeric epics assume a masculine view point throughout. Whether Homer's original audience was entirely male or was mixed male and female, it is pretty clear that these epics take a masculine viewpoint, that they are written from the male point of view. And it is possible that this sexual double standard, in which Penelope not only has to remain faithful to Odysseus but doesn't seem to mind that he was not faithful to her—at the end of the *Odyssey*, when he tells Penelope all his adventures, we are told she listens with delight to everything he tells her, and he tells her about Circe and Kalypso—it is possible that this double standard reflects a kind of wishfulfillment on the part of the male bard or his male audience. Possibly, but I think actually that explanation is probably anachronistic. I think there is something else going on here.

The culture reflected in the *Iliad* and the *Odyssey* both is an absolutely patriarchal culture. In the society that we see in the Homeric epics, like in many traditional patriarchal societies where marriages are arranged, the purpose of marriage is to perpetuate the legitimate family. The purpose of marriage is to see to it that a man's legitimate male line continues on after him. Now, if that is the purpose of marriage, if that is the main point of having marriage in a society at all—to provide legitimate male heirs for each man in the society—female infidelity threatens that entire system. It threatens the legitimacy of children; it threatens the marriage bond, since marriage exists to provide for legitimate children; and it threatens society in general, since society cannot function without marriage and children. So if a married woman in such a society is unfaithful even once, then the whole question of the legitimacy of her children is called into doubt; the whole question of her proper behavior in her marriage is called into doubt. There is no way, before the invention of DNA typing, for a man to know that the children who are growing up in his household are his children; he has to be able to trust that his wife has never, not even once, had sex with anyone else.

So if Penelope were unfaithful even now, in Odysseus' absence, that could call into question the whole legitimacy of Telemachos; that could throw doubts on the whole question of whether Odysseus was in fact Telemachos' father or not, if Penelope has ever even once been unfaithful. Odysseus, on the other hand, can spread ten thousand illegitimate children around the Mediterranean if he desires, and that in no way calls Telemachos' legitimacy into question. So male sexual fidelity is not needed for this system of marriage as female sexual fidelity is; and given that that is the kind of marriage this society very clearly deals with, Odysseus is not—it really isn't even legitimate, no pun intended, to say that Odysseus is unfaithful to Penelope. No-one ever expected male fidelity in this sort of society. Odysseus has not committed adultery in the *Odyssey*, because adultery, by definition for him, would mean seducing another man's legitimate wife, and that he has not done. So the sexual double standard that we see so clearly reflected in the *Odyssey* and in the *Iliad* both, and in many other works of Greek literature, as infuriating as seems to many modern readers—within the construct of the society that is being described here, Odysseus has not betrayed Penelope in any sense, probably, that Penelope wound recognize, let alone that Odysseus would recognize.

To get back to Odysseus and Circe; after one year, at the prompting of many of his crewmen, Odysseus decides to resume his journey. Circe tells him, however—when he asks her how he should go about it, how he should leave, where he should go—she tells him that first he has to undertake another journey. First, before he can return to Ithaka, he must travel to the land of the dead, and there he has to consult the soul of Teiresias, a great Theban seer and prophet, and Teiresias will tell Odysseus what it is that he needs to do to reach home safely. Now, a journey to the land of the dead seems to be an element that the greatest Greek heroes have in common.

Herakles journeyed to the land of the dead and back again; Theseus did as well; Orpheus did; now Odysseus will. In later literature, in the great Roman epic, the *Aenead*, Aeneas, patterned on Odysseus, will travel to the land of the dead and back again. So the ability to travel to the Underworld and come back out as a living man, to go and talk to the souls of the dead and return again, is something that marks someone out as a truly great, first-class hero.

On a more psychological reading of the myth, in the *Odyssey* itself Odysseus' journey—and this journey, by the way, is often called the *Nekuia*, from the Greek word for the dead—the *Nekuia* can be seen as marking the death of the warrior Odysseus, the death of the Iliadic Odysseus, and the rebirth of the Ithakan or Odyssean Odysseus. He goes into the land of the dead and comes back out again. This episode is almost at the center of the *Odyssey*; it makes up Book Eleven, so it is pretty close to halfway through the *Odyssey*. When he comes back out again, he is almost ready to return to Ithaka and start that half of his homecoming, start the process of returning to his proper status on Ithaka, when he actually is there on Ithaka. I usually tend to shy away from overly psychological reading of the *Odyssey* or of the *Iliad*. But this one, I think, actually makes a great deal of sense; the *Nekuia* scene is a kind of death and rebirth for Odysseus himself.

Be that as it may, within the context of the *Odyssey* the *Nekuia* serves several important narrative functions. First of all, it allows Odysseus to gain knowledge of the state of affairs on Ithaka. This is a very useful narrative device for the poet. We need to know that Odysseus knows that there is good reason to fear the suitors and Penelope's fidelity. How could Odysseus know that? We have the whole background knowledge because Homer, the narrator, has told us. Odysseus doesn't; he is out there wandering around trying to get home. Well, he knows after Book Eleven of the *Odyssey*; he knows that the suitors are threatening Penelope, he knows how much trouble there is on Ithaka, because the soul of the Theban prophet Teiresias has told him so, and he has told us that Teiresias has told him so. So, it is a device which allows Odysseus to get news of home in a way that otherwise would be hard to motivate within the narrative of the *Odyssey*.

Another point about the *Nekuia* is that it allows us, the audience, to see some of the main characters of the Trojan War, in a kind of review or reprise of the *Iliad*. We see Agamemnon, we see Aias—Odysseus talks to them—we see Achilles. So it gives us a second view of some of the characters who are Odysseus' companions in the *Iliad*, and thus provides a fitting pivotal point for the epic's turn from Odysseus' past to his future. We revisit the past one last time before we then move on to the Ithakan half of the *Odyssey*.

Also, thinking now about the audience within the narrative, rather than us, the audience for the epic outside the narrative, Odysseus' account of his journey to the land of the dead, I think, is absolutely riveting to his Phaiakian audience. Imagine this story from their point of view. There is this stranger who suddenly appeared in their palace. He has been very reticent about who he is for an entire day; finally, when he tells you who he is, it turns out that he is one of the greatest heroes of the Trojan War, whom everyone has heard about, who has disappeared for ten years, and nobody knew where he was. Then, just to top that off, he tells you "Oh, by the way, I went to the Underworld and came back alive." And this has really strong dramatic power; and picking up on my point about Odysseus as a great rhetorician, who casts his story to appeal to his audience, it is worth remembering throughout his narrative of his wanderings that he is talking to the Phaiakians and that he is trying to please them, to enchant them, to delight them, so that they will give him the best possible gifts and send him home to Ithaka.

So, Circe tells Odysseus that he must go to visit the dead and speak to the soul of Teiresias the prophet. Fair enough, but how do you get there? If someone tells you go to the land of the dead and speak to the soul of Teiresias, what is the process for getting there? Circe tells Odysseus how to do this; he should sail out onto the streams of the River Ocean she says. Now, the River Ocean refers to the idea that the earth is a flat disk, and that it is surrounded by an ever-flowing river, an ever-flowing stream of ocean. What Odysseus has to do is sail out through the Pillars of Herakles—what we call the Straits of Gibraltar—into that never-ending, ever-flowing stream of ocean. Once you sail out of the Mediterranean—the ocean, the sea, whose name "Mediterranean" means "the sea in the middle of the lands"— once you sail out of that into the stream of Ocean, normally you never come back again, normally you are lost forever. Circe tells Odysseus that he should sail out onto the streams of Ocean and let the wind carry him to Persephone's land.

Persephone's land is located only very vaguely. We are not told, really, exactly where it is; just that once Odysseus has sailed westward, out through the Straits of Gibraltar, the winds will carry him to Persephone's land, somewhere on the other side of the River Ocean. There is an entranceway to the Underworld; there the ghosts will come up and talk to him. Persephone, of course, is the queen of the Underworld, wife of the god Hades, who is the king of the Underworld. Circe also tells Odysseus that when he gets to Persephone's land he must dig a pit, sacrifice two sheep, cut their throats over the pit when he sacrifices them, pour their blood into the pit. The ghosts who come up out of the Underworld will want to drink that blood before they can speak to Odysseus.

So, Odysseus follows Circe's instructions; he sails through the Pillars of Herakles onto the streams of Ocean and is carried to Persephone's land, digs the pit, sacrifices the sheep, pours the blood into the pit, and then meets and speaks to a series of ghosts of the dead. The first main group that Odysseus speaks to during the *Nekuia* includes his comrade, Elpenor; Teiresias, the prophet whom he has gone there to see in the first place; the ghost of Odysseus' mother Antikleia; and a whole list of great heroines from the past. Let's start with Elpenor.

The first ghost who speaks to Odysseus when he arrives in Persephone's land is his young companion, Elpenor. Elpenor has always struck me as one of the saddest little characters in Homeric epic. This poor guy was so inconsequential, so unimportant, that no one had even realized he was missing until they run into him dead in Persephone's land. Odysseus looks at him and says, "What are you doing here? How did you get here, why are you dead?" Elpenor explains that he had been sleeping on the roof of Circe's palace—not at all a strange thing to do in a very hot climate, to sleep on the flat roof so the breezes can cool you off—but that he was drunk and he missed his footing in climbing down the ladder from the roof, fell and broke his neck; and apparently when Odysseus and his men set sail nobody did a head-count, nobody even noticed that Elpenor was missing. So Elpenor's body is unburied on Circe's island, as his ghost is telling Odysseus how it is that he died. Elpenor begs Odysseus to go back to Circe's island, after he leaves the Underworld and bury Elpenor; as we will see, Odysseus does in fact do that.

Now, Elpenor is able to speak to Odysseus without drinking blood out of the pit that Odysseus has dug because his body is unburied; Elpenor is not yet truly in the Underworld. He is in the status that Hektor is in at the end of the *Iliad*, or that Patroklos is in at the end of the *Iliad*; the unburied body means his spirit cannot actually go into the Underworld. The ghosts who are actually in the Underworld cannot speak or recognize Odysseus, or have any cognizance of anything, until they are given a drink of blood. Blood equating life is very clearly obvious here; the ghosts have to drink blood before they have memory, before they have speech, before they have self-awareness. Elpenor is in that kind of in-between state of being neither truly dead nor truly alive, and therefore he can still recognize Odysseus and speak to him. Teiresias, interestingly enough, is able to recognize Odysseus before he drinks the blood.

Circe has told Odysseus that Persephone granted Teiresias the boon of keeping his wits intact even after death. Apparently what Teiresias needs the blood for is to regain his prophetic abilities; as the standard every-day ghost can't even speak until he takes a drink of blood, so Teiresias can speak but can't prophesy, doesn't have his ability to foretell the future, until he takes a drink of blood. So Odysseus lets Teiresias drink the blood, and Teiresias gives Odysseus explicit instructions about what he needs to do to get home safely. Teiresias starts out by telling Odysseus that Poseidon is angry with him for blinding the Cyclops Polyphemos. "But," Teiresias says, "you might make it home, you and all your companions might actually make it home if"—and this is a very important if—"if you do not harm the cattle of the sun god, Helios. When you land on the sun god's island, if you do not harm the cattle, you might make it home alive." Teiresias says:

> If you keep your mind on homecoming, and leave these [the cattle] unharmed,
> you might all make your way to Ithaka, after much suffering;
> but if you do harm them, then I testify to the destruction
> of your ship and your companions, but if you yourself get clear,
> you will come home in bad case, with the loss of all your companions,
> in someone else's ship and find troubles in your household.

Exactly the words the Cyclops used in his curse. Teiresias, though, then adds a little detail about these troubles in Odysseus' household:

> insolent men, who are eating away your livelihood
> and courting your godlike wife and offering gifts to win her.

So, Odysseus has now heard if he leaves the sun god's cattle unharmed, he and all his men can make it home; if, on the other hand, the sun god's cattle are harmed, Odysseus will make it home only very late and will find suitors courting his wife, Penelope.

Next, Odysseus speaks to the ghost of his mother, Antikleia. Now this is an extraordinarily poignant and, I think, moving scene. First of all, just as Odysseus had not known Elpenor was dead, he hadn't known his mother was dead; there is no way he could have until he saw her ghost in the Underworld. He is desperate for news of Ithaka when he speaks to her. He asks her how she died, how his father is, how his son Telemachos is, how Penelope is doing, if she is waiting for him—and Antikleia answers everything Odysseus asks her. She answers him in reverse order; she talks to him first about Penelope, who is indeed still waiting for him. Second, she tells him about his son—Telemachos is doing very well—then about his father, who is still alive but has left the palace, retired up to the country, and is living as a poor old man out of grief over Odysseus. And then Odysseus' mother says, "And that is the same thing that happened to me," she says; "I did not die of a lingering illness, I did not die of a sudden catastrophe, but it was longing for you, Odysseus, that killed me."

Now, think about the impact of that. He had not even known his mother was dead; he sees her ghost in the Underworld; he says, "What killed you?" And she says, "You did." This is the one time in the *Odyssey* when Odysseus the fluent speaker, Odysseus the rhetorician, has no words. He says nothing in response to his mother. He tries to embrace her but can't; she slips through his arms, and as she flutters away into the background she tells him to remember all these things to tell to his wife Penelope—and we'll see at the end of the *Odyssey* he does exactly that.

Next, Odysseus describes a long list of heroines who appeared to him, heroines from the old days, mothers of kings, famous queens. Then he very abruptly breaks off his narrative, almost at the middle of sentence. He says, "I saw lots of other people too, but it is late, it is time to go to sleep; tomorrow, please give me a ship and send me home." Now, this break in the narrative, I think, accomplishes a couple of very important things. First of all, it's a way for Homer, the bard, to remind us, the external audience, of exactly where we are and what's going on. Odysseus has been speaking in his own voice—that is, Homer has been impersonating Odysseus—for about two and a half hours of performance time now. It is worth backing up for a minute and saying, "Now, remember where we are. We are in the great hall of the Phaiakian King Alkinoos; it is late at night, Odysseus is telling his own story, he is telling his story to Alkinoos and Arete to try to gain favor from them." So this break in the narrative is a way of reminding us where we are, what is going on.

It also, I think, reminds us that Odysseus is again, as always, crafting his story to appeal to the person whose interest he most wants to hold. In this case, that is still Arete; because Athena and Nausikaa had both told him that she has the real power in Scheria. Think about this long list of great heroines; who is that most likely to appeal to? This great and powerful queen, who is herself in the same position as some of the women Odysseus says he talked to.

And lastly, this break in the narrative whets the internal audience's, the Phaiakians audience's, appetite for more. Alkinoos practically begs Odysseus to continue; and again, think about it from their point of view. You have got this guest; it is the middle of the night; he is saying, "I was in the Underworld, I talked to these few people, I am in the land of the dead—but that is enough of that, let's go to bed and then send me home tomorrow." I think anyone would react as Alkinoos did—"You can't stop there, and you have got to tell us the rest of the story." Alkinoos says, "I would stay awake all night to listen to you; tell me, did you see any of your companions from Troy? What else did you see? What else did you do?" And at Alkinoos' request, Odysseus picks up the narrative again—as we will in the next lecture, when we continue discussing Odysseus' story of his adventures in the Underworld.

Lecture Six

From Persephone's Land to the Island of Helios

Scope: This lecture continues to look at Odysseus' narrative of his journey to Hades. We note elements in the Hades narrative that seem particularly designed to enchant Odysseus' Phaiakian audience, and then consider the vexed question of Odysseus' veracity in these accounts of his adventures. The lecture moves on to the final episode of the "Great Wanderings," the killing of Helios' cattle and the death of all Odysseus' remaining companions. We see how Odysseus manages to explain his status as sole survivor without losing his audience's sympathy by implying that he bears no responsibility for his companions' deaths; thus, once again Odysseus' skill in rhetoric is foregrounded by the bard.

Outline

I. At Alkinoos' request, Odysseus resumes his narrative with descriptions of speaking to the ghosts of his former comrades and to the ghost of Herakles. He then ends the *Nekuia* narrative very abruptly.

   A. Odysseus resumes his story, and tells of meeting the souls of Agamemnon, Achilles, and Aias.

   1. Agamemnon tells the story of his own murder, and warns Odysseus not to trust even Penelope.

   2. Achilles claims that he would prefer to be even a poor man's slave than king over all the dead, thus apparently rejecting the choice of fates he made in the *Iliad*.

   3. Aias, still angry over the issue of Achilles' armor, refuses to speak.

   B. Odysseus' last encounter in the *Nekuia* is with the ghost of Herakles.

   1. Herakles greets Odysseus almost as an equal.

   2. After speaking to Herakles, Odysseus was suddenly overcome with fear of the hordes of ghosts, and set sail again.

   C. The effect on the Phaiakian audience is crucial here. Odysseus presents himself as someone who has returned alive from Hades, someone whom gods and seers address, and someone whom the great Herakles himself greets as a peer.

    D. Since these adventures are all narrated in Odysseus' own voice, and since his purpose is to charm the Phaiakians so that they will give him gifts and help him home, we cannot take everything he says at face value as being unquestionably true.

    E. The whole *Nekuia* interweaves news for Odysseus with reminders of his past. Odysseus is truly "in limbo," neither dead like his comrades, nor truly living with his family.

II. Odysseus then ends the story of his wanderings with the description of the adventure in which all his remaining comrades were killed, their arrival on Thrinakia, the island of the Sun God Helios.

    A. After leaving "Persephone's land," Odysseus returns to Circe's island.

        1. Odysseus and his men bury Elpenor.

        2. Circe greets Odysseus and his comrades as twice-dying men, since they have gone to Hades.

        3. Circe tells Odysseus about the next dangers he will encounter: he must sail past the Sirens; he must navigate between the Stymplegades, or "Clashing Rocks;" and he must find a way between the monster Skylla and the whirlpool Charybdis.

        4. Circe then repeats Teiresias' warning about the cattle of Helios.

    B. In due course, Odysseus comes to Thrinakia. He wants to sail past it without stopping, but Eurylochos persuades him to stop for one night.

    C. The winds blow against them for an entire month, so they cannot leave Thrinakia. Finally, Eurylochos and the other companions kill and eat some of Helios' cattle. Odysseus shapes the account to show that he was not responsible, and could not have stopped his men.

        1. Odysseus has gone off alone to pray, and has fallen asleep.

        2. Eurylochos and the others sacrifice the cattle reverently and promise to build a temple to Helios.

        3. Odysseus wakes to the smell of roasting meat.

        4. The men eat, but Odysseus does not.

    D. The winds change and the ship sets sail. But at Helios' request, Zeus sends a storm to wreck the ship, and only Odysseus escapes

alive. Again, Odysseus includes details that stress his
blamelessness in the disaster.

1. Odysseus recounts how he knows what Helios said to Zeus;
   he heard it from Kalypso, who heard it from Hermes.
2. The storm blows the ship back to Charybdis, where it is
   destroyed and all the companions drowned. Odysseus barely
   escapes with his life, and then floats on some wrecked timbers
   to Kalypso's island.

III. Odysseus' first person narrative ends here, with his arrival on Ogygia.
Thus, halfway through the Odyssey we have circled back to its
beginning, and are now ready for another beginning, this time on
Ithaka.

Essential Reading:

Odyssey, Book XI, lines 375–end; Book XII.

Supplementary Reading:

Lillian Doherty, "Sirens, Muses, and Female Narrators."

S. Douglas Olson, *Blood and Iron*, Chapter 3.

Jean-Pierre Vernant, "Death with Two Faces."

Questions to Consider:

1. Is it possible to make sense out of the narrative of the *Odyssey* if we
   assume that every supernatural adventure Odysseus narrates in the
   Great Wanderings is a lie? Are there any elements of the story that are
   vouched for by "Homer" as narrator of the *Odyssey*? Can you work out
   any consistent standard to judge when Odysseus is telling the truth and
   when he may be lying?

2. In the proem of the *Odyssey*, the poet says that Odysseus' comrades
   were "fools," destroyed by "their own reckless actions," because they
   ate Helios' cattle. Does this seem consistent with their story as it is
   presented in Book XII?

Lecture Six—Transcript
From Persephone's Land to the Island of Helios

Hello, and welcome to Lecture Six. In the previous lecture we went from the island of Aiolos, through Odysseus' encounter with Circe, into Odysseus' visit to the land of the dead. In this lecture, we, like Odysseus, resume his narrative of his conversations with the ghosts of the dead, and follow his story through to the loss of his remaining companions and his arrival on Kalypso's island. At Alkinoos' request, Odysseus resumes his narrative of the ghosts he spoke to in the Underworld, with descriptions of encounters with several of his companions from the Trojan War. Specifically, he speaks of meeting Agamemnon, Achilles, and Aias the Greater and speaking to each of them. He then describes an encounter with the ghost of Herakles and brings the *Nekuia* to a rather abrupt and surprising ending.

As Odysseus resumes his story, he talks first about his encounters with Agamemnon, Achilles, and Aias. Agamemnon, like Elpenor and Odysseus' own mother Antikleia, is another dead soul that Odysseus meets who he had not known was dead. We, of course, as the audience, know perfectly well that Agamemnon is dead, and this has been mentioned over and over again from the very beginning of the *Odyssey*. But up until this point, Odysseus had no way to know that. And so his first reaction upon seeing Agamemnon is grief and wonder at how Agamemnon died. He asks him, "Were you drowned at sea? Did you encounter enemies who killed you?" And Agamemnon tells Odysseus the story which, again, we the audience have heard several times already at this point, of his—Agamemnon's—murder at the hands of his treacherous wife Klytaimestra and her lover Aigisthos. So, at this point, Odysseus is given this comparison to contemplate, between his own situation *vis à vis* Penelope, and Agamemnon's *vis à vis* Klytaimestra; and lest the implication be too subtle, Agamemnon specially says to Odysseus "Do not trust even Penelope." He says, "There is no trust in women; when you get home be very careful, because you cannot tell what may have happened in the time you were away."

So, Odysseus has heard from Teiresias—the prophet whom he consulted at the beginning of the *Nekuia*—he has heard that if he and his companions harm the sun god's cattle, he will arrive home to find troubles in his household; specifically, suitors courting Penelope. Agamemnon's ghost has now told him that these things do, in fact, happen in real life, and that the consequences can be devastating; in Agamemnon's case, Klytamestra's treachery cost him his life. So Odysseus has good reason to be concerned now; he's had this double warning about Penelope and what may be happening on Ithaka. And it is important for us, as the audience of the epic, to remember that the seven years' captivity on Kalypso's island take place *after* Odysseus' trip to the Underworld, in the timeframe of his story. We, of course, hear about Kalypso first, and then hear about the Great Wanderings; but remember, Odysseus is narrating in flashback. All of this—the trip to the Underworld, everything else—happened before he arrived on Kalypso's island. So those seven years, when he is sitting there, looking out over the water every day, yearning to go home—part of what is motivating that is precisely these warnings that he received from Teiresias and Agamemnon about what might be happening on Ithaka in his absence. His desperation to go home, his absolute fixated desire to go home, is in part motivated by his fear of what he might find if he gets there too late.

After talking to Agamemnon, who asks Odysseus for news of his son Orestes—and of course he can't give him any news because, he, Odysseus hasn't been back home yet—after talking to Agamemnon, Odysseus next talks to the ghost of Achilles. He describes to Achilles the great funeral that the Greeks gave Achilles; a funeral that of course does not remain in any surviving epic, but was recounted in one of the lost epics, as I mentioned in the first lecture on the *Odyssey*. Achilles responds to this recounting of his own funeral by telling Odysseus that there is no point in trying comfort him for having died, and he says that he would prefer to be the slave of a poor man than to be king to all the perished dead. Now this is a very remarkable thing for Achilles to say, because it seems to flatly contradict the choice that Achilles made in the *Iliad*, where he was told by his mother, the goddess Thetis, that he had a choice of two fates—to fight and die gloriously at Troy and have a short life but everlasting fame, undying *kleos*, or to live a long and uneventful life and leave no fame behind him but die a very old man. In the *Iliad*, Achilles chose the short and glorious life with the undying reputation to live after him. Now, in the *Odyssey*, his ghost says, "I would rather be a poor man's slave"—which is as wretched an existence as can be imagined—"I would rather be a poor man's slave than be king over all the dead."

Is Achilles being inconsistent here? I am not sure. Some people think yes, that this is simply an inconsistency; that the *Iliad* and the *Odyssey* disagree here. I think there might be another way of looking at it. I think perhaps one thing that is going on here is that, again, as I have talked about before, *kleos* is a compensation for death in the minds of the living; the living see *kleos* as a kind of immortality. The living see *kleos* as meaning that they will in some sense continue after they are dead, but apparently for the dead it is meaningless. In other words, glory, fame, reputation, only has any value in the world of the living, where it is the living who repeat glory, fame, and reputation about someone already dead. The dead Achilles finds no comfort in that, though the living Achilles might have found comfort in contemplating it before his own death.

Another way of looking at Achilles' statement here is that this is Achilles still being Achilles, as we saw him in the *Iliad*, torn between his two sides—between his mortal side inherited from his father, his divine side inherited from his mother—as we saw him balancing those two fates, saying at one point that he would choose to go home and live the long and glorious life, at another point he would choose to die gloriously. There seems to have been a sense in which Achilles was torn between two choices in the *Iliad*; perhaps he is now, even after death, still torn, thinking that he made the wrong choice, whichever one it was.

After speaking to Achilles, Odysseus moves on to talk to the ghost of Aias the Greater. Now, Aias, you'll remember, committed suicide when the armor of Achilles was awarded to Odysseus and not to him. Odysseus, when he sees Aias' ghost in the Underworld, speaks to him very humbly, very respectfully, and says that he, Odysseus, wishes he had never seen the armor of Achilles, that that armor was in no way worth the loss of so brave a companion as Aias. And yet Aias will not speak to him; Aias simply walks past him without uttering a word. This is a scene that has resonated throughout a great deal of later literature, most noticeably, perhaps, the encounter of Aeneas and the queen Dido who committed suicide for love of him in Virgil's *Aenead*. Aias will not speak, but remains angry and passes on by Odysseus.

At some point Odysseus seems to have moved from standing outside the Underworld, standing on Persephone's land and letting the ghosts of the dead come up to him, because at this point in the narrative he starts speaking as though he is in Hades. He starts describing seeing ghosts, seeing spirits inside the Underworld, so he himself is inside the Underworld looking at them. He mentions some famous criminals who are being tormented in the Underworld. Now, by and large, Homer's picture of the afterlife includes no punishment for sinners and no reward for the good. Basically, the overall picture of the afterlife is that everybody lives this kind—or everybody maintains this kind—of a bleak pointless existence, where they flitter around witless and mindless and don't even know it themselves until someone gives them blood to drink. But alongside that picture, there is the idea that there are a few—sometimes called "canonical criminals"—a few really, really major wrongdoers who are punished with eternal torment in the Underworld. Odysseus mentions seeing some of these. Perhaps the most famous one he mentioned is Tantalos, Agamemnon's grandfather as it happens, who tried to steal mortality from the gods by stealing nectar and ambrosia. He is punished by standing up to his chin in a river of water with fruit trees blowing just over his head—he is eternally hungry and eternally thirsty. But when he tries to drink the water flows away and leaves a dry riverbed; when he tries to pluck a piece of fruit to eat the wind blows it out of his grasp. So within sight and smell food Tantalos is eternally hungry and thirsty. Odysseus sees him; sees several other criminals being punished with equally fiendish torments; and then he says that he sees and speaks to the ghost of Herakles.

This is Odysseus' last encounter in the *Nekuia*. Herakles, interestingly enough, doesn't need to drink the blood; just as Teiresias recognized Odysseus without drinking the blood, so apparently does Herakles. Herakles speaks to Odysseus and greets him as, in some sense, a peer, almost an equal. He looks at Odysseus and he recognizes him, calls him by name, and says, "Then you, too, are suffering the kinds of troubles and pains that I also suffered when I was alive"—almost saying to Odysseus, "You are like me, Odysseus; you too are suffering what I suffered." This conversation with Herakles is Odysseus' last conversation in the *Nekuia*; immediately after this, he says that he was suddenly overcome with fear that the dead might overwhelm him, and he ran, he left, he set sail again for Circe's island.

Now, I think the effect on Odysseus' Phaiakian audience is crucial to consider here, particularly with what the mention of Herakles is doing in the story. Odysseus presents himself not just as someone who has returned alive from Hades—that is pretty remarkable in and of itself—but there is more than that. He presents himself as someone who has returned alive from Hades, someone whom seers like Teiresias and divinities like Circe speak to as an equal, almost, or as someone they are interested in; and he presents himself as someone whom the great Herakles himself greets as a peer. This last conversation, when Herakles says, "Odysseus, son of Laertes, you are suffering the same kinds of things I suffered"—that is a rhetorical *tour de force*. Herakles was the hero to end all heroes, the great hero of Greek culture, and for Odysseus to say, in the Phaiakians' hearing, "Herakles spoke to me almost as a brother, almost as an equal," that has got to have an enormous effect on his audience.

And this leads to a point that is important to consider throughout Odysseus' narrative of his wanderings, throughout Books Nine through Twelve of the *Odyssey*. At this point of the *Odyssey*, we have only Odysseus' word for the truth of any of these adventures. We don't have what we usually have in the rest of the *Odyssey*, the poet speaking in that presumed omniscient voice in which, if the poet says something is true, we assume it is true. In this section of the *Odyssey*, the poet is quoting Odysseus. As we'll see later in the books when Odysseus is back on Ithaka, Odysseus is a very gifted liar. On Ithaka he lies almost in preference to telling the truth, and he lies very, very well. Now, some scholars go so far as to suggest that all of Odysseus' narratives of the Great Wanderings are one big lie, that none of this ever happened. I am not quite that nihilistic about the *Odyssey*; I don't think we can go that far. For one thing, some of the adventures—the blinding of Polyphemos, the killing of the sun god's cattle, which I will get to later in this lecture—those are vouched for by the narrator elsewhere in the epic. But it is worth considering that Odysseus, as always, is crafting his narrative to appeal to his audience. He is choosing to foreground those points that make him look best, and put into the background those points that make him look worst. He is carefully, always in this section, trying to persuade the Phaiakians to help him, to give him gifts, to honor him and to remember his story and tell it to others so as to perpetuate his *kleos*. So, I don't think we have to go so far as to assume that he is flat-out lying when he says that Herakles greeted him this way. I do think it is worth considering why he chooses to foreground that episode and perhaps to put some others into the background.

Another point that is worth considering is that Odysseus, when he shapes his narrative to appeal to his audience, is doing exactly what the bard does in performance, what any bard or any storyteller does in performance. He is bringing up the details that he thinks his audience wants to hear and pushing into the background the ones that they don't want to hear, as Homer is doing for us in the *Odyssey*. Remember the opening of the *Odyssey*, when Homer says to the Muse, "Start the story at some point"; the implication being that the Muse could start the story anywhere she wanted to, i.e., that Homer could start the story anywhere he wanted to. In another version of the *Odyssey*, the *Nekuia* might have been pushed way into the background and another episode that we hear only very much in passing—say, the Laistrygones, who destroy eleven of Odysseus' twelve ships—could have been pushed into the foreground. The bard crafts his story, the bard gives more attention to some episodes, less to others, depending on what the particular audience wants to hear. Odysseus, in this section of the *Odyssey*, is acting as the bard. The bard is acting Odysseus; Odysseus is acting the bard; a very nice complementary picture there.

The whole *Nekuia*—getting back to its function within the narrative—the whole *Nekuia* interweaves news for Odysseus with reminders of his past. Through this journey to the Underworld, Odysseus sees reminders of his past and receives news of his future—the warning about Penelope; the warning about what might be happening on Ithaka; the news that his mother is dead; that his father has retired to the country; the sight of Agamemnon and Achilles. In this whole section of the *Odyssey*, Odysseus is both looking back to his past and looking forward to his future, but unable to access either of them. In a very real sense, then, he is in a kind of limbo. He is neither dead—he is not really there with Agamemnon, Achilles, and Aias— but neither is he alive; he is not with his family. And so his position as a living man in the land of the dead very clearly reflects his position in the world itself at this point; he is neither one nor the other. He is not united with the members of his past, or at home with his family as he hopes to be in the future.

He moves on after the *Nekuia*—we are still in his narrative of his wanderings—he moves on to describe the loss of the rest of his companions, when they do indeed kill the cattle of the sun god Helios, and his arrival on Kalypso's island. As we move into the sun god's cattle episode, Odysseus tells us that after leaving Persephone's land, after setting sail from the land where he spoke to the souls of the dead, he does indeed go back to Circe's island and bury the body of his comrade Elpenor, as Elpenor's ghost had asked him to do. Circe greets Odysseus and his comrades as "twice-dying men"; she refers to them as twice-dying men since they have been to Hades and returned. This fits in nicely with that psychological interpretation that I spoke of earlier about the *Nekuia*, in which you can see it as a kind of death of Odysseus and rebirth. Circe herself greets him as someone who must die twice—he has died once by going to the Underworld; he is going to have to die again when he actually dies and return there.

After burying Elpenor, Odysseus gets advice from Circe about the dangers he will encounter next. She tells him several things he has to do between leaving her island and getting home to Ithaka. He must sail past the Sirens—these are females who sit on rocks and sing absolutely irresistibly beautiful songs to any sailors who sail past them. The Sirens entice men. They lure sailors onto their rocks; the sailors crash their ships and die. So the Sirens are as threatening as any female entity in the *Odyssey* that

Odysseus is going to encounter; their song is absolutely irresistibly enticing, but obeying it, listening to their song, equals death for the mariners who sail past them. Circe tells Odysseus, if he wants to hear the Sirens' song and live, what he must do is stop all his companions' ears with beeswax so that they can't hear the Sirens, then have his companions tie him to the mast so that, as they sail past the Sirens, he can hear the song but will be unable to respond to it. This, of course, is what he does, so he becomes one of the only living men ever to hear the Sirens' song and survive—yet another moment that would undoubtedly give his Phaiakian audience shivers to think about, that this is someone who heard the Sirens and lived.

After passing the Sirens, Odysseus must navigate his way between the so-called Symplegades, a word that means the "crashing rocks," huge rocks that clash together and then bound apart; and what a ship has to do to survive them is time its sailing through perfectly, so that it goes through when the rocks are farthest apart rather than when they clash together. Now, it has been suggested that the Symplegades represent a very exaggerated mariners' tale of icebergs, which I think is a very interesting possibility— huge rock- like floating things in the ocean, that sometimes crash into one another, sometimes crash into ships, other times don't.

This is a point at which I can say a little bit about the whole question of whether Odysseus' wanderings represent any kind of reality or not. There have been all sorts of attempts to map out Odysseus' journey on the map of the Mediterranean; where is Kalypso's island, where is Circe's island, so forth. I think most of that is useless. I agree with the ancient critic who said that trying to find where the island of Kalypso was is as foolish as trying to find the cobbler who made the bag in which Aiolos tied up the winds; it is not something that has any actuality at all. And yet, it is possible that some of Odysseus' adventures represent garbled, misunderstood, exaggerated reports that had worked their way back from sailors who had sailed maybe even out past the Straits of Gibraltar and back into the Mediterranean again. The possibility that the Symplegades represent icebergs, I think, is not by any means too far-fetched. The possibility that other adventures Odysseus has may, in some way, represent some realities somewhere, I think, is not necessarily far-fetched; but trying to map out his journey exactly and say the Cyclops' island is Sicily—although the Sicilians like to say that, because it is good for selling tourists trinkets—but to try to say that the Cyclops' island is Sicily, that the Phaiakians' is Corfu—I think that is wasted effort.

After passing through the Symplegades, Odysseus must navigate his way between the monster Skylla and the whirlpool Charybdis—which of course is become proverbial for being caught between two great dangers, to navigate or sail between Skylla and Charybdis. Skylla is a six-headed monster, cannibalistic; if Odysseus sails too close to her, she will eat six of his men. Charybdis, however, is a whirlpool that will destroy his entire ship. Circe recommends that he sail a little closer to Skylla and give a wider birth to Charybdis, and that is in fact what he does. Circe then repeats Teiresias' warning about not harming the cattle of Helios, if Odysseus and his men come to the island Thrinakia.

Now, Odysseus follows Circe's advice; he narrates his journey through all the dangers Circe enumerates. Skylla does indeed eat six of Odysseus' men, but he makes it through the pass between Skylla and Charybdis without losing his entire ship, and he comes in due course to Thrinakia, the island where the sun god pastures his cattle. Odysseus wants to sail past this island without stopping, but Eurylochos, his second-in-command—the same man who led the group of half of Odysseus' companions to check out Circe's palace—Eurylochos persuades Odysseus to let them stop for a night.

The men are tired; they want to sleep on dry land, they want to cook a meal out of the provisions that Circe has given them. They don't want to sail at night, which is very dangerous. Odysseus, against his better judgment, relents, but makes the men promise that they will not harm any cattle or sheep they find on the island. He tells them about Teiresias' and Circe's warnings, and extracts a promise, an oath, from the men that they will not harm the cattle. Of course, they promise; that should not be a problem. They are only planning to stop for one night. But once they have stopped on Thrinakia, the winds blow against them for an entire month, so that they cannot leave. They eat their way through the provisions Circe had given them, and they are starving. As they are starving, finally, Eurylochos and the other companions sacrifice and eat some of Helios' cattle.

Now at this point, Odysseus carefully phrases what happened in a way that absolves him from any blame. He says that he had gone off to pray to the gods for help in getting off Thrinakia and the gods had sent sleep to overcome him, so that he was asleep when Eurylochos and the other men decided to sacrifice and eat the cattle. This is reminiscent of Odysseus saying that he was asleep when the men loose the winds out of the bag that Aiolos had given him; so that in both cases, when disaster strikes, Odysseus is asleep and cannot be held responsible for it.

Eurylochos and the other men sacrifice the cattle reverently; they promise the sun god, Helios, that if they ever make it back to Ithaka they will build him a great temple, and they start to eat the meat. And in a lovely, vivid little detail, Odysseus wakes up to the smell of roasting meat and realizes what has happened. He does not eat; his men do, but Odysseus does not. And yet the fact that it is going to be disastrous becomes obvious right away. The meat keeps lowing on the spits, the hides crawl on the ground— these cattle were immortal, and in some sense, even once they have been killed, they are still immortal; it is a very eerie scene. The winds change, once the cattle are dead, and the ships set sail. But at Helios' request, Zeus sends a thunderbolt and a storm to wreck the ship, and only Odysseus escapes alive.

Now, once again, Odysseus includes details that stress his blamelessness in the disaster. His men were not lost because he had poor skills in piloting; his men were not lost because of anything he did; and this was a direct intervention of the gods. And one point that I always like to bring out here is how marvelously and utterly in control of his narrative the bard, Homer, is at this point. In epic, in the *Iliad* and the *Odyssey* both, we are very accustomed to the bard, to Homer, telling us what the gods say to one another, what goes on Mount Olympus, the conversations the gods have. I don't think it would occur to one reader out of a hundred—if Odysseus simply said in passing, "Helios asked Zeus to destroy my companions and Zeus did so," I don't think it would occur to one reader out of a hundred to stop and say, "Wait a minute; how could Odysseus know what Helios said to Zeus?" But it occurred to Homer that one in a hundred might wonder, and he tells us—he has Odysseus tell us—how Odysseus can know what Helios said to Zeus. Odysseus tells us that Helios said to Zeus, "If you don't punish Odysseus' companions I will go down to Hades and shine on the dead men"—in other words, I will leave the world in darkness—and therefore Zeus punishes Odysseus' men. And Odysseus says, "I know this because Kalypso told me, and she said she heard from Hermes."

Now pause for a moment to admire the levels of narrative here. Homer tells us that Odysseus tells the Phaiakians that Hermes told Kalypso that Helios had told Zeus to smash Odysseus' ship. We are levels and levels deep in narrative, and who told what to whom. And yet it all works out; it is almost like an ancient analog of a footnote, that we are told how it is Odysseus can know.

So, Odysseus' last ship is smashed on the open sea, all of his men drown— the storm blows the ship back to Charybdis which is where it is smashed—

all of his men drown, Odysseus barely escapes with his life, and then floats on some wrecked timbers to Kalypso's island where Kalypso rescues him. Thus, as Book Twelve ends, Odysseus' first-person narrative ends with it, with his arrival on Ogygia, Kalypso's island. We have circled back to where we were in Book Five, halfway through the *Odyssey*, and indeed to where we were in Book One, at the very beginning of the *Odyssey*. Odysseus has told us how he came to Kalypso's island, how he happened to lose all of his companions, what it was that brought him to the Phaiakians in the state that he was in; and we are now ready for another beginning, this time on Ithaka itself. And in our next lecture we'll see that the Phaiakians give Odysseus a marvelous ship that takes him back to Ithaka, they set him down on his island of Ithaka, and we begin the second half of the *Odyssey* with Odysseus trying to figure out how to reestablish himself, on his home island of Ithaka.

Lecture Seven
The Goddess, the Swineherd, and the Beggar

Scope: This lecture begins our study of the second half of the *Odyssey* by discussing the change in pace and subject matter in the "Ithakan" books. From Book XIII onward, the narrative pace is much slower, and the challenges Odysseus faces are very different from those we have seen earlier. The lecture looks in detail at Odysseus' arrival on Ithaka, the significance for *xenia* of the formulaic lines he speaks here for the third time, his encounter with the disguised Athena, and their plan for his vengeance on the suitors. We also discuss Odysseus' arrival, in disguise, at the hut of his loyal swineherd, Eumaios, and the *xenia* he receives there.

Outline

I. The second half of the *Odyssey* differs noticeably from the first half in its pace and in the type of challenges Odysseus faces.

   A. The pace of the narrative slows down markedly. The events narrated in Books XIII through XXIV would barely fill one book of the "Great Wanderings."

   B. Odysseus is still in constant danger, but it is no longer danger from monsters and goddesses and supernatural forces. Rather, he is now in danger of being killed by Penelope's suitors.

II. Odysseus must continue to be *polutropos*, skilled at reading his interlocutors, and above all self-controlled.

   A. Once back on Ithaka, Odysseus faces a number of situations in which his own human emotions threaten to betray him. In order to reinstate himself as ruler of Ithaka, he must stay in disguise; therefore, any betrayal of emotion when he sees Penelope or Telemachos for the first time, for instance, would be highly dangerous.

   B. These new challenges are no less exacting than the swashbuckling adventures of the first half of the epic.

III. The change in pace and type of adventures means that in some sense Book XIII signals a new beginning, or a second opening, of the *Odyssey*. This is signaled by Odysseus' arrival on Ithaka.

    A. He arrives asleep. The Phaiakian sailors put him down on the shore without waking him.

    B. When he wakes, he does not know where he is.

    C. Once again, as he did on Scheria and on the Cyclops' island, Odysseus speaks the same formulaic lines about wondering where he is and if the people there know *xenia*.

        1. These three occurrences are the only times Odysseus says these precise lines in the *Odyssey*.

        2. This is an excellent example of how a bard working in a formulaic tradition can use that tradition to give heightened effect to his work.

IV. Athena appears in disguise and tells Odysseus he is on Ithaka. He responds by lying to her, pretending to be a stranger to the island, which pleases her. She then tells him who she is and says that she had always been looking out for him.

    A. Athena's identification of Ithaka is the first emotional trial Odysseus faces. As Athena herself says, anyone else would have immediately run to see his wife and palace, but Odysseus contains himself and is cautious.

    B. Athena explicitly says that Odysseus' craftiness, and skill in lying are why she favors him. She then reveals her identity to him, saying that she is known for *mêtis* (wisdom, skill, craft) among the gods as he is among mortals, and that she will devise a *mêtis* (plan) for him to defeat the suitors.

    C. Athena says that she always watched over Odysseus. Odysseus' response, that he was not aware of her after they left Troy, and her answer are indicative of the gulf between gods and humans.

        1. To Odysseus' objection that she had left him alone for nearly 10 years, Athena simply responds that she did not want to argue with her father's brother Poseidon, and that she knew Odysseus would reach Ithaka some day.

        2. However, Athena's anger over the rape of Kassandra caused her to abandon all the Greeks. During this time, Odysseus blinded Polyphemus and incurred the wrath of Poseidon. Thus, her answer is not entirely straightforward.

  3. The difference, in human terms, of reaching Ithaka 10 years earlier or 10 years later seems utterly lost on Athena.

V. Together, Athena and Odysseus plot how he will regain his kingdom.

  A. Athena disguises Odysseus as an old beggar and advises him to go stay with his loyal swineherd, Eumaios. This will help Athena engineer a meeting between Odysseus and Telemachos.

  B. As a beggar, Odysseus will be able to enter his own palace unnoticed by the suitors, and without raising any suspicions about what he is doing there.

VI. Odysseus is received with proper *xenia* by the swineherd Eumaios. The two men tell one another their stories; Odysseus lies, saying that he is from Crete. Eumaios recounts that he himself is a king's son, kidnapped in early childhood.

  A. The *xenia* Eumaios offers Odysseus works on two levels. On the surface, the slave entertains the beggar; on a deeper level, the king's son entertains a king.

  B. As one of the few loyal slaves left in Odysseus' household, Eumaios serves as a foil for the disloyal slaves and the hubristic suitors.

  C. Eumaios' descriptions of the state of Odysseus' household and Ithaka in general work both within the narrative, to provide crucial information to Odysseus, and outside the narrative, to remind the audience of how badly Odysseus is needed on Ithaka.

VII. Meanwhile, while Odysseus and Eumaios talk, Athena has traveled to Sparta to summon Telemachos home. The scene is thus set for the reunion of father and son.

Essential Reading:

Odyssey, Books XIII–XV.

Supplementary Reading:

Jenny Strauss Clay, *Wrath of Athena*, Chapter 4. This reading provides a close analysis of Athena and Odysseus' meeting on Ithaka in Book XIII.

S. Douglas Olson, *Blood and Iron*, Chapter 6 (on Eumaios).

Laura Slatkin, "Composition by Theme and the Mêtis of the *Odyssey*."

Questions to Consider:

1. Compare Athena's conversation with Odysseus with gods' interactions with humans in the *Iliad*. What similarities and differences do you see?

2. Odysseus lies about who he is to Athena, and again to Eumaios. What do you make of his willingness to resort to lies as soon as he is back on Ithaka? Does it have any significance for our understanding of Odysseus' character in the first half of the *Odyssey*?

Lecture Seven—Transcript
The Goddess, the Swineherd, and the Beggar

Hello, and welcome to Lecture Seven of the *Odyssey*. In Lecture Six we saw how Odysseus closed his narrative of the Great Wanderings, his travels from Troy to Kalypso's island, by describing the wreck of his last ship, the loss of his remaining companions because they had slaughtered the sun god's cattle, and his final arrival on Kalypso's island. With the story of Odysseus' wanderings complete, we are now ready to turn to the second half of the *Odyssey*, which describes his adventures on Ithaka itself. This lecture will begin by discussing the change in pace and subject matter in the Ithakan books, that is Books Thirteen through Twenty-Four of the *Odyssey*. We will look in detail at Odysseus' arrival on Ithaka; the significance for the concept of *xenia* of the formulaic lines he speaks here for the third time in the *Odyssey*; his encounter with the disguised Athena and how they plot together the way in which he can take vengeance on the suitors. We will also discuss Odysseus' arrival in disguise as a beggar at the hut of his loyal swineherd Eumaios and the *xenia* that he receives there, at the swineherd's hut.

So, to begin with, the second half of the *Odyssey* differs noticeably from the first half both in the narrative pace and in the type of adventures and challenges that Odysseus faces once he is back on Ithaka. The pace of the narrative slows down remarkably; the entire course of events narrated in Books Thirteen through Twenty-Four of the *Odyssey* would barely be enough to fill one book of the so-called Great Wanderings, of the adventures that Odysseus narrates in Books Nine through Twelve. Really, all that happens once Odysseus is back on Ithaka is, he arrives back; Athena disguises him as a beggar; he makes his way back into his palace in disguise; with the help of his son Telemachos and two loyal slaves, he kills all the suitors and is reunited with Penelope. That's it; that's the narrative of the second half of the *Odyssey*; and yet that basic storyline fills half of the epic. So, clearly, the bard has slowed down remarkably, has changed the narrative pace, has changed his approach to his material; now we are focusing, in much more minute detail, on Odysseus' emotions and on the very delicate way that he has to maneuver in order to reinstate himself in power in Ithaka.

Similarly, another difference between the first half of the *Odyssey* and the second half is that, from here on out, the chronology is straightforward. We don't have any more of this moving backwards and forwards; no more flashbacks. The only chronological oddity at all in the second half of the *Odyssey* is that in Book Fifteen we follow Athena to Sparta, where she goes to fetch Telemachos back home again. But aside from that, the chronology is completely straightforward, and the scene is set entirely on Ithaka aside from the one visit to Sparta in Book Fifteen.

Now, Odysseus also, from this point on, faces an entirely different sort of challenge and an entirely different sort of danger than we have seen in the first half of the *Odyssey*. He is still in grave danger; perhaps even in more danger than he has been in most of the first half of the *Odyssey*, because if the suitors realize who he is before he has managed to make a plan and find a way to overpower them—if the suitors realize who is they will undoubtedly kill him. You will remember, at the end of Book Four, we left the suitors; the last time we saw the suitors, they were waiting in ambush to kill Telemachos when Telemachos returned from visiting Menalaos at Sparta. If the suitors were willing to kill Telemachos, how much more willing would they be to kill Odysseus, in order to cement their chances of taking over the power in Ithaka? So Odysseus is, without question, in danger of his life, but it is a different kind of danger that he is in, this second half of the *Odyssey*. It is a human-to-human, almost mundane danger; he is not going to have any more encounters with cannibalistic monsters, or with goddesses who want him to be their husband, or with supernatural forces. He will still interact with Athena—in fact, he'll interact more directly with Athena than we have seen previously in the *Odyssey*— but with the exception of Athena's aid, everything else that Odysseus encounters on Ithaka is every-day, mundane, normal human activities and normal human situations. We are through with the monsters and the sorceresses and all of the supernatural adventures that made up Books Nine through Twelve of the *Odyssey*.

However, Odysseus must continue to be *polutropos*, to show his skill, his cleverness, and the many turnings of his mind, as that word describes. He must continue to be skilled at reading his interlocutors, at figuring what is best to say to a particular person to whom he is talking, and above all, he must be cautious and self-controlled on Ithaka even more than we have seen previously in the *Odyssey*. On Ithaka, Odysseus faces a series of what I like to call emotional tests or emotional trials, a series of situations, that is, in which his own human emotions threaten to betray him. Early on in the second half of the *Odyssey* in Book Thirteen, Athena disguises Odysseus as a beggar, as I will describe a bit later in this lecture. In order to reinstate himself as ruler of Ithaka, he must maintain this disguise no matter what any one says to him, no matter what happens. That means that any betrayal of emotion—for instance, when he sees his son, Telemachos, for the first time, when he sees his wife Penelope for the first time after twenty years, when he overhears a disloyal slave say something about how glad he is that Odysseus is dead—any betrayal of emotion in any of those situations would be horrifically dangerous. And so the main challenge that Odysseus faces in this second half of the *Odyssey*—before the challenge of actually killing the suitors, that is—the main challenge he faces is to maintain his disguise, to stay in disguise—to stay "in character," to use a theatrical term, as the beggar—no matter what happens, to show no emotion. And we will see him go through a series of situations in which almost anyone but Odysseus would be incapable of maintaining his disguise and hiding his emotions. So, these new challenges, these emotional trials as I like to call them, are no less exacting and no less dangerous than the challenges he faced in the first half of the *Odyssey*. They are different; he is not being shipwrecked and having to swim for his life, he is not having to talk his way out of a goddess's bedroom, but they are no less dangerous and no less exacting than the swashbuckling adventures of the first half of the *Odyssey*.

This change in pace and change in type of adventures and type of challenges Odysseus faces in some sense signal that Book Thirteen is, in fact, a new beginning or a second opening of the *Odyssey*. We are almost starting all over again, with a new introduction to Odysseus and with a new type of Odysseus. And in fact, this is stressed by the bard in a few lines when he describes Odysseus being carried back to Ithaka on the ship of the Phaiakians. The bard does a little recap, almost, of the opening lines of the *Odyssey*. He reminds us that Odysseus is a man who has suffered many pains and gone through many troubles and crossed the sea many times, but now he is being carried back to Ithaka on the ship of the Phaiakians—lines that recall, verbally and in terms of imagery, the opening lines of the *Odyssey*, in which the bard talks about the many pains Odysseus suffered and his many crossings of the sea. So we get almost a second little proem near the beginning of Book Thirteen. However, the bard also tells us that Odysseus is asleep on the ship of the Phaiakians; when he comes to Ithaka he is asleep. And the Phaiakian sailors lift him gently off their ship, still sleeping, still wrapped in his blankets; carry him onto Ithaka; set him gently down, still asleep; and pile around him all the gifts that they have given him, that Alkinoos, Arete, and all the noble Phaiakians have given him—gifts we are told that equal the booty he would have brought back from Troy, so he has not lost anything financially, so to speak, by his twenty years of wandering.

He arrives on Ithaka asleep; and this, I think, is a very important detai, because it seems to me that it helps set a tone that I, at least, find pervasive in the second half of the *Odyssey*—a tone of melancholy, for lack of a better word, of irrevocable loss. Remember how it has been stressed through the first half of the *Odyssey* that Odysseus is longing to see his day of homecoming. Athena tells Zeus, and us, in Book One that he is longing to see even the smoke rising from Ithaka. We are told that he sits on Kalypso's island looking out over the water, longing to see a sight of his own country. He says to Kalypso, "What I want is to see my house and my day of homecoming." Odysseus never does see these things; he never has that experience that any returning exile would want, standing in the ship seeing Ithaka appear on the horizon, seeing the harbor come nearer and nearer, recognizing landmarks, watching the ship pull into harbor, stepping off the ship—he never gets that. He never actually "sees his day of homecoming." He is asleep when the Phaiakian sailors put him down on the island of Ithaka, and when he wakes up he does not recognize where he is.

Part of the reason he does not recognize it is because Athena has covered the island with mist. Now she does this not just to torment him. Athena is capable of tormenting him in a somewhat friendly way; but here, she is not trying just to torment him. She wants him not to recognize Ithaka until she has a chance to appear to him, to disguise him, to work out a plot for killing the suitors with him. She doesn't want him immediately overwhelmed with joy at being at Ithaka, to start going to the palace and maybe run into someone who would recognize him, and that would be that. So, Athena has a good motivation for disguising the island. But nevertheless, Odysseus wakes up on his own land, in his own country; not only has he not had the experience of seeing his approach to Ithaka, but he doesn't even know where he is. And he says—when he wakes up, he says those same lines that we have heard twice before. He wakes up and looks around Ithaka, and he says to himself:

> Ah me, what are the people whose land I have come to this time,
> and are they savage and violent, and without justice,
> or hospitable to strangers and with minds that are godly?

Now that you have heard Odysseus say these exact same lines three separate times, we are in a position to talk about why he says those particular lines in those particular circumstances, and what the bard is doing with this. These three lines, just to remind you, are said three times—when Odysseus arrives on Scheria, where the Phaiakians are going to give him the best possible *xenia* that any traveler could ever hope for; when he arrives on the land of the Cyclops, when he is narrating his adventures to the Phaiakians he tells them and us that he said this when he arrived on the Cyclops' island, where of course he got the exact opposite of *xenia*, the worst travesty of *xenia* any one could imagine when the cannibalistic Polyphemos ate several of Odysseus men. Now, back on Ithaka, he says these same lines again, and let's think about that for a minute. Ithaka is the one place in the world where Odysseus should not have to depend on *xenia*; he is home, he is not a *xenos*—a stranger, a guest, a foreigner, a wanderer any more, he is home on Ithaka. He should not need *xenia* any more.

And yet, because of the disorder in Ithakan society, he is going to have to use the conventions of *xenia* in order to re-establish himself in his own homeland. He is going to have to present himself as a *xenos* to the swineherd Eumaios, he is going to have to use the convention of that ritualized guest-host relationship to get himself back into his own proper position on Ithaka—and why is Ithaka so disordered? Because, as we talked about earlier, because of the misuse of *xenia* by the suitors. So what the bard has done here, with the repetition of these formulaic lines, is give us sort of a full picture of how *xenia* functions in the *Odyssey*; beautifully with the Phaiakians, completely non-functionally with the Cyclops, and now, back on Ithaka, what Odysseus has to use in order to correct the misuse of that very thing, *xenia*.

I like to spend some time talking about these lines, because I think they are an absolutely astonishing example of how a bard working in a formulaic tradition—that is, a kind of poetry that is created by the repetition of set phrases and set lines—these lines are an example of how a bard working in such a tradition can use that tradition to heighten the effect of his work, to underline particular points, to highlight important themes. The fact that the *Odyssey* grows out of a formulaic oral tradition does not therefore necessarily mean that the bard who put it into shape was in any way uncreative or unoriginal; his creativity consisted in using these oral formulaic building-blocks of his verse to highlight the themes that he wanted to highlight. Odysseus could have said these lines every time he arrived anywhere. He could have said these lines on Aiolos' island; he could have said them on Circe's island; he could have said them when he arrived at the Laistrygones' island. He says them only these three times. And I think it is safe to say he says them only these three times because Homer knew what he was doing in composing this poem.

Athena, at this point, appears in disguise and tells Odysseus he is on Ithaka. And Odysseus responds, interestingly enough, not by jumping for joy and running off to the palace but by lying to Athena, claiming to be a stranger who has heard of Ithaka but giving Athena a very complicated circumstantial lie to explain who he is and what he is doing there. Interestingly enough, his lie pleases Athena; she then tells him who she is and says she has always been looking out for him. Let's look at those points in a little more detail. Athena's identification of Ithaka, Athena appearing in disguise—as a young shepherd boy, this time—and saying to Odysseus that this is Ithaka, that is the first emotional trial that he faces. As Athena herself says, anyone else would have run off immediately to see his wife and his palace and his son, but Odysseus contains himself. The bard tells us that he rejoices he is home on Ithaka, but he contains himself; he doesn't react with joy because, of course, he doesn't know he is talking to Athena. He thinks this is just some strange shepherd boy, and he wants to find out what the situation is. Remember, Agamemnon and Teiresias had both warned him about what he might find when he got back to Ithaka. We see his caution, thus, in this scene; we see his ability to restrain his emotions and be cautious.

We also see his skill in rhetoric coming to the fore again, which we talked about so much in the first half of the *Odyssey*. In the second half, in the Ithakan books, Odysseus' skill in rhetoric plays itself out for the most part in telling really, really convincing lies to all sorts of different people. The first lie we hear him tell is to Athena, when he says he is a stranger who had heard of Ithaka when he was once on Crete. Now, Odysseus' lying character became problematic in later Greek literature, and certainly in Roman literature. By the fifth century, when the great tragedies were written in Athens, some Greek authors at least were uncomfortable with Odysseus, a great hero, also being a great liar; and he shows up as an untrustworthy, devious, often even almost villainous character in later literature. Certainly by the time you get to Roman literature, to Virgil's *Aeneid*, to Ovid's *Metamorphoses*, Odysseus—or Ulysses, as the Romans called him—is almost the paradigm for someone who cannot be trusted, for someone who is a vicious liar, who is almost evil in his use of lies.

But in the *Odyssey* itself, Odysseus' lying seems to be taken as a good thing. Athena certainly approves of it; she explicitly says to Odysseus—after he lies to her, she reveals herself as the goddess Athena and explicitly says to him—that it is precisely his craftiness and his skill in lying that make her care for him, that make her interested in protecting him. She says, in fact, that just as she is known for *mêtis* is the Greek word—wisdom, skill, craft, cleverness—among the immortals, so he is known for that same thing, *mêtis*, wisdom, skill, craft, cleverness—including cleverness in lying—

among humans, and that is why she is interested in him. She also uses the same word, *mêtis*, when she says that together they will devise a plan; so the word that means "wisdom, skill, craft" can also mean "plan," in the concrete sense that they will devise a plan, a *mêtis*, for how he can overcome the suitors.

She says one other very interesting thing in this scene in the *Odyssey*. She tells Odysseus that she was always looking out for him at Troy and later; she says she was always watching out for him and taking care of him and making sure that he was all right. Now, Odysseus responds in some very, very interesting lines; he comes as close to reproaching Athena, as close to criticizing a god, as any character I know of Greek literature—at least, of any character who gets away with it, who does not anger a god by such criticism. Athena says, "I always looked out for you; I always took care of you." And Odysseus' responds, more or less, "Oh did you really? I am surprised to hear it." This is what he says:

> This I know well: there was a time when you were kind to me
> in the days when we sons of the Achaians were fighting in Troy land.
> But after we had sacked the sheer citadel of Priam,
> and went away in our ships, and the gods scattered the Achaians,
> I never saw you, daughter of Zeus, after that, nor did I
> know of your visiting my ship, to beat off some trouble
> from me, but always with my heart torn inside its coverings
> I wandered.

In effect he says, "Well, where have you been for the last nine years? You say you were always taking care of me—not so *I* noticed it."

Athena's answer is no less interesting and is indicative, I think, of the great gulf of perception between gods and humans; because to Odysseus' objection that she had left him alone for nearly ten years—and what a ten years they were! The time in which he blinded the Cyclops and that brought down Poseidon's wrath on him; the seven years when he was a captive of Kalypso—to his complaint that she left him alone and did not help him for those ten years, Athena simply responds that she did not want to argue with her father's brother, Poseidon, and that she knew Odysseus would make it home someday. Let's look at each of those points in turn.

She didn't want to argue with Poseidon; fine, once Odysseus has blinded the Cyclops, Athena is in a sort of difficult position. She has to either go against Poseidon and say, "Leave my favorite, Odysseus, alone," or she has to let Odysseus suffer for a while, while Poseidon works out his anger at

Odysseus. But why didn't she help Odysseus *before* he blinded the Cyclops? There, I think, is one of the key points in the *Odyssey* where we have to know the background story to understand why there was that window of missed opportunity in which Odysseus could blind Polyphemos the Cyclops. Remember, during the Sack of Troy, Aias the Lesser raped the Trojan princess, Kassandra, in Athena's temple; and I have mentioned before that that called down the wrath of the gods, particularly the wrath of Athena. Other authors tell us that, at that point, Athena was so angry over Aias the Lesser's crime that she withdrew her protection and her interstet from all of the Greeks—and I think that is what caught Odysseus. Athena's anger over what Aias had done allowed a space of time in which she was not looking out for Odysseus, and it was in that space of time that he blinded Polyphemos. Once that had happened, then even when Athena remembered that Odysseus had not been guilty of the crime that Aias the Lesser had committed, it was too late, in the sense that Poseidon was already angry at Odysseus.

But what about her comment—and this is what I really want to think about a bit—what about her comment that she didn't want to anger Poseidon and she knew Odysseus would get home some day? That is where I see this great gulf of perception between gods and humans. Athena more or less seems to say, "Well, I knew you would get home eventually; ten years earlier, ten years later, what does it matter, what is the difference?" She, after all, is immortal and ageless; what does time mean to her? Ten years to her is nothing; but to Odysseus, ten years? If he had gotten home ten years earlier, Telemachos would have been only ten years old; the suitors would never have started courting Penelope; he and Penelope would have had time to have more children. From the human point of view, ten years makes all the difference in the world; it makes an inconceivable difference. And Athena, to use a modern idiom, seems just to "not get it"—she just doesn't understand what she has just said to Odysseus. He doesn't respond to this comment in any way; this is the only explanation he ever gets from Athena and he leaves it at that.

Together, Athena and Odysseus plot how he will regain his kingdom. She disguises him as an old beggar. They sit down under an olive tree, by the way, leaning their backs against the tree to plot out what they'll do to the suitors, and I think it is significant that it is an olive tree, because of course the olive is Athena's symbol, it is her sacred tree. They plot that she will disguise Odysseus as an old beggar and that will let him infiltrate his palace, so to speak, and she will continue to give him advice throughout the rest of the *Odyssey*. She, meanwhile, will go to Sparta to fetch Telemachos, to bring Telemachos home, and she will tell Telemachos not to go directly to the palace, to avoid the main harbor of Ithaka where the suitors are waiting to kill him. Rather, Athena will tell Telemachos to go to the hut of the old swineherd, Eumaios; meanwhile, Odysseus will also have gone to the hut of the swineherd Eumaios. So Athena is engineering the possibility of a private meeting between father and son.

The disguise as a beggar is an absolutely stroke of genius, because as a beggar, Odysseus will be able to enter his own palace, in effect, unnoticed by the suitors and without raising any suspicions of what he is doing there. If he came into the palace as a man of royal rank, or even of high rank, people would look at him, they would pay attention to him, they would wonder who he was and what he was doing; their suspicions might be raised. But a beggar can go anywhere, and no one really looks at him. It makes perfect sense for a beggar to come to a palace where a great many people are feasting; that is what beggars do, basically, go around at feasts and ask for table scraps, in effect. And this, I think, is an equally important point; nobody really looks at a beggar, just as we don't really look at homeless people who ask us for change on the street. If you were asked two days later to recognize someone who had panhandled from you two days before, most of us probably couldn't do it; we don't look at those people. The suitors will not really look at an old beggar. So, Athena has devised a way in which Odysseus can get into the palace, and no-one will think it at all odd that he is there.

She sends him to stay with his loyal swineherd Eumaios, and the two men tell one another their stories. Odysseus, of course, shows up as a beggar and asks for *xenia*. The swineherd Eumaios, who is a slave of Odysseus, takes the beggar in, and they tell each other their stories. Odysseus once again tells a lie, saying that he had come from Crete. Eumaios, however, recounts that he himself was born a king's son but was kidnapped and sold into slavery in early childhood; and I think that is a very remarkable little detail, because it means that, if you think about it, the *xenia* that Odysseus receives from this swineherd Eumaios works on two levels. On the obvious level— what anyone would see if they walked into the hut—a slave is entertaining a beggar. But look under the surface, and a king's son is entreating a king. So it works on both levels.

It is also an interesting point that, as I am sure any reader of the *Iliad* and the *Odyssey* has noticed by now, these epics take clearly the aristocratic point of view. They are written for aristocrats; they assume that slaves and commoners are only there to further the aristocrats' desires and to make their lives easier. Eumaios is one of the view slaves, in either the *Iliad* or the *Odyssey*, who is painted in some detail and is treated with great respect and great admiration, even by the bard; and I think perhaps we are given this detail that Eumaios was born a prince to help explain how a slave can be so admirable as Eumaios, in fact, is in this story. As one of the few loyal slaves left in Odysseus' household, Eumaios serves as a foil, as a comparison to the disloyal slaves who we'll meet later, and of course the hubristic suitors who are destroying Odysseus' household and livelihood.

Also, Odysseus is able to ask Eumaios for details about the state of his household. Just as a curious traveler would want to know who rules this country, what goes on here, what is happening, he is able to get information from Eumaios about the suitors, about Penelope, about the fact that Telemachos has gone away on a ship and nobody is quite sure where he is or if he'll ever come back. All of those details provide crucial information for Odysseus about how things are on Ithaka, right now, this very instant. They also, as we have seen so often in the *Odyssey*, remind us, Homer's audience, of exactly what the state of affairs is, of exactly how bad the suitors are, and how desperate Penelope is becoming in Odysseus' and now Telemachos' absence.

Meanwhile, as Odysseus and Eumaios talk, Athena, as I said, has traveled to Sparta to summon Telemachos. We get one last look at Helen and Menalaos entertaining Telemachos at Sparta. Telemachos is presented with wonderful gifts, to remind us of how a good host ought to treat a guest. He returns home and, as Athena advises him, he does not go straight to the main harbor but he will return through another harbor and go to the house of Eumaios the swineherd; and thus the scene is set for the reunion of father and son which we'll see in Book Sixteen.

So, in this lecture we have seen Odysseus arrive home to Ithaka at last; we observed how, even here, he still has to be cautious, he still has to enact that epithet *polutropos* that was used of him in the first line of the *Odyssey*. He has to be clever, he has to be versatile, and he has to be skillful in rhetoric, though his rhetoric in these books normally takes the shape of out-and-out lies. The theme of his emotional trials, of the emotional tests that he faces and the necessity for him to hide his emotions, will continue in full force in Books Sixteen and Seventeen, and that is where we'll begin our next lecture, with the reunion of Odysseus and Telemachos.

Lecture Eight
Reunion and Return

Scope: The two books covered in this lecture, XVI and XVII, include Odysseus' reunion with his son Telemachos and his entry, still disguised as a beggar, into his own palace. Throughout this section of the *Odyssey* the poet stresses Odysseus' emotional trials; he must not show joy at the sight of Telemachos, anger at the evil goatherd Melanthios, or sorrow at the death of his dog Argos. Each encounter reiterates Odysseus' supreme self-control and moves him closer to his utmost danger, being in the palace with the suitors, and his utmost trial, reunion with Penelope.

Outline

I. Book XVI opens at dawn in Eumaios' hut. Following Athena's instructions, Telemachos arrives and is fondly greeted by Eumaios.

   A. Homer stresses the emotional impact on Odysseus' of Telemachos' arrival in two main ways.
      1. A simile compares Eumaios' reaction to a father's reaction upon seeing his son.
      2. Telemachos calls Eumaios *atta* ("papa"), and refers to Odysseus as a *xenos* (stranger).

   B. Odysseus behaves properly for a beggar, and Telemachos behaves graciously in return.

   C. Odysseus asks Telemachos to describe the situation in the palace to him.
      1. Telemachos says that Penelope can neither bring herself to marry nor bring an end to the matter.
      2. He adds that the suitors are devouring all his goods and destroying his household.

II. Telemachos sends Eumaios to the palace to tell Penelope that he has returned safely. This leaves father and son alone.

   A. Athena appears to Odysseus and summons him out to the courtyard.

   B. She instructs him to reveal his true identity to Telemachos.

    C. She taps him with her wand, and he becomes younger and handsome again.

III. Odysseus goes back into the hut, and tells Telemachos who he is.

    A. Telemachos is astonished at Odysseus' changed appearance, and thinks that he must be a god.

    B. In a remarkably short and straightforward speech, Odysseus tells his son "I am your father."

    C. Telemachos refuses to believe him at first.

    D. Odysseus can offer no proof; Telemachos has to decide to accept him "as is."

IV. Telemachos accepts Odysseus' identity, and the two weep in each other's arms.

    A. This is the first time on Ithaka that Odysseus lets his emotions show.

    B. Another remarkable simile stresses what Odysseus and Telemachos have lost. Their weeping is compared to the cries of birds whose young have been stolen from their nest.

V. Odysseus begins to plot his return to the palace. He invests great trust and responsibility in Telemachos.

    A. Odysseus asks how many suitors there are, and if he and Telemachos can fight them alone or will need more help.

    B. Odysseus tells Telemachos to return to the palace the next morning and wait for him there; he will come later, in disguise, with Eumaios. He gives Telemachos three crucially important instructions.

        1. If the suitors abuse Odysseus, Telemachos must not react.

        2. When Odysseus looks at Telemachos and nods to him, Telemachos must remove the weapons that hang on the walls of the great dining hall and put them away in a storeroom.

        3. Telemachos must not tell anyone at all, not even Penelope, that "the beggar" is Odysseus.

    C. These instructions imply that Odysseus accepts Telemachos as fully mature, trustworthy, and capable of restraint and cunning equal to his own.

VI. Book XVII brings Odysseus at last to his own palace. On the way, he has two significant encounters.

   A. Odysseus and Eumaios meet the disloyal goatherd Melanthios on their way into town. This meeting has two functions; it is another emotional trial for Odysseus, and it provides him with information about Melanthios' disloyalty.

   B. In the courtyard of his palace, Odysseus sees his aged dog Argos, lying on a heap of dung. Argos dies the instant he sees Odysseus. Again, this meeting has two primary functions.

   1. Again, it is an emotional trial. Odysseus dares not show any emotion at the sight of his loyal dog. Argos is too weak to crawl, but he wags his tail and lays his ears back. Odysseus secretly wipes away a tear, walks past Argos to enter the palace, and Argos dies.

   2. The Argos scene also reminds us of the state of Odysseus' palace and society. Odysseus asks Eumaios about the dog, and Eumaios says he is neglected because the servants are careless in their master's absence.

   3. The once-splendid dog dying on a dungheap is a visual representation of what has happened to Odysseus' palace in his absence.

   4. Argos' death the instant Odysseus enters his palace stresses the irrevocable consequences of that entry.

VII. Once inside his palace, Odysseus begins to interact with the suitors. Antinoos abuses Odysseus by throwing a footstool at him, and this gains Penelope's attention.

   A. Penelope summons Eumaios, and asks him to send the beggar to her.

   B. Odysseus sends back a message that he will speak to her later, in the evening.

Essential Reading:
Odyssey, Books XVI and XVII.

Supplementary Reading:
S. Douglas Olson, *Blood and Iron*, Chapter 4.

Questions to Consider:

1. Do symbolic readings, such as my explanation of the Argos scene, depend on there being one "author" of the *Odyssey*? Could such symbolism develop in a traditional system such as posited by the Analysts?

2. Why does Odysseus say so little to Telemachos when he identifies himself? Would this not be a time for a long, fluent, rhetorically brilliant speech if ever there was such a time?

Lecture Eight—Transcript
Reunion and Return

Hello, and welcome to Lecture Eight. In our previous lecture we discussed Odysseus' return to Ithaka and his encounter with Athena, how she disguised him as a beggar and sent him to stay with his swineherd Eumaios until he could make his way back to his own palace. We also discussed the emotional trials that Odysseus faces on Ithaka, and the dangers they pose to him. This lecture, which covers Books Sixteen and Seventeen of the *Odyssey*, will continue to focus on that theme of emotional trials, as we see Odysseus encounter his son Telemachos for the first time; meet a disloyal slave, the goatherd Melanthios; and finally encounter his aged dog Argos when he returns to his own palace.

Book Sixteen opens at dawn, in Eumaios' hut. Following Athena's instructions, Telemachos arrives at the swineherd's hut and is very fondly greeted by Eumaios. Now this scene—in which Telemachos arrives at Eumaios' hut, Eumaios greets Telemachos, Odysseus is there in his disguise as the beggar—this is one of the most profoundly difficult scenes, emotionally speaking, that Odysseus faces; because of course Odysseus, in character as a beggar, cannot in any way show that he recognizes anything significant about this young man, who he is, that he is anyone that the beggar should particular notice of, even. And Homer addresses the emotional impact on Odysseus of Telemachos' arrival in two main ways.

First, he uses a beautiful simile to describe how Eumaios reacts to the sight of Telemachos, how it delighted Eumaios the swineherd to see Telemachos again. Telemachos appears in the doorway of the hut, Eumaios goes to him, runs up to him, kisses him, kisses his head, kisses his eyes, kisses his hands; and then Homer says:

> And as a father, with heart full of love, welcomes his only
> and grown son, for whose sake he has undergone many hardships
> when he comes back in the tenth year from a distant country,
> so now the noble swineherd, clinging fast to godlike
> Telemachos, kissed him even as if he had escaped dying.

In other words, Eumaios' emotion on seeing Telemachos is compared to the emotion that Odysseus is feeling. A father welcoming his only, grown son, when he comes back after many hardships in the tenth year of wandering—it is very clear that here we are seeing Odysseus' emotion projected onto Eumaios.

Secondly, more subtly but, I think, also more importantly, Telemachos calls Eumaios "father." Actually, he calls Eumaios *atta*, a Greek word which is, in effect, baby-talk. It means, more or less, "papa," or "daddy," or something like that. It is a word that can be used to express respect to an elder to whom you are unrelated, as is the case in so many languages; if you are speaking to an older person, an older man whom you are not related to, you can call him "father," you can call an older woman "mother." We don't do that in English any longer, but many languages do. So it makes sense that Telemachos would use this term of affection and respect for Eumaios. But think of it from Odysseus' point of view. The first words Odysseus hears Telemachos say—after Eumaios has greeted him by saying, "You have come back, Telemachos," so Odysseus knows who this young man is—the first words he hears Telemachos say, after Eumaios has asked him to come into the hut and stay for a while, Telemachos says:

> So it shall be, my father; but it was for your sake I came here,
> to look upon you with my eyes, and to hear a word from you,
> whether my mother still endures in the halls ...

So Odysseus is sitting there in the background. He hasn't seen Telemachos since Telemachos was an infant too little to crawl; in the first words he ever hears Telemachos say, Telemachos says "Papa," and he says it to somebody else—and Odysseus must not show any emotion whatsoever.

Odysseus manages to show no emotion; in fact, he even remembers how he ought to be acting, in character as the beggar. He does what a beggar ought to do, when a young man of obviously superior social rank comes into the house—Odysseus gets up from his seat. And I think this is yet another moment of intense emotion for Odysseus, because—how will Telemachos act? Odysseus has heard about these suitors; he has heard about how wanton and reckless and ill-behaved they are. Suppose Telemachos, his own son, just brushes him aside and sits down on the seat and pays no attention to him? Telemachos could be as ill-behaved as the suitors. In fact, Telemachos acts perfectly. He speaks very graciously to the beggar— definitely in the tone of a superior speaking to an inferior, but he tells the beggar, "No, no, sit back down; Eumaios will get me another chair," and Odysseus does sit back down. So, yet another moment of extreme emotional tension; will Telemachos know how to behave or won't he? Has he grown up to be a proper young man or hasn't he? Another such moment passes, and Odysseus must show no emotion whatsoever.

Then, just to turn the knife a little bit more in the wound, Homer has Telemachos speak to Eumaios again, and this time Telemachos says to Eumaios, "Atta—Papa—where did this *xenos* come from?" Now, there are two people in the room with Telemachos. One of them is his father; the other—if you think back to the last lecture when I talked about how Eumaios is of royal birth—the other one is appropriate to be a *xenos*, to be a guest-friend to Telemachos and Odysseus. So, when Telemachos says, "*Atta*, father, where did this *xenos* come from," he is speaking a sentence that is perfectly appropriate for the situation, but he is reversing the terms. He is saying *atta* to Eumaios, and referring to Odysseus, his own father, as his *xenos*. Once again, Odysseus cannot and does not show any emotion.

In fact, Odysseus strikes up a conversation with Telemachos. He asks him to describe the situation in the palace; he asks him to tell him about the suitors. What are they doing there? He says, "Do you suffer their insolence willingly? Why don't you get rid of them? Don't you have any one to help you?" He coaxes Telemachos to tell him, to describe the situation to him, and thus Odysseus hears Telemachos say in his own words that Penelope can neither bring herself to marry nor put an end to the matter. That reminds us—and I think it is a very salient reminder at this point—of precisely what a desperate situation Penelope is in, as I brought out in the first lecture on the *Odyssey*; how she is caught between two conflicting duties. If she is a wife she must not remarry; if she is a widow she must remarry; and still in Book Sixteen, just as we discussed in Book One, there is no way for Penelope to know which duty to follow. Telemachos puts this very clearly—she cannot bring herself one to marry one of them; she also cannot put an end to the matter. So Odysseus and we are both reminded that Penelope is in desperate straits and really needs Odysseus to come back. Telemachos also remarks that the suitors are devouring all his goods and destroying his household, a similar reminder both to Odysseus and to us of just how outside the bounds of decent behavior the suitors have put themselves.

Telemachos then sends Eumaios to take a message to Penelope to tell Penelope that he, Telemachos, is returned safely home. This leaves Odysseus and Telemachos alone together, and Athena, who apparently is watching over everything that happens, appears in the courtyard of the swineherd's hut. Only Odysseus can see her; in a rather eerie little detail, we are told that the dogs can see her as well, but Telemachos can't. Athena nods to Odysseus—gives him a signal by nodding; he goes out into the courtyard, and she tells him,

"Now would be a good time to tell Telemachos who you are." Not only does she give him permission to tell Telemachos who he is, she had told him in Book Thirteen not to reveal himself to any one until she gave him permission to do so. Not only does she tell him that now he may tell Telemachos who he is; she also taps him with a wand that she is carrying, and suddenly, instead of looking like the old ugly beggar that she had disguised him at the end of Book Thirteen, suddenly he looks younger and handsomer and his clothing is clean. At the end of Book Thirteen, we are told she wrinkles his skin and grays his hair and blears his eyes and makes him look not just different but older; now she makes him younger and handsome again and he walks back into the hut to talk to Telemachos.

Now, Telemachos is, understandably enough, astonished at Odysseus' changed appearance. Remember, Telemachos did not see Athena; from Telemachos' point of view what has happened is the old beggar gets up for no obvious motivation, wanders out into the courtyard, stands there a minute, turns around, and comes back in again—and looks twenty years younger and much handsomer. Telemachos, understandably enough, thinks this must be a god. Human beings don't do that; gods do that all the time. Gods disguise themselves as a human being, and then suddenly put off the disguise, at least to some extent, and look much more glorious than they had looked before. So Telemachos, very understandably, says, "You must be a god," and asks this god, whoever he is, to be propitious to him. Now, Odysseus tells Telemachos who he is in a remarkably short, for Odysseus, and straightforward speech. He doesn't wrap this speech up in fancy rhetoric and try to lead into it gently. He simply says to his son:

> "No, I am not a god. Why liken me to the immortals?
> But I am your father, for whose sake you are always grieving
> as you look for violence from others, and endure hardships."
> So he spoke, [says the narrator] and kissed his son, and the tears running
> down his cheeks splashed on the ground. Until now, he was always unyielding.

So, at this moment, Odysseus lets his emotion out. I think perhaps the shortness of the speech is meant to indicate that he can't say any more, that he is overwhelmed with weeping at this moment of telling Telemachos who he is. Ironically enough—and it is a beautiful irony—this one time in the second half of the *Odyssey* when Odysseus speaks the straightforward, unvarnished, unadorned truth, what reaction does he get? Telemachos says, "You are not my father"; Telemachos does not believe him. People believe him when lies; when he speaks the truth he gets the reaction, "No, you are not."

Now, Telemachos' reaction is, of course, very understandable; how could this be his father? He has just changed appearance; human beings don't do that. Once Odysseus explains that it is Athena who made him change appearance like this, then Telemachos accepts that this is in fact his father. Odysseus can offer Telemachos no proof; there is no way he can prove to Telemachos who he is. Telemachos doesn't remember his father; Telemachos can't see any resemblance; Odysseus can't remind Telemachos of anything they had ever done together; they do not know each other. Odysseus can offer no proof whatsoever. All he can do is say what he does say: "I am the only Odysseus that will ever come back to Ithaka," is how he puts it; "I am the only Odysseus who will ever come back to you." And once he has explained the odd anomaly of his changed appearance, Telemachos makes, in effect—to borrow a term from another context—a leap of faith, and accepts that this is in fact his father and then they weep in one another's arms. Once Telemachos has accepted that this is Odysseus they embrace, and the two of them weep together.

Homer uses a remarkable simile to describe their weeping and to describe their emotion at this point. The bard says:

> They cried shrill in a pulsing voice, even more than the outcry
> of birds, ospreys or vultures with hooked claws, whose children
> were stolen away by the men of the fields, before their wings grew
> strong; such was their pitiful cry and the tears their eyes wept.

This simile, I think, stresses a couple of things in this scene. I always like to ask students in the classroom, "Why are Odysseus and Telemachos weeping? Aren't they happy to see each other? What are they crying for, and what does this simile tell us about why they are crying?" The answer I always get from several students is, "Well, obviously, they are crying over the lost years," and I think that is exactly right. They are crying over everything they have lost, that cannot be given back to them; and I think what this simile does to underline that is very, very important. They are weeping like birds weep whose children, whose young, have been stolen from their nest. But the bard uses the word for children, not for the word for the young for animals. And it is very accurate to say that Odysseus' child was stolen from him. Odysseus never has a child; he leaves an infant, and he comes back to a young man. He never has a baby, he never has a toddler, he never has a five-year-old, he never has a young adolescent—all of that is

113

gone, and all of that is irrevocably lost. Odysseus' child was stolen from him, just as Telemachos' father was stolen from him while Telemachos was a child, and I think that is what the simile comparing their weeping to these birds is meant to tell us.

And I also like, at this point, to look again at Athena's words in Book Thirteen, when she says, "I knew you would make it home someday; what did it matter if it was now or ten years earlier?" In human terms, as I have already said, the difference is incalculable; and that shows us the gap between gods and humans. For Odysseus and Telemachos, those ten years would have made all the difference in the world; for Athena they are negligible. And once again, this ties into that tone of melancholy, irrevocable loss, that, I, at least, see so clearly in the second half of the *Odyssey*. Of course Telemachos and Odysseus are happy to be reunited, but nothing will ever give them back those twenty years.

Immediately after they stop weeping, Odysseus jumps into action and starts plotting; "how are we going to kill the suitors?" Telemachos wants to know, "How did you get here, who brought you here, how did you come back, why are you here now?"—all the questions that Telemachos would obviously want to ask. Odysseus answers very, very briefly. "Phaiakian men brought me here," is about all he says, and then he says, "Tell me about the suitors; how many are there? Can you and I together kill all of them?" Telemachos' reaction at this point, I always think, can be summed up best in the one word, "Wow!" This is just wonderful. Here his father is; he says, "I have always heard what a great fighter you are, but this is incredible; you've awed me." And then he counts up the number of suitors, and tells Odysseus there are actually 108 suitors and they have ten servants, so that is a total of 118 men ;and Telemachos says, "There is no way; we can't kill them." Odysseus responds by saying, more or less, "One hundred and eighteen? I think we can manage that. We might need to get a couple other people to help us, but with Athena and Zeus, we can manage that." And at this point, Telemachos more or less says, "Okay; that is fine with me, if you think we can do it."

Odysseus immediately starts giving Telemachos instructions. He tells Telemachos to return to the palace the next morning and wait for him there. Odysseus and Telemachos will not go to the palace together; they will arrive separately, and he doesn't want to draw any attention to the fact that Telemachos already knows this beggar. He will come later, after he gets back into disguise as the beggar with Eumaios. And Odysseus gives Telemachos three crucially important instructions at this point. He says, "If the suitors abuse me, if anyone does anything awful to me at all, if they throw things at me, if they revile me, if they abuse me, you must not react. I am just an old beggar, you must not react." He also tells Telemachos, "When I look at you and nod to you, when I give you the signal, you take down the weapons that are around the walls of the great dining hall, take them down, take them to an inner storeroom of the palace and lock them away; and if anyone asks you why you are doing that," he says, "tell them that the weapons have been grimed by the smoke in the dining hall and you are taking them off to be cleaned." Obviously, the idea is you don't want the suitors to be able to grab weapons off the walls. Thirdly, Odysseus tells Telemachos that he must not tell anyone at all, not even his mother Penelope, that the beggar is Odysseus.

Now, what Odysseus is doing here with these instructions, I think, is extremely important. He is, in effect, accepting that Telemachos is a fully responsible, mature adult; he is trusting Telemachos to be as self-contained, as cautious, as he himself is. "Show no emotion, no matter what anyone does to me," Odysseus says; "don't tell your mother I am back"—he is trusting that his son is capable of restraint and cunning no less impressive than his own. He is putting enormous trust in Telemachos.

And so as we move on into Book Seventeen, Telemachos does indeed go back to the palace first, and Book Seventeen also brings Odysseus at last to his own palace. On the way there he has two very significant encounters. First, Odysseus and Eumaios meet a disloyal slave, a goatherd named Melanthios, on the path. Melanthios acts hatefully to the old beggar, just out of spite. He abuses him verbally, he abuses Eumaios verbally, and he kicks Odysseus. Melanthios kicks the old beggar, trying to knock him out of the path. This is an emotional trial for Odysseus in a couple of ways. First of all, a king is not accustomed to being kicked by a slave, and we are told that Odysseus briefly considers picking Melanthios up and breaking his head on the ground like breaking a pottery jug, but decides he'd probably better not do that, so he retrains himself from his immediate reaction to this insult from Melanthios. Also, as Eumaios laments Melanthios' cruelty to this poor old beggar—and remember, Eumaios doesn't know this is Odysseus; Eumaios is simply shocked that anyone would mistreat a poor old beggar so badly—as Eumaios laments Melanthios' cruelty, Melanthios says something to the effect of "Odysseus is dead, and I am glad that he is dead; and I wish you would die, too; and I wish that the gods would kill Telemachos as surely as they killed Odysseus." So Odysseus has been given information about Melanthios that will be very important in the rest of the

Odyssey—that Melanthios is treacherous, disloyal, wishing for Telemachos' death, undoubtedly in league with the suitors.

Once Odysseus reaches the courtyard of his palace, he has yet another emotional trial, his encounter with his aged dog Argos. As Odysseus walks into the courtyard, he is about to enter his own palace, about to go through the door for the first time in twenty years, and there lying on a heap of dung, a heap of manure in the courtyard, is the ancient dog Argos. Now this is obviously a very old dog indeed. He had to have been old enough, when Odysseus left to go to war, that he could already hunt, because we are told, when Eumaios describes the dog, that he could already hunt when Odysseus went off to war. So he would have had to be six or eight months old at a bare minimum then. Odysseus has been gone for some twenty years, so this is a twenty-one or twenty-two-year-old dog; very, very old. Not impossible, I am told; dogs can actually live to be that old. When Odysseus sees the dog, once again this is an emotional trial for him. The dog, Argos, recognizes Odysseus and dies as he sees Odysseus, so Argos' life, which has been extended waiting for his master to come back, ends at the instant he sees his master.

Now, at first sight, it may seem like this is merely a rather frivolous little sentimental detail; Odysseus sees his old dog and the dog dies. I think there is more going on here, as there so often is in Homeric epic. I don't think this is a trivial episode at all; in fact, I think it has some fairly significant points to be brought out of it. As I said, it is an emotional trial; obviously, Odysseus cannot, dares not show any emotion at all at the sight of this dog. It is just a dog; why would the old beggar care about it? But he does ask Eumaios to tell him what this dog is doing here; he says, "Why is this dog lying on a dung heap outside the palace?" And Eumaios says, "This was Odysseus' favorite dog, but once the master is gone, the slaves are careless; nobody takes care of the dog, unfortunately. The dog was splendid in his youth, but now he is ignored and in very bad shape." Odysseus cannot show any emotion at any of this. Argos is too weak even to crawl, but he lays his ears back and wags his tail; and Odysseus surreptitiously wipes away a tear, making sure that Eumaios can't see him weep, and this is when he asks Eumaios about the dog. And as Odysseus walks past Argos, as he passes by Argos to step into his palace, that is the instant when Argos dies. So, clearly there is an emotional chord being tugged at here in Odysseus, that he can't pat the dog, he can't speak to him, he can't do anything that would call attention to the fact this dog recognizes him.

But on a more important level, I think the Argos scene also reminds us of the state of Odysseus' palace and society. When Odysseus asks Eumaios about the dog, as I already said, Eumaios says Argos is neglected because slaves are careless in their master's absence. This once splendid dog, dying on a dung heap, is almost a visual symbol, almost a summing-up, of the state of the palace and the state of Ithaka. The dung heap right there by the palace door, that should have been taken out to the pastures and spread for manure on the fields—the very fact that it is there is an indication of how careless the slaves are in their master's absence. But more than that, the dog himself, I think, is a symbol of the entire state of affairs in Ithaka; and many years ago, one of the first times I taught the *Odyssey*, when I was going through this scene in the classroom, a student who had not said a single word during the whole term, always sat in the very back row of the classroom, suddenly sat bolt up right and said, "Yes, and the ticks are draining Argos' life-blood, just as the suitors are draining the substance of the palace"—and then he sat back and never said another word the rest of the course. The clearest example of the Muse striking that I have ever seen in my life, and I think he was absolutely right. We are told that Argos is covered with ticks and they are draining his life's blood, and that is just the way the suitors are draining the substance of the palace.

Argos' death the instant Odysseus steps into his palace, I think, stresses the irrevocable consequences of that entry. The palace is in disarray; Ithaka is in disarray; Argos symbolizes that. The instant Odysseus crosses the threshold, the instant the master is back in his palace, Argos dies; the instant Odysseus is back is in his palace, the state of affairs in Ithaka is on its way to being rectified, though nobody knows that yet. And so, in short, I think this whole scene with Argos has reverberations that go much deeper than one might immediately, the first time through, recognize in reading it. It is, of course, also on purely the surface level simply a very touching little scene. We have all known loyal animals; the idea of the dog waiting all those years for his master, dying when he sees Odysseus, and Odysseus not even being able to stop and pat him, to acknowledge him in any way—it is a very touching and very emotionally moving scene.

Once Odysseus is inside his palace, he begins immediately to interact with the suitors, in the character of the old beggar. And the second main ringleader of the suitors—whom I don't think I have mentioned by name before—Antinoos abuses Odysseus, first verbally, and then throws a footstool at him, hits him with a footstool. The other ringleader of the suitors, Eurymachos, of course is the one who was so disrespectful to the prophet Halitherses in Book Two of the *Odyssey*. Eurymachos and Antinoos are the two main gang-leaders or ringleaders of the suitors. Antinoos throws a footstool at Odysseus, and the noise and uproar that results from this, the suitors shouting and so forth, gains Penelope's attention. Penelope sends for Eumaios, asks him what is going on—she is not actually there in the room, she is in her own chamber—she asks Eumaios what is going on, and requests Eumaios to send the beggar to her. She wants to talk to this beggar; she wants to find out who he is. We get the impression that Penelope questions any traveler who comes through Ithaka, that whenever any stranger arrives, comes to Ithaka, Penelope wants to talk to him, wants to find out, "Have you ever seen Odysseus, do you know Odysseus, do have any news of my husband?"

So, by throwing a footstool at Odysseus, Antinoos got Penelope's attention, made Penelope realize that there is a stranger, there is a beggar, in the palace. Now she asks Eumaios, "Send him to talk to me." Eumaios takes this message to Odysseus and, in what might be seen as a rather surprising display of independence for a beggar, Odysseus sends the message back telling Penelope to wait until after nightfall, to wait until evening. He says that he doesn't want to enrage the suitors by speaking to the queen when the suitors are around. When the suitors all go off to sleep wherever they sleep—that is left a little bit vague, back to their own houses or somewhere—after nightfall, then, Odysseus says through Eumaios, then the beggar can speak to Queen Penelope. On a more subtle level, looking at the narrative, I think it is worth considering that Odysseus is simply trying to see to it that Penelope doesn't see him in the full light of day; if they wait until after evening it is more likely that she won't recognize him. As we'll see in the remaining books of the *Odyssey*, Odysseus' disguise seems a little permeable, a little malleable; sometimes people comment on how much this beggar resembles Odysseus, other times they don't seem to see any resemblance whatsoever, and I think it is worth considering that Odysseus simply doesn't dare let Penelope see him in anything other than the darkness of evening and the flickering light of the fire.

So, as Book Seventeen ends, we have established that Odysseus and Penelope will meet and will talk sometime later that evening. We have seen Odysseus come from Eumaios' hut all the way into his own palace. We have seen him reunited with Telemachos; then we have seen him encounter Melanthios and Argos; now he is in the palace in character as the beggar, and we are ready in our next lecture to discuss the actual reunion of Odysseus and Penelope, and to discuss the over-arching question of the next few books of the *Odyssey*—does Penelope realize that this beggar is her husband or doesn't she? That is where we will take it up in the next lecture.

Lecture Nine
Odysseus and Penelope

Scope: This lecture looks in close detail at the two lengthy conversations between the disguised Odysseus and Penelope in Book XIX, and the scene that separates those conversations, in which Eurykleia recognizes Odysseus. It analyzes the setting of Odysseus' and Penelope's encounter, and the implications of the fact that they are not alone as they speak. Turning to the Eurykleia scene, the lecture offers an interpretation of it that explains the significance both of Odysseus' scar and of his name, and the importance of his name's meaning ("Giver/Receiver of Pain") for the entire *Odyssey*. Finally, the lecture addresses the great critical issue of Book XIX: whether or not Penelope recognizes that the beggar is her husband.

Outline

I. Book XVIII builds the suspense between Penelope's request to speak to the beggar and her actual meeting with Odysseus. The book also introduces the character Melantho, sister of Melanthios and lover of Eurymachos; it also reiterates the suitors' insolence and their corruption of Odysseus' slaves.

   A. Penelope comes downstairs to beguile gifts from the suitors; this is Odysseus' first sight of her.

   B. Telemachos tells the suitors to go home for the night. They are astonished at his assertion, but they do as he suggests.

II. Book XIX opens with Telemachos and Odysseus storing away the weapons from the great hall. After this, Penelope comes downstairs and speaks to Odysseus.

   A. The time and place of this first conversation between Odysseus and Penelope are crucial in several ways.
      1. They are sitting on either side of their hearth, the symbolic center of the household.
      2. Since it is evening, the likelihood of Penelope immediately recognizing Odysseus is less.

    3. They are not alone in the room. Eurykleia, Eurynome, Melantho (sister of Melanthios, the unfaithful goatherd) and, quite possibly, other female servants are there.

  B. Penelope begins by asking "the beggar" who he is.
    1. He tells her to ask him anything else, but not to ask his identity.
    2. She responds with a description of her own troubles, including the famous weaving trick which allowed her to keep the suitors at bay for over three years, and then asks again who he is.
    3. He responds with a lying story, saying that he comes from Crete and that he met Odysseus before the Trojan War.

  C. This conversation is the most intense emotional trial that Odysseus has yet encountered. This is stressed by a simile describing Penelope's weeping and his reaction.

  D. Penelope then offers Odysseus a bath; he responds by asking for an "aged woman" to wash only his feet. Penelope summons Eurykleia to wash the guest's feet.

III. Eurykleia bathes Odysseus' feet, and recognizes him by a scar on his thigh.

  A. Eurykleia's sight of the scar leads to a long description of how and when Odysseus got both the scar and his name, the two essential signs of his identity.
    1. While visiting his grandfather, the young Odysseus took part in a boar hunt and was wounded by the boar's tusk.
    2. This grandfather had given Odysseus his name, a name which seems to mean "giver/receiver of pain."
    3. The physical sign of Odysseus' identity, the scar, thus enacts the meaning of his name.

  B. Odysseus' name is enacted throughout the *Odyssey*. In all his adventures, he both suffers and causes physical and/or emotional pain.
    1. We see this very obviously with the Cyclops.
    2. But we also see it even with good characters such as the Phaiakians, whom Poseidon punishes for their encounter with Odysseus.

      3. Eurykleia's reaction here stresses the same idea; she is seized by grief and joy together as she recognizes Odysseus.

IV. One of the great critical questions of the *Odyssey* is whether or not Penelope recognizes the beggar as her husband. Their entire conversation in Book XIX, especially the part following the foot-washing scene, can be interpreted to support either interpretation, that she does or that she does not.

    A. Since the two are not alone, even if Penelope suspects that the beggar is Odysseus she must be very careful in her words to him.

        1. At the very beginning of their conversation, she tells him about her weaving trick, and the anguish that the suitors have caused her. This makes good sense if she knows who he is, but is harder to explain if she does not.

        2. She presses him to reveal his identity and to tell her if he has ever seen Odysseus. Her copious weeping at his reply makes good sense if she does not know who he is, but is harder to explain if she does.

    B. The most important conversation for this question is Penelope's account of her dream, and Odysseus' reaction.

        1. Penelope says that she had a dream that an eagle killed her pet geese, then spoke to her and said that he was Odysseus and the geese were the suitors. She asks her guest to interpret the dream for her.

        2. Odysseus tells her that the dream can bear only one meaning; Odysseus is about to return.

        3. Penelope then immediately suggests an archery contest with Odysseus' old bow, to determine which suitor she should marry.

        4. If we assume Penelope knows who the beggar is, this scene can be read as a kind of coded plan, in which she ascertains his intentions and provides him with a weapon.

        5. If she does not know, the scene still makes sense; she is setting the suitors a test which she has good reason to think they cannot pass.

    C. The ambiguity itself—"what does Penelope know and when does she know it?"—provides a large part of the interest and drama of this section of the *Odyssey*.

Essential Reading:

Odyssey, Books XVIII and XIX.

Supplementary Reading:

Norman Austin, *Archery at the Dark of the Moon*, Chapter IV. This reading examines similarities in the scenes between Telemachos and Helen, Odysseus and Nausikaa, Odysseus and Arete, and finally Odysseus and Penelope.

Jenny Strauss Clay, *Wrath of Athena*, Chapter 2, pp. 54–74. Clay provides a close analysis of the significance of Odysseus' name in the scar episode, taking the basic meaning of the name as "curse" rather than "pain."

Uvo Hölscher, "Penelope and the Suitors."

S. Douglas Olson, *Blood and Iron*, Chapter 7.

Questions to Consider:

1. Since Odysseus' scar is so distinctive and Eurykleia is bound to recognize it, many readers have been troubled by Odysseus' asking for "an old woman" to wash his feet. Can you think of an explanation?

2. Choose one side of the "what does Penelope know and when does she know it?" controversy and construct the strongest argument you can to support your position. Is there any narrative element still left unaccounted for by your analysis?

Lecture Nine—Transcript
Odysseus and Penelope

Hello, and welcome to Lecture Nine. In our previous lecture we saw Odysseus reunited with his son Telemachos, and then discussed his return to the palace and his two significant encounters with the goatherd Melanthios and with his old dog Argos on the way back to his palace. In this lecture, we turn to Odysseus' conversations with his wife Penelope, as well as looking at the scene in which Odysseus' old nurse Eurykleia recognizes him by a scar on his thigh. We will discuss the significance of this recognition scene with Eurykleia and of the scar itself, and then finally the lecture will address the great critical issue of Book Nineteen of the *Odyssey*, whether or not Penelope suspects that the beggar is in fact her husband, Odysseus.

Book Eighteen builds the suspense between Penelope's request to speak to the beggar, when she sends Eumaios to ask the beggar to come speak to her face to face, and her actual meeting with Odysseus. Book Eighteen also introduces another crucial character, the slavewoman, Melantho, sister of Melanthios and lover of the suitor Eurymachos. So, Book Eighteen, which I am not going to spend much time on at all, reiterates the suitors' insolence in their encounters with Penelope, and reiterates their corruption of Odysseus' slaves, since Melantho is not the only serving-woman who has become a concubine of one of the suitors. Also, in Book Eighteen, Penelope is motivated by Athena; Athena puts the idea in Penelope's mind to go downstairs and show herself to the suitors and speak to them, to try to encourage them to give her gifts. Before she goes downstairs, Athena beautifies Penelope; she makes her taller and thicker—which tells you something about ancient standards of beauty—and whiter than sawn ivory, and in this newly beautified state Penelope goes downstairs and shows herself to the suitors, who are all overwhelmed with passion at the sight of her.

It is significant also, however, that this is Odysseus' first sight of Penelope in twenty years; so when Odysseus first lays eyes on his wife, Athena has made her look more beautiful for him as well. So the beautification of Penelope in Book Eighteen serves two purposes; it encourages the suitors, when she says, "Give me gifts; suitors are supposed to give gifts to the woman they are courting. You have just been destroying the substance of my household; if you really want to marry me, give me some presents." Her beauty encourages them to respond favorably to that suggestion; it also lets

Odysseus see her as utterly desirable, not at all less than she used to be despite his twenty years of absence. Interestingly, Odysseus listens to the speech in which Penelope tries to wheedle gifts from the suitors, and the narrator says he is pleased to hear his wife beguiling gifts from the suitors "when her mind has other intentions." We are not told how Odysseus knows that Penelope has other intentions in mind, that she is just trying to get gifts from the suitors but not really planning to marry one of them. Apparently, Odysseus just takes it for granted that Penelope is doing this as a kind of trick, a kind of wile, that she is not seriously planning to marry whichever suitor gives her the best gifts.

Finally, at the end of Book Eighteen, Telemachos tells the suitors to go home for the night, rather forcefully. They are astonished, once again, that Telemachos asserts himself as an adult and a person in authority over the palace, but they do as he suggests; they all leave for the night. This clears the way, in Book Nineteen, for Odysseus and Penelope to meet and to speak to one another without the suitors all around. Book Nineteen, which I am going to focus on for the rest of this lecture because it is a remarkably rich book, opens with Telemachos and Odysseus storing away the weapons from the great hall. You will remember, in the last lecture, I mentioned that Odysseus tells Telemachos, "When I give you a signal, you should store away the weapons"—that never actually happens. Rather, Telemachos and Odysseus together, at the beginning of Book Nineteen, take the weapons down from the walls of the great dining hall and store them away in a storage chamber, so that they will be unavailable to the suitors when the actual fighting starts, whenever and however that occurs. After this scene in which Telemachos and Odysseus store away the weapons, Penelope comes downstairs to speak to the old beggar.

Now the time and place of this first conversation between Odysseus and Penelope is very important in several ways. First off, let's consider the setting where they actually are. When Odysseus and Penelope first speak to one another, they are sitting on either side of the fireplace, in their own great hall. The hearth, in Greek culture as in so many cultures, was the symbolic center of the home, we still in English have the fossilized phrase "hearth and home," which gives something of that same sense of the emotional significance, the symbolic centralness, of the hearth. Of course this makes all the more sense in preindustrial societies, where the fireplace is the source of light, the source of heat, the source of cooking, really the one essential element that allows civilized life to take place, therefore the one essential element of a home. The hearth is the symbolic center of the home, and in this first conversation that

Odysseus and Penelope have in twenty years they are sitting on either side of the fireplace, of their own hearth, looking at one another in the firelight. Let's consider the timing of this conversation; as I already mentioned in the last lecture, since it is evening, since the firelight and perhaps a few lamps here and there, or a few torches, are the only light available, it is less likely that Penelope will spontaneously recognize that the beggar is in fact Odysseus, and that may be part of why Odysseus engineered this conversation to take place after dark.

Thirdly, and perhaps the most important detail to bear in mind when we consider their conversation with one another, Odysseus and Penelope are not alone in the room. Penelope herself says, in Book Eighteen, that she would never go downstairs to talk to men without attendants accompanying her. No married woman in this culture that we see in the *Odyssey* would talk to men without attendants accompanying her. And in fact we know, in Book Nineteen, that at least three women servants are present at all times when Odysseus and Penelope speak to one another. Eurykleia, Odysseus' old nurse, is there; she is right there, able to be summoned to wash Odysseus' feet, in about the middle of Book Nineteen. Eurynome, a housekeeper, is also there; and most importantly, Melantho, that treacherous sister of Melanthios the treacherous goatherd, is present during Book Nineteen. Before Odysseus and Penelope speak to one another, each of them has a brief conversation with Melantho, and the bard never says anything about Melantho leaving, which I think means it is safe to assume she is still there. So, in the whole conversation that Odysseus and Penelope have with one another, there are people listening and at least one of those people, Melantho, is treacherous. There may be other serving-women in the room as well; we are not told specifically, but Melantho is there, Melantho is treacherous, Odysseus has spoken to her and knows that she is treacherous. Therefore, Odysseus must be more than ever on his guard not to let any hint show that he is in fact Odysseus. If Penelope recognizes him and acknowledges him, Melantho will undoubtedly, immediately, run off to Eurymachos and say, "The beggar is Odysseus in disguise; you and the other suitors come and kill him." So the danger level is ratcheted up a notch here, through Melantho's presence.

In the conversation with the beggar, Penelope begins by asking the beggar who he is. Quite reasonably, she wants to know if he has ever encountered Odysseus, if he has ever had news of Odysseus; and surprisingly enough, Odysseus responds by saying, "Ask me anything else, but don't ask me who I am." This is another question that I always throw out to students in the classroom—why does he say that? And some critics would think this is too naive and too psychologizing a response, but the response I always get is "Well, it is obvious he doesn't want to lie to Penelope"; and I think that is perhaps exactly what is going on here. When it actually comes to it, when his wife, sitting across their hearth from him, says, "Who are you?" he says, "Don't ask me that." Now, as we'll see, he does in fact lie to her; but perhaps we are meant to see here that, in the first instance, he just simply doesn't want to have to lie to Penelope of all people.

When he says, "Don't ask me who I am," she responds, also surprisingly at first glance, with a description of her own troubles. She pours out her heart to this old beggar; she describes the famous weaving trick, which was mentioned by one of the suitors in Book Two of the *Odyssey*, the trick whereby she wove a shroud for Laertes every day, unwove it every night, and thus managed to keep the suitors at bay for three years, since she said she would marry one of them once she finished the shroud. She mentions that to the old beggar; she says now she can't think of another trick, she can't think of another way to hold the suitors off; Telemachos is a grown man, she says, and should take over the household now—she doesn't know what to do. And then, at the end of this speech, when she has poured out her heart to this old beggar, then once again she says, "Tell me who you are," and at this point—maybe he has had time to gather his wits, maybe he has had time to remember that he must lie—Odysseus does in fact respond with a long and involved lie, saying that he comes from Crete and that he did in fact meet Odysseus, but he met Odysseus when Odysseus was on his way to the Trojan War.

So the beggar, whom Penelope is talking to, we have to assume, in the hopes of getting recent news of Odysseus, can only say to her, "Yes, I saw him twenty years ago"; that does her no good at all. And she responds by weeping copiously, out of disappointment, we must assume, that there is no more recent news to be had of Odysseus. This conversation, I think it is fair to say, is the most intense emotional trial we have seen Odysseus undergo yet. There they are, together in their own house; he can't tell her openly who he is, and now she sits and weeps for him; the bard says she weeps for her husband, who is sitting right there beside her. Her weeping is described in a simile; her tears are compared to snow melting on a mountain in the copiousness of their flow down her cheeks. And as Odysseus pities her, the bard tells us, but can't show any emotion, the bard says that Odysseus hides his own tears and continues to deceive his wife.

After Penelope stops weeping she offers her guest a bath; it is not the old beggar's fault that he has no good news to tell her so she, in her role as gracious hostess—very superior hostess here, since he is just a beggar—she offers him a bath. Now he refuses an entire bath, but he says he would like to have his feet washed, and he asks specifically for some old woman, some aged woman who, he says, has gone through as many troubles as he himself has to wash his feet for him. Penelope thereupon summons Eurykleia, Odysseus' old nurse, to come and wash the beggar's feet. And this is one of the points where the disguise seems to be getting a little bit permeable, because Penelope comments to Eurykleia—she says, "By this time Odysseus probably looks about like this old beggar" (Athena has made him look old and ugly again, by the way). And Eurykleia, when she comes over to wash the beggar's feet, says, "I have never seen anyone who looks as much like Odysseus as you do; you have his hands, you have his feet, you look very much like Odysseus." Odysseus says, "Yes, that is what everyone says who has seen Odysseus and me both." So, the disguise, the degree of the disguise, is questionable in this part of the *Odyssey*. How much does Odysseus look different from himself, and how much does he just look like a much older version of Odysseus? So, Eurykleia bathes Odysseus' feet, and this washing of his feet leads to one of the crucial and most important scenes in the entire *Odyssey*, the scene in which Odysseus' old nurse, the old woman who had cared for him when he was a baby and a child, sees a distinctive scar on Odysseus' thigh and recognizes that this old beggar is in fact her master.

The scar is described in a long portion of the narrative that describes not only how Odysseus got this scar, but also describes how Odysseus got his name. And if you think about it, those two things are two essential markers of Odysseus' identity. In this culture, as we saw in the scene with the Cyclops, when the Cyclops, Polyphemos needed to know Odysseus' name in order to be able to curse him, the name is bound up with a person's identity in a very deep and profound way. Polyphemos could not curse Odysseus without knowing his name; the name is in some sense the essence of the person. So, Odysseus' name is one essential attribute of who and what he is, one essential marker of his identity. What about the scar? Well, in a society that has no other means of proving identity, no fingerprints, no dental records, no photographs, no DNA typing, none of that, how would you know, when someone returns after twenty years, that he is who he says he is? People can change out of all recognition in twenty years; some people look very much the same, some look so different that you really would not recognize them. In that kind of a society, a scar, an identifiable idiosyncratic scar, is one of the few absolute proofs of identity that exists; a birthmark of course would be the same sort of thing. If someone shows up in Ithaka, looking very much like Odysseus, knowing a lot of what Odysseus knew, but does not have this distinctive scar on his thigh, that person is not Odysseus, no matter what he says. On the other hand, if someone shows up on Ithaka not looking much like Odysseus, but has this absolutely distinctive scar on his thigh, that person is Odysseus, all appearances to the contrary notwithstanding. So, in this scene in which we are told how Odysseus gets his scar and how Odysseus gets his name—and I will get back to exactly how those things happen in just a second—we have got the two crucial identifying marks of Odysseus, of who he is—his scar, his name—interweaved in a story about how he got both of them.

How did he get them? While visiting his grandfather, the young Odysseus—he was a teenager at the time—took part in a boar hunt, and was wounded in the thigh by the boar's tusk. The boar stabbed Odysseus in the thigh with his tusk at the exact instant that Odysseus stabbed the boar with his sword and killed it. So, in the instant when Odysseus killed the boar, the boar inflicted this scar upon his thigh, gave him this essential mark of his identity. Now, this grandfather, whom Odysseus was visiting at the time, Penelope's father, had given Odysseus his name when Odysseus was an infant, and Odysseus' name, interestingly enough, seems to be related to the Greek word for pain; his name seems to mean, in effect, he who gives and receives pain; giver and inflictor of pain, or almost just "pain-man," if you like, or even just pain itself. There is some controversy about this. Some scholars think that his name is related, instead, to a verb that means "to be angry at," "to cause vexation to." Other scholars think that his name should be traced to a word that means pain. I like the reading that says this name means pain, because it works so very well in this essential scene where we are told both about his name and about his scar. Think of how I just described Odysseus getting the scar. The instant in which he receives his scar, he inflicts pain on the boar, the boar inflicts pain on him—the scar thus enacts the meaning of his name.

Another aspect of the meaning of his name is how this plays out throughout the *Odyssey*. Odysseus is the man who inflicts and receives pain, both physical and emotional, really everywhere he goes. Almost every adventure, if not every adventure, he has, somebody suffers either physical or emotional pain through encountering Odysseus, and he usually suffers it in return. We see this very obviously with, say, the Cyclops Polyphemos. Odysseus inflicts grievous physical pain on the Cyclops by blinding him;

Odysseus also sufferers emotional pain through the loss of his crewmen. But we see this also even with good characters such as the Phaiakians. I haven't yet talked about what happens to the Phaiakians after Odysseus leaves, and I am afraid it is nothing good. The Phaiakians are punished by Poseidon for helping Odysseus. The extent of their punishment is ambiguous, because this is one of the few places where different manuscripts read a crucial line a little bit differently, and any editor of the *Odyssey* has to decide which reading to go with. But at the very best, Poseidon asks Zeus if he may do two things to the Phaiakians, if he may turn the ship that brought Odysseus to Ithaka into stone in the harbor of Scheria, and Poseidon also wants to hide the city of the Phaiakians under a great mountain. So he wants to kill all of them for helping Odysseus.

Zeus' response is the line that reads two different ways in different manuscripts of the *Odyssey*. Zeus says either, "Turn the ship to stone and hide their city under a great mountain," or he says, "Turn the ship to stone and do not hide their city under a mountain." So if you are an editor of the *Odyssey* you have to choose how badly the Phaiakians suffer for helping Odysseus; most editors go with the second reading, because, I think, it is almost unbearable to think that Alkinoos, Arete, Nausikaa, all of them die because of helping Odysseus. But at the very least, the ship is turned to stone; those sailors who so carefully carried Odysseus onto land, laid him down so gently while he was sleeping, surrounded him with gift—they are dead, they are turned to stone because they helped Odysseus. Odysseus didn't mean to harm the Phaiakians, but simply by being Odysseus, by encountering them, he caused them suffering and distress. Our last view of them in Book Thirteen, Alkinoos is praying to Poseidon; now, Alkinoos has heard a prophecy that this suffering will come to the Phaiakians someday, because of their helping of Odysseus. He is praying to Poseidon not to destroy them, and that is the last we see of the Phaiakians. We don't know, we are not told exactly what happens next. But Alkinoos says, in his prayer to Poseidon, "We will never again help shipwrecked travelers home." So by encountering the Phaiakians Odysseus has ruined them; he has changed their society; they will never any longer give the kind of *xenia* to others that they gave to Odysseus.

We see this again and again; every encounter Odysseus has, he causes pain, whether he means to or not. This enacts again and again, throughout the *Odyssey*, the meaning of his name, "the person who gives and receives pain." Even in Eurykleia's reaction, Eurykleia stresses the same idea; the bard says she is seized by grief and joy at the same time, when she realizes

129

that this is in fact her master. She starts to turn to Penelope to say, "This is Odysseus"—two things happen. Athena turns Penelope's attention away so Penelope doesn't see what is going on with the foot-washing, which is a pretty remarkable lapse on Penelope's part—Eurykleia has dropped Odysseus' foot in the basin and the basin has been knocked over, water is all over the floor, and Eurykleia is obviously very excited, but Athena makes Penelope just not notice this. Also, Odysseus grabs Eurykleia by the throat and says, "Are you trying to kill me? Be quiet," swears her to secrecy, and of course Eurykleia understands the situation. After all, Melantho was still in the room, and Eurykleia is trustworthy; she keeps her silence. But she now knows this is in fact Odysseus.

After Eurykleia has washed his feet, Odysseus goes back and speaks more to Penelope, and one of the foremost critical questions, not just of Book Nineteen but of the whole second half of the *Odyssey*, is, does Penelope or does she not recognize the beggar as her husband? Does she even suspect that this beggar is her husband? Their entire conversation in Book Nineteen can be interpreted—and believe me, has been interpreted, in many books and articles—to support either viewpoint: that Penelope has no idea that this beggar is her husband; that she knows perfectly well that this beggar is her husband; or that she maybe suspects but isn't sure. Since the two are never alone, if Penelope does suspect that the beggar is Odysseus, it still makes excellent sense that she doesn't say so. If she suspects, she is quickwitted, just as he is; she has read the situation; she knows Melatho is there; she can't just come right out and say, "Odysseus, you have come back." She must choose her words very carefully if she does suspect who this is.

Now, think back to their very opening conversation, when Penelope tells Odysseus about her weaving trick, tells him that she cannot think of another trick to hold the suitors now, that she is desperate, that she doesn't know what to do. Her unburdening herself this way to the old beggar makes very good sense, if she suspects that this is in fact her husband; she is saying, "Thank the gods you are here, you are back just in the nick of time, I didn't know what to do. I have remained faithful to you, I kept them at bay for three years, I don't know what to do now; it is in your hands." That scene in which she unburdens herself to this strange old beggar makes less sense if she doesn't know who he is; it is a little bit hard to think of why she would pour her heart out in this way to a beggar, who has actually just been rather disrespectful by saying, "Please don't ask me who I am." On the other hand, right after that, Penelope presses Odysseus to reveal his identity and tell her if he has ever seen Odysseus; he says, "I saw Odysseus twenty years ago," and she responds by weeping like snow melting on a mountain. That makes perfect sense if she does not know who the beggar is. Her copious weeping is perhaps harder to explain if she does. And you can go through their entire interactions with one another, throughout the rest of the *Odyssey*, this way and find some scenes that seem to indicate she does know who he is, some that seem to indicate she doesn't.

The most important conversation for this question comes after the foot-washing scene, near the end of Book Nineteen, when Penelope recounts a dream that she had, and we see her tell about her dream, and we see Odysseus' reaction to that dream. In this scene, Penelope says that she had dreamed that an eagle swooped down and killed her pet geese; that she had pet geese eating grain in the courtyard, and an eagle swooped down and killed them. Penelope was weeping over the death of her pet geese, and then the eagle perched on the roof, spoke with a human voice, and said, "Don't cry; this dream is symbolic. I, the eagle, am Odysseus; the geese are the suitors; Odysseus is going to come back and kill the suitors." Then Penelope says to the beggar, "Please interpret this dream for me." Well, if ever a dream did not need to be interpreted, clearly this is such a dream; the dream is very clear, and Odysseus says, "The dream is very clear; Odysseus himself has told you what is going to happen. He will come back and kill the suitors." Now, Penelope immediately responds to his words, saying "this is very clear," Penelope immediately responds by saying, "Well, some dreams are true and some dreams are false; it is impossible to know which is which," and then she right away says, "I am going to set a contest for the suitors tomorrow. I will get Odysseus' great bow, which only he could string, and whichever suitor can string that bow most easily and can then perform a magnificent feat of archery with it, shooting an arrow through twelve ax-heads,"—we'll talk more about in the next lecture''—"whichever suitor can do that, I will marry."

Okay, let's think about what is going on in this conversation. If we assume that Penelope knows who the beggar is, then you can read this conversation as almost a kind of coded making of a plan. She says to him, in effect, "Are you planning to kill the suitors? Is that what you are planning to do, now that you are back?" And he says, "Absolutely; no-one can interpret this dream in a different way. Odysseus will kill the suitors; yes, I am planning to kill the suitors." She says, "Good; I will get your bow out of storage and get it down into the great hall where you and the suitors are. Then you will have to figure out how to get it into your own hands, but at least it will be there." And of course a bow is the one weapon that one man trying to kill

108 men most needs, because a bow allows him to stand apart from his victims and shoot them in rapid succession. So, if we assume that Penelope knows who the beggar is, then this whole scene is a kind of coded plan in which she ascertains his intentions and provides him with a weapon.

If she doesn't know who he is, however, the scene still makes sense. She honestly wants to know how this dream strikes someone else; she wants validation for what she would like to think the dream means, and by setting the suitors this test I think she is setting a test which she has good reasons to believe the suitors cannot pass. Now a lot of critics are very troubled by Penelope, at this point, saying, "I am going to marry whichever suitor can string the bow." A lot of people take this as very odd, that Penelope at this very instant decides, "All right, tomorrow I will choose which man I am going to marry." I see it a little differently. I think by picking a bow that only Odysseus was ever able to string, Penelope is actually doing another kind of delaying tactic. If she offers the suitors the chance to string this bow and none of them can do it, then she can say, "Well, none of you are worthy to marry me; none of you are the man Odysseus was." Maybe they still won't go away, but at least maybe she has delayed the process of having to choose one of them a little bit. So, I think she is intentionally picking a test that she knows they cannot pass, by saying [she will marry] whichever suitor can string the bow of Odysseus.

So, once again, this scene, the scene in which she tells Odysseus her dream and asks him to interpret it for her, can be read to support the idea that Penelope knows, or at least suspects, that the beggar is Odysseus. It can be read to support the idea that Penelope has no idea at all that the beggar is Odysseus. You have to weigh the alternatives and decide which seems more likely to you, as a reader of the *Odyssey*. The third possibility, the third critical camp here, is of course that the ambiguity is in itself what we are supposed to get out of this whole section of the *Odyssey*. Homer cannot change the ending of the story; his audience knows perfectly well that Odysseus will in fact kill the suitors, that Odysseus and Penelope will in fact be reunited. How does a bard—working in that kind of tradition, where the storyline is set—how does a bard engage his audience's interest, build some kind of suspense, keep the story interesting, when the outcome is already known? This kind of technique, leaving us wondering what is going on in Penelope's mind—does she recognize Odysseus, does she know that the beggar is her husband, does she maybe suspect that the beggar is her husband?—this kind of ambiguity is part of what builds the suspense, builds the interest, keeps the audience engaged with the story.

So as Book Nineteen comes to an end, we have been told that the very next day Penelope will set the great contest of the bow; we know that Odysseus will try to get that bow into his own hands so that he can use it against the suitors. We have seen Eurykleia recognize Odysseus; he now, that means, has one more ally, someone he can trust to help him if he needs her to help him. Furthermore, the whole ambiguity of this question—what I like to refer to as the "what does Penelope know and when does she know it" question—this whole ambiguity provides part of the interest and part of the driving narrative force of this section of the *Odyssey*. In our next lecture, we'll turn to looking at the actual contest of the bow, when Penelope does indeed bring Odysseus' great bow out of storage, give it to the suitors, and challenge them to try to string it to decide which one of them will marry her. We'll see the suitors try and fail to string the bow, and we'll then move on into discussing Odysseus' actual slaughter of the suitors.

Lecture Ten
Recognitions and Revenge

Scope: This lecture, which covers Books XX–XXII, examines the "contest of the bow," Odysseus' revelation of his identity to the loyal slaves Eumaios and Philoitios, and the slaughter of the suitors. We continue our consideration of Penelope's knowledge and motives, as well as focusing on the narrative strategies the bard uses for increasing the sense of inevitability as the suitors' doom approaches. The importance of *xenia* is noted once again, as we consider whether Odysseus' slaughter of the suitors and the disloyal slave women is justified or not.

Outline

I. The bow contest which Penelope proposed in Book XIX is actually undertaken in Book XXI. Thus, Book XIX creates narrative suspense and heightens the inevitability of the suitors' doom.

   A. Penelope brings Odysseus' bow down from the storeroom. She weeps as she holds it.

   B. Penelope tells the suitors that she will marry whichever one of them can string the bow most easily and shoot an arrow through 12 axes.

   C. Telemachos sets up the axes.

II. The suitors try to string the bow, but fail.

   A. Telemachos tries first, and would have succeeded on the third attempt had Odysseus not caught his eye.

   B. Leodes, a young suitor, tries next, and tears his soft palms in the attempt.

   C. Antinoos warms the bow by the fire and rubs it with tallow to soften it, but even so cannot string it.

   D. There is magnificent irony in this scene of the suitors conditioning the weapon that will kill them.

III. While the suitors are engaged with the bow, Eumaios goes outside, accompanied by Philoitios (a loyal oxherd). Odysseus goes out to join them, and reveals his identity to them.

A. He proves his identity by showing them his scar.

B. He promises to free them and give them houses and wives if they succeed against the suitors.

C. He gives each of them instructions.

    1. Eumaios should bring the bow to Odysseus, and then should tell the women servants to bar the door from the hall into the rest of the house.

    2. Philoitios should bolt the door into the courtyard.

    3. Thus, the suitors will be unable to escape from the hall.

IV. Odysseus reenters the house, to find the suitors still unable to string the bow. He asks to be given a chance with it.

    A. Eurymachos remarks that he does not so much regret missing marriage with Penelope as he is ashamed at the thought that "men unborn" will be told of the suitors' inability to string the bow. He is clearly concerned about his *kleos*.

    B. Odysseus asks to be given a chance, and the suitors are highly indignant at the idea.

    C. Penelope intervenes, and says to let the beggar try. Once again, her words are capable of double interpretation.

        1. If she does not know the beggar is Odysseus, letting him try is simply a show of contempt for the suitors.

        2. If she does know, she is ensuring that he will get the bow into his hands.

        3. Either way, the audience would find a wonderful irony in her words.

    D. Telemachos speaks up and claims authority over the bow. He tells Penelope to go upstairs and tend to her own, womanly duties.

V. Eumaios brings the bow to Odysseus, who strings it easily. The poet compares Odysseus' stringing of the bow to a bard's stringing of a lyre. He plucks the bowstring and Zeus' thunder strikes fear in the hearts of the suitors.

    A. Odysseus shoots through the axes, and nods to Telemachos, who comes to stand close beside him.

    B. Odysseus then shoots Antinoos.

VI. The suitors do not immediately realize that this is Odysseus, but he declares himself to them.

    A. Odysseus' words to the suitors stress their position as "beyond the pale" due to their violations of *xenia*.

    B. Eurymachos blames all the suitors' wrongdoing on Antinoos, and offers to pay recompense to Odysseus.

    C. Odysseus refuses to accept the offer; it is too little, too late.

VII. With Athena's help, Odysseus and Telemachos kill all the suitors.

    A. While Odysseus holds the suitors at bay with his arrows, Telemachos runs to get armor for himself, Odysseus, Eumaios, and Philoitios. By mistake, he leaves the door to the storeroom open.

    B. Melanthios climbs through the vents in the wall to get armor for the suitors.

    C. Telemachos admits to Odysseus that it was his mistake in leaving the door open that allowed Melanthios access to the armor. This moment can be seen as Telemachos' final maturation.

    D. Odysseus sends Eumaios and Philoitios to overpower Melanthios, while he and Telemachos hold off the suitors.

    E. After appearing briefly disguised as Odysseus' friend Mentor, Athena makes most of the suitors' spear-throws useless. The ones that do hit cause only minor injury, such as a scratch on Telemachos' wrist.

    F. Finally Odysseus and his comrades kill all the suitors. At Telemachos' request, Odysseus spares the bard Phemios and the herald Medon, who had been forced to cooperate with the suitors.

VIII. In the aftermath of the slaughter, Odysseus cleanses his palace and kills the disloyal female slaves.

    A. Odysseus sends Telemachos to fetch Eurykleia. She starts to rejoice over the dead suitors, but Odysseus stops her. Eurykleia reports that of the 50 female slaves, 12 were disloyal.

    B. The disloyal women are forced to clean the hall and carry the suitors' bodies outside.

    C. With Eumaios' and Philoitios' aid, Telemachos hangs the women in the courtyard.

D. Odysseus purifies the palace with fire and sulphur.

IX. The killing of the suitors, and especially of the disloyal slavewomen, strikes many readers as too grim; at this point they lose sympathy for Odysseus. But within the context of the society the *Odyssey* depicts, these actions are justifiable.

    A. From their very first entry into the epic, the suitors have been portrayed as knowingly disregarding proper behavior and being unamenable to reason.

    B. The *Odyssey* takes for granted that slaves owe obedience to their masters, as subjects do to their king. The disloyal women have betrayed Odysseus in both those aspects.

Essential Reading:

Odyssey, Books XX–XXII.

Supplementary Reading:

Norman Austin, *Archery at the Dark of the Moon*, Chapter V. Austin presents a very interesting reading of the bow-contest based on the positions of the sun and moon.

Richard Seaford, *Reciprocity and Ritual*, Chapter 2, Section D (pp. 53–65).

Questions to Consider:

1. I argued in the lecture that Odysseus' punishment of the suitors and the disloyal women is justified, considered within the context of the epic itself. Do you agree, or does the vengeance seem excessive to you?

2. Consider the effect of Athena's intervention in the battle, where she makes the suitors' spearcasts useless but ensures that Odysseus' and his comrades' are lethal. Does Athena's involvement here make the outcome seem all the more inevitable (cf. the gods' interventions in the *Iliad*), or does it take away from Odysseus' credit?

Lecture Ten—Transcript
Recognitions and Revenge

Hello, and welcome to Lecture Ten. In our previous lecture, we examined Odysseus' conversations with Penelope in Book Nineteen, the scene in which Eurykleia recognizes him—Odysseus—by a scar on his thigh while she is washing his feet, and we discussed the question of whether or not Penelope recognizes Odysseus. We ended with a reference to the archery contest that Penelope says she will set up for the suitors on the following day. This lecture, which covers Books Twenty through Twenty-Two, will examine the contest of the bow and Odysseus' revelation of his identity to two loyal slaves, Eumaios and the oxherd Philoitios. We'll then move on to talking about the slaughter of the suitors, and we'll finish with noting, once again, the importance of *xenia* as a motivating narrative motive in the *Odyssey*, and we'll consider whether or not Odysseus' slaughter of the suitors and the disloyal slave women is in fact justified.

Book Twenty is really there in the *Odyssey* to provide delaying of the action between Book Nineteen and Book Twenty-One. Nothing new happens in Book Twenty; the suitors come back from wherever they have spent the night after Book Eighteen and we see the suitors' insolent and inappropriate behavior reiterated in Book Twenty, particularly in its motivation by Athena. Athena, we are told, will not let the suitors stop acting outrageously; this stresses, I think, the sense of inevitability. The suitors are doomed to be killed by Odysseus; nothing at this point that they can do will change that doom, and Athena makes it even more certain by seeing to it that they continue to act outrageously. To take just one example in Book Twenty, one of the suitors throws an ox-hoof at the old beggar, at Odysseus, for really no reason except just to be hateful. So Book Twenty reiterates the idea that the suitors are inevitably doomed; it causes narrative suspense by delaying the actual enactment of the bow contest that Penelope has suggested in Book Nineteen; and it moves us on into Book Twenty-One with a heightened sense of the inevitability of the suitors' doom.

In Book Twenty-One, we actually see the bow contest, which Penelope had proposed in Book Nineteen. Penelope goes to the storeroom where Odysseus' bow is kept, takes the bow, holds it on her lap for a while, and weeps over it. Once again, the question of why Penelope is weeping, and what we take that to mean about her knowledge or lack of knowledge of the beggar's identity, is important here, and once again the scene can be read in both ways. If Penelope does not know that the beggar is Odysseus, then clearly she is weeping at this poignant reminder of her former husband, and at the thought that she might actually have to marry one of the suitors, if one of them does in fact manage to string bow and thus prove that he is as good a man as Odysseus was. On the other hand, if Penelope does know that the beggar is in fact Odysseus, then I think there is an equally obvious explanation for her weeping. This is an extremely dangerous moment for Odysseus. He may be able to overwhelm and kill all the suitors, once he gets hold of his bow that Penelope will bring downstairs. But by far the most likely outcome—for people who do not know, as we do, the foreordained end of the story—by far the most likely outcome is that the suitors will kill Odysseus. So, either way, Penelope is at a point that may lead to catastrophe for her, and a forced marriage with one of the suitors.

Penelope comes downstairs with the bow, and she tells the suitors that she will marry whichever one of them can most easily string the bow and can then shoot an arrow through twelve axes. We are then told that Telemachos takes the axes and sets them up in order. Now, what exactly is meant by shooting an arrow through twelve axes, is yet another one of the problems in the *Odyssey* that has been discussed at great length and hasn't ever been definitively solved. I think one possibility has to be excluded right away. This is not a magic bow; these are not magic arrows; Homer is not suggesting that the arrow will actually go through the metal of the ax-heads.

Probably what we are supposed to picture is double-bladed axes with a hole in one side, through which a thong could be tied so that the warrior could carry the ax at his belt that would make sense. If the axes are set up in a row, the trick would be to shoot the arrow through those holes in the ax-heads. Other people think that we are talking just about ax handles here, or that, rather, there is a hole at the end of the ax handle, that the axes are set head down, and the arrow is to be shot through the handles. It doesn't really matter all that much for our purposes. The point is that this is a significant feat of archery, to be able to shoot an arrow through a hole in twelve axes set up in a row without the arrow wavering or missing or getting caught in the axes.

So, Telemachos sets up the axes for this contest, and the suitors then try to string the bow. Each one of them fails miserably. Telemachos tries first, and on the third attempt he was about to string the bow when, the bard tells us Odysseus, caught his eye and signaled with his brows—some sort of frown or raising his eyebrows or something—to his son, don't do that. Telemachos is about to ruin the whole scheme by stringing the bow himself. Telemachos comes to his senses, hands the bow over to the suitors, saying, "Well, I am just young and a weakling; you, who are so much stronger than I, surely you can string this bow." The first suitor to try is a young suitor named Leodes. Homer tells us that he was the only one of the suitors who did not approve of the way the suitors were behaving, the only decent man among them, in effect. He tries first to string the bow and we are told that he tears his soft palms up on the string as he is trying. He can't even begin to bend Odysseus' bow. The others suitors try; none of them can string it. Eventually Antinoos warms the bow by the fire, rubs it with tallow to soften it, and still cannot string it. Now, once again, Homer is, I think, stressing the inevitability of what is going to happen to the suitors, in a rather ironic and actually rather ghastly way. These suitors are conditioning the weapon that will kill them. They are bending it—it is stiff from having been stored away for twenty years—they are trying to bend it, they are softening it with tallow in front of the fire, they are doing everything to make this bow workable; and this is the bow that will in fact kill them. A magnificent irony going on there.

While the suitors are thus engaged with the bow, trying and failing to string it, Eumaios goes outside. He is accompanied by a character I haven't mentioned yet, the other loyal slave whom Odysseus finds in Ithaka, Philoitios, an oxherd. Just to recap, Eumaios is the swineherd, Melanthios is the goatherd, Philoitios is the oxherd. Philoitios was introduced in Book Twenty, and when we first see him he speaks very kindly to the old beggar, treats the old beggar in an extremely friendly way, and also, in Book Twenty, Philoitios prays that Odysseus might come home. So just as Melanthios spontaneously said to the old beggar, "I wish the suitors would kill Telemachos as surely as Odysseus is dead," Philoitios spontaneously says to the old beggar, "How I wish Odysseus would come home and set his household in order." So, when Eumaios and Philoitios go outside, Odysseus gets up goes out to join them. And notice how the suitors pay no attention whatsoever to the comings and goings of two old slaves and an old beggar; they don't care what these people do. This gives Odysseus an opportunity to plot with Eumaios and Philoitios, plot the suitors' destruction, while the suitors are right there inside the hall but paying no attention whatsoever to what the old beggar is doing.

Odysseus goes out to join Eumaios and Philoitios and he asks them, "What would you do if Odysseus came home? Would you fight for him, or would you fight for the suitors?" Eumaios and Philoitios both react by saying if only that could happen, of course they would fight for Odysseus; at which point Odysseus reveals his identity to them. He proves who he is by showing them his scar, and he says that they are the only two of his slaves whom he has heard praying for his homecoming, the only two that he can trust really wanted him to come home. After he proves his identity, after he shows them his scar, he also promises that if they will fight beside him and Telemachos, if they will help him and Telemachos overcome the suitors, he says that he will free each of them, give them each a house and a wife, set them up as free men, and honor them as he honors Telemachos.

Now, as I have mentioned a few times in passing, the *Odyssey* takes it absolutely for granted that slavery is the only system by which society can operate; there is never any hint in the *Odyssey*, or for that matter in the *Iliad*, that there could be another arrangement other than slavery. And yet Homer doesn't sentimentalize slavery; he doesn't assume that slaves like being slaves, or that even slaves who are very loyal to their master enjoy slavery. The best thing Odysseus can offer Eumaios and Philoitios is their freedom; it is simply taken for granted that any slave would want to be free. So, since Odysseus is asking them to risk their lives in what is, by any reckoning, a fairly desperate encounter in which they quite likely will be killed, he has to make it worth their while by saying, "If you survive, I will free you and set you up with a house and little bit of land and a wife," so that they will have an opportunity to make a life for themselves as free men.

He also gives each of them instructions. When they go back inside—and he says, "Let's go in separately"; he'll go in first, they should come in after him; he doesn't want to draw any attention to the fact that they have been talking to one another—when they go back inside, he says, Eumaios should bring the bow to Odysseus. At some point, Odysseus will suggest, "Let me try stringing the bow; the suitors," he says, "will of course be very indignant at this, but Eumaios, bring the bow to me any way. Just take it and bring it over to me." And then, he says, "Eumaios, tell the women servants to bar the door that leads from the great dining hall into the rest of the house." The great hall is the first room you come in to when you come in through the courtyard; there is a doorway at the far end that leads to the rest of the house. So, Eumaios' responsibility is to see to it that the door into the rest of the house is barred. Philoitios, meanwhile, should bar the door to the courtyard, so that the suitors will be trapped; they won't be able to get out of the great hall in either direction. Then Odysseus re-enters the house; after giving these instructions to his two loyal servants, Eumaios and Philoitios, he re-enters the house to find the suitors still unable to string the bow. They are still trying; they are still passing it around and trying to string it, but they can't do it. And this is when Odysseus asks to be given a chance; the old beggar asks to be given a chance to string the bow.

Now, the suitors have pretty much given up on the bow, and Eurymachos makes a very interesting comment at this point. Eurymachos remarks that he does not so much regret missing marriage with Penelope as he is ashamed at the thought that men unborn will know that he and the other suitors failed to string this bow. Suddenly Eurymachos is thinking about his *kleos*, about his reputation, about what people will say about him. Suddenly Eurymachos is worried that people who are not yet born will hear this story and will know that he, Eurymachos, could not string the bow of Odysseus. This is what I would like to call an "extra-textual moment," a moment that moves right outside the text and almost looks back in on it from the outside, because what Eurymachos says he is afraid of is exactly what Homer is doing. We are listening to a story that tells us that Eurymachos could not string the bow, and within that story Eurymachos says, "I am really worried that you people as yet unborn will hear that I couldn't string the bow." And once again, that reminder of what we are listening to, I think, is another narrative strategy that stresses the inevitability of the suitors' doom. The suitors themselves realize that they will become a laughingstock throughout all eternity. As long as epic survives, people will be saying Eurymachos could not string Odysseus' bow.

Odysseus asks to be given a chance and, as one might suspect, the suitors are highly indignant at the idea. They are young noblemen, and this bow has been offered to them as a means of winning the hand of Penelope, and suddenly this old disreputable-looking vagabond says, "Well, let me try to string the bow." They are indignant on two accounts. First of all, how dare he even think he could, when they can't and he is so much older than they are? And second, how dare he suggest that he should take part in the contest, which would win the hand of Penelope? Penelope herself intervenes at this point, and says let the beggar try; and she makes a very interesting comment. She says, "If he strings the bow he is not going to take me off to his house and make me his wife; he has no such thought of anything like that; he just wants to see if he can string it."

Now, again, as so frequently before, her words can be interpreted either to imply that he doesn't know this is Odysseus, or to imply that she does. If she doesn't know that this is Odysseus, what she has just done is a beautiful expression of contempt for her suitors—"I will let this old man, this old beggar, try to string the bow, and I think he might be able to do it." That is a fairly harsh statement to these young men who have failed to string the bow, that she holds them in such low regard that she thinks an old beggar might succeed where they failed. If she does know this is Odysseus, of course, she is insuring that he gets the bow into his hands; she is intervening in the action at the exact moment when it would be most helpful for her to intervene, to see to it that Odysseus actually gets his hands on this bow. Either way, the audience would find a wonderful irony in her words when she says, "If he succeeds, do you think he is planning to take me to his house and to make me his wife?" He is in his house and she is his wife. So, there is not a process involved here; he is not going to take her anywhere and he is not going to make her his wife, no matter what happens. And either way, her words also stress that Odysseus will get the bow into his hands; the sense of inevitability is underlined yet again.

At this instant, Telemachos suddenly speaks up and asserts authority over his mother. He says, basically, "This is my house, this is my bow, and you go back upstairs and pay attention to your womanly duties and leave men's business to the men." Now, this is yet another instant where I always throw the question out on the floor to my students and say, why does Telemachos do that? And someone always comes up with what I think is the right answer; he is desperate to get Penelope out of there. He pulls rank on her, he pulls authority on her, at this exact instant because Telemachos, without question, knows that the beggar is Odysseus, realizes what is about to happen. Odysseus is about to get hold of the bow, he is about to start shooting the suitors, there is going to be blood, gore, death in this hall any instant now, and unlike us, Telemachos does not know the foreordained outcome. The most likely outcome is that Telemachos and Odysseus will both be killed; and I think Telemachos does not want his mother to see him die. He is trying to spare her, and to remove her from danger, by getting her out of the way and doing it in a way that he knows will work—because the last thing in the world Penelope would do to Telemachos, in front of the suitors, is in any way shame him or question his authority. She is not going to say to him, "How dare you speak to me like that, young man?" When he says, "Mother, go upstairs and tend to your womanly duties," she is going to do exactly what she does do, obey him silently and leave.

So, when Eumaios actually brings the bow to Odysseus, Penelope has left; Telemachos is on guard for what is going to happen next. Eumaios hands the bow to Odysseus and Odysseus strings it with the greatest of ease. There is nothing to it; he simply bends the bow and strings it. The poet compares Odysseus' stringing the bow to a bard's stringing a lyre. He says, "As someone who is skilled in playing the lyre easily pulls the string over the peg of the lyre, so easily Odysseus strung the bow." Once again, another little extra-textual moment, in which the bard says, in effect, "Odysseus was as skillful at handling his bow as I, the bard, who is strumming a lyre and singing to you, am at handling a lyre." Odysseus plucks the bowstring; it gives off a musical twang; Zeus thunders on high; and great sorrow seizes the suitors—all sorts of extremely ominous things happening all at once.

Odysseus, now that he has strung the bow, shoots an arrow through the axes—again, nothing to it; almost as an afterthought, he picks an arrow, shoots through the axes, and nods to Telemachos. Telemachos comes and stands close beside him. Odysseus then, the next instant, shoots and kills the suitor Antinoos. Now the moment when Odysseus shoots and kills the suitor Antinoos is actually near the beginning of Book Twenty-Two; the stringing of the bow ends Boo Twenty-One. This is a good point to remind you that these book divisions are absolutely artificial; they are a later addition to the *Odyssey*, not part of the original bard's original conception. So as I am recounting the story, Odysseus strings the bow, shoots the arrows, nods to Telemachos, and shoots Antinoos; that is how the narrative flow would have gone in the original performance.

The suitors, interestingly enough, do not immediately realize that this is Odysseus; they still do not quite realize what is happening to them. They think the beggar has either gone crazy, or that it was a mistake; they thnk he shot one arrow through the axes and was aiming at something else, and hit Antinoos by mistake. And they tell him that this is an extremely bad mistake that he has made, and that he is going to suffer for it. But he declares himself to them; he says to the suitors—when they are scolding him and remarking how grievous a mistake he has just made for himself by shooting Antinoos—Odysseus says to them:

> You dogs, you never thought that I would any more come back
> from the land of Troy, and because of that you despoiled by household,
> and forcibly took my serving women to sleep beside you,
> and sought to win my wife while I was still alive, fearing
> neither the immortal gods who hold the wide heaven,
> nor any resentment sprung from man to be yours in the future.
> Now upon all of you the terms of destruction are fastened.

So he runs through everything that the suitors have done wrong at that point. They have disregarded *xenia* by despoiling his household; they have forcibly taken his serving women, which is, in a slaveholding society, another outrage against his property, against what should be done in his household. They sought to win his wife while he was still alive—now, to be fair to the suitors, they couldn't have known he was still alive, but that doesn't really matter in Odysseus' opinion—they sought to win his wife while he was still alive; and remember Eurymachos speech to Halitherses, all the way in Book Two. They did exactly what I said then Eurymachos shows that they did; they feared neither the immortal gods nor any bad opinion among humans. In other words, they set themselves entirely outside the moral pale of their own society; they violated just about everyone of their society's mores, as we have talked about before. And therefore, Odysseus says, "the terms of destruction are set on you."

Now, the suitors, being the suitors, still try to see if there isn't some way they can get out of this. Eurymachos, in fact, says to Odysseus, "Well, actually, Odysseus, there *was* one man who did all those things you said; it just happens that Antinoos, the guy you already killed, was responsible for everything, so you have killed the right man. The rest of us are really sorry; why don't we give you some gifts, and we'll let bygones be bygones?" So, Eurymachos tries to put all the blame on Antinoos, which cuts no ice whatsoever with Odysseus; he refuses to accept the offer. In fact, he says, "If you gave me all the possessions your father has and more than that, it wouldn't matter." The situation has gone beyond any kind of material recompense; only the suitors' death will work at this point, and there is nothing they can do now.

And with Athena's help, Odysseus and Telemachos do in fact manage to kill all of the suitors. While Odysseus holds the suitors at bay with his arrows, Telemachos runs to the storeroom to get armor for himself, Odysseus, Eumaios, and Philoitios. Odysseus has only so many arrows in his quiver, and also the element of surprise and shock is only going to hold the suitors back for so long; it won't be too long before they realize that they could rush Odysseus in a mass and overwhelm him, even though he does have a bow and they have no weapons. So Telemachos goes quickly to get armor for himself, his father, and the two helpful slave men. By mistake, Telemachos leaves the door to the armor storeroom open; and that is a very bad mistake, a mistake that could in fact have been fatal, because Melanthios, the treacherous Melanthios, climbs through vents in the wall— apparently there are ventilation ducts in the wall of this palace—he climbs through them to get to the floor where the storeroom is, and then starts supplying armor for the suitors.

So, there is a moment when Melanthios is bringing armor and spears to the suitors; Telemachos has brought armor and weapons back for his father and his confederates, and yet it looks like the battle could go in exactly the wrong direction, because Melanthios is arming the suitors. Odysseus, seeing this, thinks one of the serving women must have opened the storeroom somehow and let Melanthios in; and Telemachos—at this moment when they think they are about to die because of this mistake—Telemachos admits that the mistake was his. I like to see this as the moment of Telemachos' final maturation; when his father says, "One of the serving women has betrayed us, Melanthios is bringing armor to the suitors," Telemachos says, "No, I did that; that was my mistake. There is no one else to blame, Father; I did it." And that, as I said, I think is the moment when Telemachos really claims his full maturity and his full adulthood, when he admits that mistake to Odysseus.

Odysseus sends Eumaios and Philoitios to overpower Melanthios in the storeroom; that means, of course, that Odysseus and Telemachos are left holding off the suitors by themselves for a while, while Eumaios and Philoitios go overpower Melanthios and tie him up. But Athena steps in to help; she appears briefly as Odysseus' friend, Mentor, to encourage him. Odysseus knows it has to be a god; for one thing, how could Mentor suddenly be there in the locked hall, how could he get in, what would he be doing there? Athena also, more importantly, sees to it that the suitors' spear-throws are useless. So the suitors are throwing their spears at Odysseus and Telemachos; Athena simply turns them aside, or she lets a few of them hit but only inflict very minor injuries. For instance, Telemachos gets a scratch on this wrist, which is not much of an injury when an enemy throws a spear at you. And finally, Odysseus and his comrades manage to kill all of the suitors.

Leodes—the young suitor who tried first to string the bow and tore his palms on it—Leodes begs Odysseus for mercy, and tells Odysseus, "I never violated any of your serving women; I never did any thing wrong. Please spare my life." But Odysseus says, in effect, "Just by being one of the suitors you must have wished that I was dead, and you were trying to take over my household"; and therefore no plea for mercy can take effect at this point. So, even the one suitor that we are told was actually not evil, even Leodes, is killed. Odysseus does, however, spare his own bard, Phemios, and his herald, Medon, only because Telemachos tells him that those two men helped the suitors out of compulsion; not because they wanted to, but because the suitors forced them to. So, at Telemachos' request, Odysseus spares Phemios and Medon; in his own fury, we are left with the impression Odysseus would have killed them as well.

The aftermath of the slaughter requires cleaning the palace, both literally and ritually speaking. Odysseus sends Telemachos to fetch Eurykleia. Eurykleia comes in and starts to rejoice over the dead suitors; she starts to raise a cry of triumph when she sees the suitors dead. It is Odysseus who stops her and tells her it is not appropriate to rejoice over dead men. Odysseus also asks Eurykleia how many of the slave-women were treacherous and how many were loyal, and Eurykleia says that of the fifty female slaves, twelve were intentionally disloyal. Odysseus then sends Telemachos to kill those twelve disloyal female slaves. Telemachos, Eumaios, and Philoitios hang the treacherous female slaves in the courtyard, after first forcing them to clean up the slaughterhouse that the great hall has become, to wash it down, to carry the suitors' bodies out into the courtyard. Now, remembe,r these disloyal women had become the suitors' lovers, so they are being asked to clean up the bodies of the their own dead lovers. It is a pretty vicious thing that they're forced to do. After the hall has been cleaned, literally speaking, Odysseus purified it, ritually speaking, with fire and sulfur.

Now, this whole scene, the killing of the suitors and especially the killing of the disloyal servant women, sits very ill with some modern readers. A good many modern readers find this too grim, too much, too harsh a reaction; all the suitors, even Leodes who begs for mercy, are killed, the serving women are killed, and Odysseus and Telemachos seem to glory in committing this slaughter. Despite our modern sensibilities, however, I think within the context of the *Odyssey* itself, within the context of the society the *Odyssey* depicts I think these actions can be seen as justifiable. Once again, from their very first entry into the epic, the suitors have been portrayed as knowingly disregarding proper behavior and at being unamenable to any kind of reason. In a point I didn't mention, in Book Sixteen, when Eumaios has informed Penelope that Telemachos is back on Ithaka, Eurymachos assures Penelope that nobody will ever hurt Telemachos. He says, "I feel loyal to Telemachos because I remember Odysseus from when I was a small boy. Odysseus used to hold me on his lap and be kind to me, and therefore I will protect Telemachos; don't worry, Penelope." But then the bard tells us Eurymachos said this, but was actually planning himself to spearhead the murder of Telemachos. So over and over again, we are reminded how completely immoral, amoral even, the suitors are. And in a society that has no law courts, no legal system, no system of punishment for wrong-doing except personal vengeance, what do you do with a group of people who have intentionally set themselves outside the boundaries of their own society's moral code? So, I think within the society depicted by the *Odyssey*, killing the suitors is justifiable.

Killing the slave-women; again, this goes against our modern sensibilities in all sorts of ways, one of which, of course, is that we don't—we very rightly disapprove entirely of slavery, and so we don't have any sense that slaves owe loyalty to their master. But again, within the *Odyssey* itself, it is taken as absolutely a given, without question, that slaves owe obedience to their master, just as subjects owe obedience to their king. The slave-women, therefore, have betrayed Odysseus in a double aspect. As subjects they have betrayed their king; as slaves they have betrayed their master; as female slaves they have betrayed their male authority figure; and once again, I think, within this society that means that they must be killed. There is nothing else to do with them. It is grim; it is, from our point of view, quite unpleasant; and yet, I think, within Homer's society as depicted in this epic, the slaughter both of the suitors and of the serving women is justified.

In our next lecture we'll move on to the end of the *Odyssey*, in which Odysseus and Penelope are finally truly reunited, with no question that she recognizes who he is, and we'll then talk about the final scenes of the *Odyssey* and the way Homer draws this epic to a close.

Lecture Eleven
Reunion and Resolution

Scope: This last lecture on the *Odyssey* discusses the final reunion of
Odysseus and Penelope in Book XXIII, and the resolution of
several themes in Book XXIV. The lecture analyzes the famous
"sign" of Odysseus' and Penelope's bed in detail, and considers
the symbolic and narrative importance that it holds. Moving on to
Book XXIV, the lecture addresses the issue of whether or not that
book belongs to the original *Odyssey*, and identifies several key
ways in which Book XXIV resolves issues that would otherwise
be left incomplete. After looking briefly at the "Second *Nekuia*"
that opens Book XXIV, the lecture concentrates on Odysseus'
encounter with his father, Laertes, and discusses the two forms of
proof Odysseus uses to establish his identity in all his reunions.
Finally, we look at the ending of the *Odyssey*, and discuss whether
or not it is effective.

Outline

I. Book XXIII begins with Eurykleia going to tell Penelope that
Odysseus has returned and has killed the suitors.

   A. Penelope refuses to believe Eurykleia, but says that some god must
   have killed the suitors.

      1. However, she will come downstairs to see the dead suitors and
      the man who killed them.

      2. Neither Eurykleia nor Penelope is shocked by the sight of the
      slaughter of the suitors.

   B. This scene is the strongest evidence that Penelope does not
   recognize the beggar as her husband before this point.

II. When Penelope comes downstairs, she sits down across from Odysseus
and looks at him rather than immediately greeting him.

   A. Telemachos scolds her for this, but Penelope says that if he is truly
   Odysseus, they have ways of recognizing one another that only
   they know.

   B. Odysseus tells Telemachos to have Phemios play his lyre and have the slaves dance, so that any passers-by will think the suitors are alive and celebrating Penelope's choice to marry one of them.

III. Odysseus bathes, and Athena makes him look younger and more beautiful. He then returns to sit by Penelope again, and reproaches her for not recognizing him. She sets him a test which leads to their true reunion.

   A. Odysseus repeats Telemachos' words of reproach, and then asks Eurykleia to make a bed up for him outside the bedroom.

   B. Penelope responds by telling Eurykleia to move "his own bed, which he himself built," outside their bedroom and make it up for him.

   C. Odysseus reacts with anger, and describes the bed he made in terms that prove his identity.

      1. The bed was constructed around a living olive-tree, which serves as one of its posts.

      2. Odysseus built his bedchamber around the bed and his house around the chamber.

      3. The bed serves as a symbol of Odysseus' and Penelope's marriage, of Athena's patronage, and of Penelope's fidelity.

   D. Penelope recognizes that this is indeed Odysseus, rushes to him, and kisses him. She asks him not to be angry at her caution, explaining that she was always afraid someone would deceive her into believing he was Odysseus.

   E. The bard uses one of the most famous similes in the *Odyssey* to describe their reunion.

IV. Odysseus and Penelope, reunited at last, go to bed together and then lie awake telling one another their stories.

   A. Athena lengthens the night so that they will have time for sex, talk, and sleep.

   B. Odysseus tells Penelope of Teiresias' prophecy about his future travels (Book XI).

   C. Eurykleia and the housekeeper Eurynome make up the bed, and Odysseus and Penelope go to bed together.

   D. After making love, they lie awake talking.

      1. Penelope tells Odysseus about the suitors.

2. Odysseus tells Penelope all his adventures, in order, just as he told them to the Phaiakians.
3. Penelope listens "with delight," again indicating the sexual double standard assumed by the poet.

E. Finally they fall asleep.

V. Some critics have argued that the *Odyssey* originally ended here, with Odysseus' and Penelope's reunion. But there is one more book, which ties up many themes of the epic.

A. Book XXIV opens with a "Second *Nekuia*," which begins with a conversation between Achilles and Agamemnon and then shows the souls of the suitors arriving in Hades.
1. Some critics think this is spurious, since it shows the ghosts in Hades conversing with one another, unlike the picture we saw in Book XI.
2. However, it picks up once again, and puts to rest, the parallel between Agamemnon and Odysseus, as Agamemnon himself praises Penelope.

B. After the scene in the Underworld, the poem turns back to Ithaka, where Odysseus goes to visit his father, Laertes.
1. When Odysseus sees his father, he is distressed at how unkempt the old man looks, and sheds tears for him.
2. However, instead of immediately identifying himself to his father, Odysseus lies to him, saying that he is a traveler who met Odysseus five years ago.
3. When Laertes reacts with grief, Odysseus identifies himself. Once again, we see him enacting his name by giving and receiving pain.
4. Laertes refuses to believe him without proof, so Odysseus shows him his scar and describes the trees they planted together when Odysseus was small.

VI. In all the recognition scenes we have seen, Odysseus has two available strategies for identifying himself: his scar and shared emotional memories.

A. Eurykleia, Eumaios, and Philoitios recognize him through the scar alone.

B. Penelope recognizes him through a shared emotionally significant memory alone.

C. Laertes is offered both types of proof, the scar and a shared memory.

D. Only Telemachos is offered no proof at all, but has to accept his father on trust.

VII. After their reunion, Laertes and Odysseus return to town, where with Telemachos, they battle the suitors' relatives. Athena allows Laertes one kill, but then brings the battle to a halt.

A. Athena requires both sides to pledge peace.

B. The conflict is thus ended, but in a rather artificial manner, which some critics find unsatisfactory.

Essential Reading:

Odyssey, Books XXIII and XXIV.

Supplementary Reading:

Jenny Strauss Clay, *Wrath of Athena*, Chapter 5. A thought-provoking summary of the interaction of gods and humans in the *Odyssey*.

Steven Lowenstam, *Scepter and Spear*, Chapter 3, Sections 6 and 7, pp. 207–244.

Sheila Murnaghan, "The Plan of Athena."

Michael N. Nagler, "Dread Goddess Revisited."

Richard Seaford, *Reciprocity and Ritual*, Chapter 2, Sections A–B (pp. 30–42).

Froma Zeitlin, "Figuring Fidelity."

Questions to Consider:

1. If Penelope has recognized the beggar as her husband, her refusal to believe Eurykleia's words at the beginning of Book XXIII is very puzzling. Can you think of any way to reconcile that refusal with an interpretation arguing that Penelope has already recognized the beggar?

2. When Odysseus encounters Laertes, there is no longer any danger and no longer any need for him to be careful or deceitful. Why, then, does the bard make Odysseus decide to lie to his father?

Lecture Eleven—Transcript
Reunion and Resolution

Hello, and welcome to Lecture Eleven. In our previous lecture we discussed the contest of the bow and Odysseus' actual killing of the suitors. In this final lecture on the *Odyssey* itself, we will look at the actual reunion of Odysseus and Penelope in Book Twenty-Three, when they are finally reunited as husband and wife. We'll analyze the famous sign of their bed, and why that bed is a fitting emblem of their relationship and its patronage by the goddess, Athena. Moving on to Book Twenty-Four, we will consider the issue of whether or not that book belongs to the *Odyssey* or is a later addition, and identify several key ways in which Book Twenty-Four repeats issues and closes issues that otherwise would be left hanging in the *Odyssey*. After looking briefly at the second *Nekuia*, the second journey to the Underworld that opens Book Twenty-Four, we'll concentrate on Odysseus' reunion with his father in that book; and finally we'll look at the ending of the *Odyssey* and discuss whether or not it is an effective closing for the epic.

So Book Twenty-Three, where we will start, begins with Eurykleia going upstairs to tell Penelope about the slaughter of the suitors, and to tell her that the beggar is in fact Odysseus, that the beggar is the man who killed the suitors and that he is in fact Odysseus. Now, when Eurykleia gives Penelope this news, Penelope at first refuses to believe Eurykleia. She says that it is not Odysseus who killed the suitors, but rather some god must have come in and killed them in the guise of the beggar. However, she says that she will come downstairs to see the men who courted her lying there dead, and to see the man who killed them.

It is worth noting—both in the scene where Eurykleia comes in after the slaughter of the suitors in Book Twenty-Two and in this scene in Book Twenty-Three—it is worth noting that neither Eurykleia nor Penelope shows the slightest disgust at the sight of blood and gore, the slightest shrinking from viewing dead bodies, the slightest reaction of horror or of being appalled at the aftermath of violence. Both of these women seem to actually enjoy looking at the dead bodies of the suitors. Eurykleia is going to raise a cry of joy over them until Odysseus stops her. Penelope—even when she says she doesn't believe that the beggar is Odysseus, that she thinks some god killed them—says that she actually wants to come downstairs and look at their bodies. So, again, our modern sensibilities are very different. The idea that someone would be appalled by or revolted by the sight of slaughter just doesn't seem to be there in the *Odyssey*.

This scene—in which Penelope reacts to Eurykleia's announcement by saying, "No, that is not Odysseus; some god has killed the suitors,"—this scene is the most difficult of interpretation for critics who want to say that Penelope has recognized the beggar as Odysseus, or suspected that the beggar is Odysseus. Critics who want to take that reading have to do some rather fancy interpretive work here to explain why Penelope suddenly says, "No, nurse, you are wrong, Odysseus is not back; some god killed the suitors." I suppose the most frequently offered argument to explain this is that this is the kind of very common human inability to believe that something you have longed for has really happened; almost a sense of, "If I believe it, I may somehow jinx it"—so that when Eurykleia finally tells Penelope what Penelope has been waiting all these years to hear, even if Penelope has already pretty well figured out that the beggar is Odysseus, she stills says, "No, that can't be true." Of course, an easier way of reading it is to say that she never suspected the beggar was Odysseus at all, and therefore, when she says now that he can't be, there is nothing to be explained away; it is simply consistent, if you think that she never knew who the beggar was in the first place.

Either way you take it, when Penelope comes downstairs, she hesitates before speaking to or recognizing Odysseus. In fact, she sits down across from him—once again, they are sitting on either side of their hearth, either side of the fireplace—Penelope sits down across from Odysseus, and simply looks at him. She doesn't say anything; she doesn't do anything; she just looks at him. And Odysseus, in return, says nothing to her; he simply looks down at the ground while Penelope looks at him. And so there is this kind of silent scene, in which the two of them are sitting across their fireplace from one another, neither one saying anything; Penelope simply gazing at Odysseus. Telemachos, who is present, finds this absolutely unbearable and, in fact, scolds his mother. I always feel a little sorry for Telemachos in this scene, because all these years when he undoubtedly has been waiting for his father to come home, imagining the great reunion, imagining his mother flying down the stairs, throwing herself into his father's arms—what happens? Penelope comes, sits down and looks at Odysseus, and says nothing. Telemachos, in fact, bursts out at Penelope and says to her that she is acting totally unnaturally in not recognizing the beggar. He says:

> My mother, my harsh mother with the hard heart inside you,
> why do you withdraw so from my father and do not

sit beside him and ask him questions and find out about him?
No other woman, with spirit as stubborn as yours, would keep back
as you are doing from her husband who after much suffering,
came at last in the twentieth year back to his own country.
But always you have a heart that is harder than stone within you.

Now Telemachos may well be right that no other woman would restrain herself, would hold back in this way, when she was told her husband was finally home after twenty years; but it is exactly this aspect of Penelope's character—her ability, which matches Odysseus' ability, to be cautious, to make sure of the circumstances before she does anything—it is exactly that ability on her part that has enabled her to wait for twenty years. Probably no other woman would have done that either. So what Telemachos is reproaching in Penelope here is precisely the character trait that makes her Penelope, that is summed up by her most common epithet, "circumspect Penelope," Penelope who considers things, who looks carefully before she leaps, Penelope who is not going, at this very last moment, to be deceived or tricked by anyone. After holding out for twenty years, the last thing in the world she would want would be to make a mistake now, at the very end, and accept the wrong man as Odysseus.

Odysseus is not concerned over Penelope's silence. First, Penelope tells Telemachos that if this is indeed Odysseus, they have ways of recognizing one another that only they know. And Odysseus smiles, tells Telemachos, basically, not to worry about it but give Penelope time, and then Odysseus sends Telemachos off to tell the bard Phemios—whose life Odysseus had spared, you remember, at Telemachos' request—Odysseus sends Telemachos to have Phemios play his lyre, and to tell the slaves to dance while Phemios plays and sings. The idea here is that any passersby who walk past the palace, and hear the sounds of lyre-playing and dancing feet, will assume that in fact Penelope has chosen a husband out from among the suitors, and that there is a celebration going on. Odysseus wants to avoid any strange silence around the palace that would indicate the suitors had been killed. So Telemachos leaves to give these instructions to Phemios and that means, in the scene in which Penelope and Odysseus really do have their final reconciliation and reunion, Telemachos isn't there. So he never gets to see the sight of his parents actually reunited, in that first glorious moment when they recognize one another.

After Telemachos leaves, Odysseus bathes, and as he comes out of the bath, Athena once again makes him look younger and more beautiful; she beautifies him one last time in the *Odyssey*. He then returns to sit by

Penelope again and, repeating Telemachos' words about the hardness of her heart, he reproaches her for not recognizing him. She at this point sets him a test, which leads to their true reunion. After Odysseus reproaches Penelope and says how hardhearted she is, he asks Eurykleia to make a bed up for him somewhere outside his and Penelope's old bedroom, because clearly, he says, Penelope is not going to accept him as her husband. He is exhausted—I suppose slaughtering 108 suitors plus a few servants is very hard work; he wants to go to sleep. He asks Eurykleia to set up a bed for him somewhere outside the bedroom. Penelope responds by telling Eurykleia to move the bed, which he himself built, his very own bed, out of the bedroom and set that bed up for him.

These words of Penelope's move Odysseus to react with anger, and to describe the bed as he himself had built it. The bed itself is immoveable; Odysseus tells us how he constructed the bed around a living olive tree. He says there was an olive tree growing in his courtyard; he planed away the branches and leaves on the olive tree but left it still rooted in the ground. Then, using that as one post, he built his bed around the tree, his bedchamber around the bed, his house around the bedchamber. Therefore, he wants to know—when Penelope says to Eurykleia, "Move the bed that he himself built out of the bedroom for him"—he wants to know who has damaged his bed, who has come in and cut away the olive trunk right above the roots so that the bed can be moved.

Now this whole idea of this immovable bed, this rooted bed, obviously works symbolically on various different levels. First and most clearly, the stability, the immovability, of this marriage bed is very clearly a symbol for the stability of Odysseus' and Penelope's marriage. The marriage bed, as a symbol of the marriage itself, is a fairly transparent symbol, an easy one to see; the bed cannot be moved, just as no one has been able to really interfere with Odysseus' and Penelope's marriage, throughout all these years. Another point to bring out is that since the rooted tree, the stillrooted tree that forms a post of the bed, is an olive tree, once again Athena comes into the picture—Athena as the goddess who stands behind, who sanctions, this marriage more than any other, Athena who is Penelope's patron no less than she is Odysseus' patron. Penelope is, of course, very skilled at weaving, which is the craft among women's crafts that Athena is most associated with; Penelope is as intelligent, as cautious, as able to plan ahead as Odysseus; and so Athena is an appropriate patron for her no less than for Odysseus. Similarly, the bed serves, obviously, as a sign of Penelope's marital fidelity. If anyone has been in the bedroom, and able to cut away the trunk of the olive tree and move the bed, by implication that person has been inappropriately intimate with Penelope; what else would he have been doing in the bedchamber? Odysseus puts this in terms that make that very clear; he says, "What man has moved my bed?" Not "what persons," but "what man has moved my bed?" He assumes that anyone who had gotten into the bedchamber and interfered with the bed had been there for the purpose of sexual relations with Penelope. So the bed is a symbol of the marriage; it is a symbol of Athena's patronage; it is a symbol of Penelope's fidelity. And it also, of course, is the sign by which Penelope recognizes that this is in fact Odysseus; because, as she tells us, only she, Odysseus, and one old serving woman whom she had brought with her at her marriage knew about this particular feature of the bed's construction.

Now, this is a point at which I always remind my students that there are times in any myth—and the *Odyssey* is, among other things, a myth—there are times when it doesn't do to try imagine things too literally. The idea that this house could have been built in this very odd way—that you build the bed first, then you build the bedchamber, then you build the house, and yet nobody ever knew why Odysseus constructed his house in that odd way; the idea that no other servants had ever been in the bedchamber and noticed that you can't move this bed to sweep under it or anything like that; this is not logically very likely. And yet, within the course of the narrative itself, none of those objections, I think, would ever occur to anyone. The symbol works so beautifully to do what it needs to do, to reiterate the solidity of this marriage, and to give Penelope a means of recognizing that this man is indeed her husband, Odysseus. He knows about the bed, he must be Odysseus. And at this point, she recognizes him fully, accepts that he really is Odysseus, rushes to him, kisses him, does all those things that Telemachos was hoping to see—but of course, Telemachos is not there at this point to see them. And Penelope asks Odysseus not to be angry at her for being so cautious. She says, very significantly, that she had always been afraid someone would come and trick her, she says, that someone would come and deceive her with words into thinking that he was Odysseus when he was not, and that was why she held back, to make absolutely certain that this is indeed her husband before recognizing him.

Far from being angry at her, Odysseus, I think, understands and appreciates exactly what she was doing. The two of them embrace and weep, and we get one more of these wonderful similes that the bard uses to such magnificent effect in the *Odyssey*. We are told that Odysseus "wept as he held his lovely wife, whose thoughts were virtuous," and here comes the simile:

> And as when land appears welcome to men who are swimming,
> after Poseidon has smashed their strong-built ship on the open
> water, pounding it with the weight of wind and the heavy
> seas, and only a few escape the gray water landward
> by swimming, with a thick scurf of salt coated upon them,
> and gladly they set foot on the shore, escaping the evil;
> so welcome was her husband to her as she looked upon him.

Now, throughout the *Odyssey*, we have really had these two parallel stories running at the same time: Odysseus trying to get home, suffering shipwreck, barely managing to make it to land, shipwrecked because Poseidon kept smashing his ship or his raft or whatever—Odysseus barely making it alive to land, and Penelope at home waiting for Odysseus to get back to her. In this simile, at the moment when they are actually reunited, the bard unites those two halves of the *Odyssey*, and does it in an even slightly more subtle way that you might expect. This simile starts by saying, "He wept as he held his wife; and as welcome as land is to a swimmer"—then you expect the end of it to be, "so welcome was his wife to him." But the bard turns the terms of the simile in mid-flow, so to speak, and says, "so welcome was her husband to her." So Penelope's emotions upon embracing the returned Odysseus are compared to Odysseus' joy at finally reaching land after shipwreck; the two tales, the two stories, the two strivings to be reunited, are themselves united in this simile, an absolutely masterstroke.

Once they have been reunited, Odysseus and Penelope are able at last to go to bed together, and then to lie awake recounting their stories throughout a very, very long night. In fact, the bard says that dawn would have risen on their weeping, if Athena had not intervened. It is very nice to have a goddess on your side. Athena realizes that Odysseus and Penelope need time to do three things. They need time to go to bed and make love with each other; then they need time to talk about their adventures; then they need time to sleep. And so Athena simply holds back dawn; she arranges for the horses of the dawn not to gallop out of their stable until after Odysseus and Penelope have had time to do these three things. She lengthens the night for them.

While Eurykleia and Eurynome are making up the famous bed, are putting bedclothes on it, making it ready for Odysseus and Penelope, Odysseus tells Penelope of a prophecy that the prophet Teiresias had given him in Hades.

Back in Book Eleven of the *Odyssey*, we are told that when Teiresias prophesied to Odysseus about how he will find the suitors in his house and he'll have to kill them, Teiresias goes on and says something else. He says that after Odysseus has killed the suitors, he will then have to make yet another journey in order to propitiate Poseidon; that Odysseus will have to travel inland until he meets people who do not know what the sea is. And once he has done that, he should plant his oar in the earth, make sacrifices to Poseidon, and then Poseidon will be reconciled to him, and he can return home and live out the rest of his life there. So, Odysseus tells Penelope—in this moment of their reunion, he tells her—that the news is not entirely good; he is going to have to leave again on another journey. So throughout this closing of the *Odyssey*, with the reunion of Odysseus with Penelope, with Telemachos, with Laertes, there is again this underlying bittersweet sense that there is another journey waiting for Odysseus; this reunion is at this point only temporary.

Well, Eurykleia and the housekeeper Eurynome have made up the bed by this time, and Odysseus and Penelope do retire to bed together. After making love, they lie awake talking; they tell each other their stories. Penelope tells Odysseus about the suitors and all her trials and tribulations with the suitors; how hard she had to strive to keep resisting them and not be overcome by them. Odysseus tells Penelope all his adventures, in order, just as he told them to the Phaiakians. In other words, we are left to assume that Odysseus renarrates the Great Wanderings, because the bard runs through in order every single episode Odysseus mentions in the Great Wanderings, just naming each one; a magnificent *tour de force* again. I am not sure I could, off the top of my head, name them all in exact order but the bard does; and so, if it took us about four hours to listen to Odysseus tell the Great Wanderings to the Phaiakians, we can assume it takes about four hours for him to tell them to Penelope. He tells them in order, and we are told that Penelope listens with delight to everything he tells her.

And of course, as I mentioned in a previous lecture, he does not censor out the fact that he spent a year living with Circe or the fact that the slept with Kalypso. He tells Penelope those details along with all the others, and she listens with delight. This can be seen as once again indicating the sexual double standard of the *Odyssey* that we talked about before; on the other hand, there is another side to it as well. Odysseus tells Penelope that Circe and Kalypso both were very taken by him, that Kalypso in particular wanted to keep him as her husband and make him an immortal; by implication, Odysseus is saying to Penelope, "But I chose you; a goddess wanted me for her husband, a goddess wanted to make me immortal, spare me from death, make me a god—but I chose to come home to you." That is a pretty powerful compliment for a husband to pay a wife. So, Penelope's delight, I think, can be understood in that way as well. Finally, Odysseus and Penelope fall asleep, and when they have slept long enough, Athena lets dawn go and the next day begins.

Now some critics have argued that the *Odyssey* originally ended here, with Odysseus' and Penelope's reunion. However, we have one more book of the *Odyssey*, Book Twenty-Four, which some critics think was added on later, was not part of the original conception—whoever had the original conception of the *Odyssey*. I tend to think that Book Twenty-Four is genuine, because it ties up, revisits, and closes several issues that are important throughout the *Odyssey*.

First off, Book Twenty-Four opens with what is often called a "Second *Nekuia*," a second visit to the Underworld, which begins with a conversation between the ghosts of Achilles and Agamemnon, discussing their pasts and past events, and then shows us the souls of the dead suitors just now arriving in the Underworld. Now, the thing that bothers many critics about this second *Nekuia* is it seems so obviously inconsistent with the picture of the Underworld we were given in Book Eleven. These souls are conversing with one another; they are talking with each other; they have their wits, they have their intelligence, they know who they are; they can speak, even though there is no-one there giving them a drink of blood. This seems completely contradictory to the picture of the Underworld that we saw in Book Eleven.

Some people have tried to explain this away in various rather subtle and clever ways. For instance, perhaps we are supposed to understand that ghosts can talk to one another in the Underworld, but can't talk to a living person until they are given a drink of blood. Perhaps; or perhaps we are not supposed to think about it in that way at all. I prefer to look at it in terms of what Homer is accomplishing with these journeys to the Underworld in the different parts of the epic. The point here is not to give us a detailed, guidebook-type description of what happens in the Underworld, either in Book Eleven or here in Book Twenty-Four. In both cases, there is another narrative point to be stressed; Odysseus charming the Phaiakians, impressing them with what a truly magnificent and unusual hero he is; or in Book Twenty-Four, I think, what the bard is doing with this second journey to the Underworld is showing us one more time that parallel that has been so important throughout the *Odyssey*—that Penelope was to Odysseus as

160

Klytaimestra was to Agamemnon, that what happened to Agamemnon on his return home could have happened to Odysseus, had Penelope been a different woman than she was. Because in this final look at the Underworld, the suitors' spirits come and talk to Agamemnon. Agamemnon asks them who they are and what they are doing there, and one suitor, who hasn't been very important before, a suitor named Amphimedon, tells Agamemnon the story of how they were all killed. After Amphimedon has recounted the story of their deaths, Agamemnon himself restates, and puts to rest, that theme of "Penelope could have been another Klytaimestra." He talks about how fortunate Odysseus was in Penelope; he says that Penelope was a truly virtuous woman, and he says, "Klytaimestra did not act like that when she killed me." So we have a kind of recognition, by Agamemnon himself of all people, that this parallel possible ending, this possible ending in which the wife is unfaithful and kills her husband, did indeed not happen; and I think it is a very useful narrative device to look at that comparison one more time, and to look at it through Agamemnon's eyes.

After the scene in the Underworld—which ends with Agamemnon saying how lucky Odysseus was and how different Penelope was than Klytaimestra—after that scene, the poet turns back to Ithaka and we see Odysseus go to visit his father, Laertes, the one member of his family with whom he has not yet been reunited; his father Laertes, who is living up in a small hut in the countryside, as though he were a poor man, as though he were a poor private citizen. When Odysseus sees his father, Laertes is out in a field tending his plants and dressed very poorly. Odysseus stands and weeps; he is distressed at how unkempt his father looks, he is saddened at how age and hardship have changed his father, and he stands and sheds tears for Laertes. However, instead of immediately identifying himself to Laertes, instead of walking up to him and saying, "I am home, I am Odysseus, I am back," Odysseus, surprisingly enough, lies to Laertes, and introduces himself as a traveler who had met Odysseus five years in the past. First, he says he met Odysseus; Laertes asks, "When did you see my son?" Odysseus says, "Five years ago," and Laertes begins to weep and grieve, because that is so long ago that it can't really give him any hope that Odysseus is still alive. When Odysseus sees his father reacting with grief, then he says, "Father, I am he, I am Odysseus, I am back."

Once again, in this scene, we see Odysseus enacting his name. First he causes grief to Laertes by lying; then he experiences grief and pain himself in his father's reaction; only then does he do what you would expect him to do in the first place, and tell his father who he is. Laertes, however, refuses to believe that Odysseus is his son without proof. Laertes says, "If indeed you are Odysseus, give me some proof that you are Odysseus," and Odysseus gives him two kinds of proof. He shows him the scar on his thigh, and he refers to when he and Laertes had planted the trees in this very orchard, when Odysseus was a little boy.

Now, I think there is a very interesting pattern at work here, in the recognition scenes we have gone through in the *Odyssey*. Odysseus has really two available strategies for proving that he is who he says he is, to anyone on Ithaka whom he wants to be recognized by. He can show his scar, the visual tangible proof of his identity, or he can refer to a shared emotionally significant memory. And look at whom he uses which of those strategies with. Eurykleia, Eumaios, and Philoitios, the slaves, are only given the scar as proof. Eurykleia inadvertently—Odysseus didn't mean for her to recognize him; with the other two, Eumaios and Philoitios, he uses the scar. So, slaves get the physical, tangible proof. Penelope is given only a shared emotional memory. My students sometimes ask me, "Why on earth doesn't Odysseus show Penelope his scar?" and aside from the obvious answer—that that would fall rather flat in the narrative, that that is not how we want them to be reunited—there seems to be a sense in which the referring to an emotionally significant memory, their bed and what their bed means to them, is more appropriate for Penelope's recognition that just saying, "Look, here is my identity card," in effect. Laertes—who is, after all, an older male, Odysseus' father, therefore in some sense a position of authority over Odysseus—he and only he gets both kinds of recognition. Odysseus shows him the proof, the tangible proof, the scar; Odysseus also refers to a shared emotional memory that Laertes will remember.

There is one person, of course—well, there is also the dog Argos—but there is one person who stands right outside this system, and that is Telemachos. As we saw with Telemachos, Odysseus can offer neither the visual proof of his scar—Telemachos doesn't know what that scar looked like—nor a shared emotional memory. They have no shared emotional memories; Telemachos was an infant. Telemachos has to accept his father on trust; he has to accept Odysseus as his father because Odysseus says so. And in a sense, Telemachos is therefore in the position that all sons are always in with all fathers. No son ever knows who his father is; no child ever knows who its parent is; we all have to accept our parents on trust. Telemachos just has to do so at age twenty, instead of at age two or three.

After the reunion between Laertes and Odysseus the two, father and son, return to town where, with Telemachos, they battle the suitors' relatives. By this time the murder of the suitors has been discovered; the suitors' relatives want to take vengeance on Odysseus. As I mentioned before, we are in a society where justice is enacted by private vengeance, and the suitors' relatives want to kill Odysseus and Telemachos for killing the suitors. Athena holds off until Laertes is allowed one kill; Laertes gets to kill one person, the father of the suitor Antinoos as it happens, so that at the end of the *Odyssey*, we see the three generations of the Ithakan royal family—Laertes, Odysseus, Telemachos—standing side by side, fighting a battle. Once Laertes has been able to kill a relative of the suitors, then Athena brings the battle to a halt. She makes both sides pledge peace, and the conflict is thus ended.

It is ended in a rather artificial manner; Athena just steps in and says, "Stop, no more fighting," and some critics find that somewhat unsatisfactory, this artificial ending of the *Odyssey*. On the other hand, how else can you end a vengeance-based conflict? By definition, that goes on generation after generation, as relatives on both sides keep killing in vengeance for their own relatives. And on another level, I think this rather arbitrary, in some sense unsatisfactory, ending is actually the perfect ending for the *Odyssey*, because it stresses again that sense of ambiguity, of bittersweetness, of irrevocable loss, that I have talked about so much. Odysseus is reestablished, but he must leave again. Ithaka is still missing, now, two whole generations of men—the fathers who went off to war, and the suitors who have been killed. It is not a happy ending; there are reunions, there are reconciliations, but there are still a lot of things left up in the air, a lot of things left unresolved. How will Ithaka be governed while Odysseus is off on his next journey? How will Telemachos maintain the rule, with the suitor's families full of resentment? So rather than a purely happy ending, in which they all have a great feast and live happily ever after, we have an ending that, I think, is consonant with the *Odyssey*'s overall tone of the irrevocability of time and of loss.

Lecture Twelve
The Trojan War and the Archaeologists

Scope: In this final lecture, we turn to the question of whether the Trojan War has any historical basis. After looking at the history of this question, the lecture recounts the story of Heinrich Schliemann's 19th-century excavations at Hisarlik and Mycenae, and examines some of the issues still left unresolved by those excavations. We touch briefly on some of the reasons for Schliemann's controversial status both in his own day and among modern archaeologists, and then trace the later discoveries made at Troy by Dörpfeld, Blegen, and the current excavators.

Outline

I. Was there ever a Troy, and a Trojan War?

   A. The ancient Greeks themselves assumed that the story was historical.

   B. The Romans considered the Trojans their ancestors through Aeneas, a Trojan prince.

   C. The assumption of historicity continued throughout the Middle Ages. But after the Renaissance, scholars were no longer certain that the Trojan War had ever occurred.

   D. By the 18th century, many scholars believed that the Trojan War was purely mythical, while others were certain that there was a historical basis to the legend.

II. The general location of Troy, whether mythical or historical, was never in doubt. The city was in the Troad, the northwest corner of Turkey, near the Dardanelles (or the Hellespont, as it was called in the ancient world).

   A. Around 700 B.C.E., Greek colonists built a small town on Hisarlik, a large flat-topped hill on the Trojan plain. They called their town "Ilion," another name for Troy. Much later, the Romans built a town there called "Ilium Novum," or "New Ilion."

B. Ancient visitors to the site included the Persian king Xerxes in the early 5th century B.C., Alexander the Great in the late 4th century, and Julius Caesar in the 1st century.

C. Interest in finding the exact site began in the 18th century but came into its own only in the 19th century, with the development of archaeology.

III. The burgeoning science of archaeology made it feasible, for the first time, for scholars to study the possible sites of Troy and try to determine where, if anywhere, the ancient city had stood.

   A. In 1822, Charles McLaren suggested that Hisarlik, the site of the Greek Ilion and Roman Ilium Novum, was the site of Homer's Troy as well. His suggestion received little attention from classicists.

   1. One problem was its size.

   2. Another problem was the existence of other equally likely sites for Troy.

   B. In the 1860s, Frank Calvert, a British subject who lived at Troy and owned part of Hisarlik, began preliminary excavations on the site. He found artifacts from a period later than the Homeric era.

   C. In 1870, perhaps at Calvert's suggestions, Heinrich Schliemann, a self-taught German archaeologist, began extensive excavations at Hisarlik.

IV. Heinrich Schliemann is widely recognized as the discoverer of Troy. Controversial in his own day, he remains so today. However, there is little doubt that he correctly identified at Hisarlik the remains of the major prehistoric city of the area, with layers dating back to c. 3000 B.C.

   A. Schliemann is controversial for several reasons.

   1. It has been demonstrated beyond question that he lied about many of the details of his own biography and about the details of his excavation of Hisarlik.

   2. Some scholars have even questioned the authenticity of some of his most spectacular finds, both at Hisarlik and at the Greek site of Mycenae. However, the balance of scholarly opinion seems to indicate that the objects Schliemann found are genuine, though perhaps the circumstances in which he says he found them have been exaggerated.

3. Schliemann's method of excavation was highly destructive and would never be tolerated on a modern archaeological dig. However, archaeology was in its infancy during his excavations, and he cannot fairly be faulted for not abiding by guidelines that did not yet exist.

4. Schliemann can be faulted for unscrupulousness in his dealings with the Turkish government. He smuggled many of his finds, including the "Treasure of Priam," out of Turkey despite having explicitly agreed to turn over any artifacts to the Turkish government.

B. Without question, Schliemann found the remains of a great and important civilization. He was looking for Homer's Troy; both there and at Mycenae, he found the first evidence of prehistoric Bronze Age civilization.

1. Schliemann's excavations at Hisarlik uncovered a site that was constantly occupied from around 3000 B.C. to around 1100 B.C. The traditional date for the Sack of Troy most commonly accepted by ancient Greeks was 1184 B.C.

2. Schliemann interrupted his excavations at Troy to excavate Mycenae, the Greek site traditionally associated with Agamemnon. There too he found evidence of a great prehistoric civilization.

V. Schliemann had thus found evidence of flourishing civilizations at Troy and at Mycenae; but had he found "Homer's Troy"? Opinion is still divided on that question.

A. The successive settlements at Hisarlik are numbered Troy I through Troy IX, starting at the bottom with the oldest and working up.

B. Schliemann thought that Troy II was Homer's Troy; actually, it is nearly 1,000 years too early.

C. Schliemann's first successor, Wilhelm Dörpfeld, identified Troy VI (c. 1270) as the Homeric city. However, this site apparently was destroyed by an earthquake, not a siege.

D. Dörpfeld was succeeded by Carl Blegen, who found evidence that Troy VI was destroyed by an earthquake, not a siege. Blegen identified Troy VIIa, which was destroyed by fire c. 1190 B.C., as the city of Priam.

E. Excavations have been resumed at Hisarlik, under the auspices of the University of Tubingen and the University of Cincinnati. Attention is once again being paid to Troy VI and its possible interactions with the Mycenaeans.

F. One other strand of evidence concerns 13th-century B.C. Hittite documents that contain references to kingdoms called Ahhiyawa and Wilusa, and imply that the two went to war.

    1. Some scholars think these names represent "Achaia" (one of Homer's terms for Greece) and "Ilios," another name for Troy.

    2. Other scholars reject these identifications. The relevance of the Hittite documents to the Trojan War thus remains uncertain.

VI. Most modern scholars agree that Schliemann found the city that gave rise to the legends of the Trojan War.

    A. But controversy remains about whether the war itself ever took place.

    B. Notwithstanding, our appreciation of the *Iliad* and *Odyssey* does not depend on the historicity of the city of Troy.

Supplementary Reading:

Susan Hueck Allen, *Finding the Walls of Troy*.

J. Lesley Fitton, *The Discovery of the Greek Bronze Age*, Section 2, Chapter [3], "Schliemann at Troy and Mycenae."

Oxford Classical Dictionary; "Mycenae," "Troy."

Michael Wood, *In Search of the Trojan War*, Chapters 1–2, 6, 8, Postscript.

Questions to Consider:

1. Does it matter for our appreciation of the *Iliad* and the *Odyssey* whether or not the Trojan War ever actually happened?

2. If Schliemann had not romanticized his descriptions of his findings at Troy and Mycenae, would those findings have excited so much interest?

Lecture Twelve—Transcript
The Trojan War and the Archaeologists

Hello, and welcome to Lecture Twelve. In this final lecture of the course, we are going to take a different approach and turn to the question of whether or not the Trojan War has any historical basis. We'll start with a synopsis of the history of this question, and then turn to Heinrich Schliemann's nineteenth-century excavations, in Turkey at a place called Hisarlik and in Greece at the citadel of Mycenae. We'll discuss some of the issues left unresolved by those exactions, and the lecture will also review some of the reasons for Schliemann's controversial status, both in his own day and among modern archaeologists. Finally, we'll consider some of the discoveries made at Troy by Schliemann's successors, Dörpfeld, Blegen, and current excavators.

Was there ever a Troy, and if so, did the people of that city ever go to war with people from Greece, in what could be called a Trojan War? The ancient Greeks themselves assumed that the Trojan War was a historical fact. They thought that it was an actual episode in the past of their own ancestors; they no more questioned its truth, its historicity, than they questioned the historicity of, say, the great Persian Wars that took place in 490 and 480 B.C. In fact, in the fifth century in Athens, and later, there were families who traced their decent from great heroes of the Trojan War—from Agamemnon, Achilles, and others—and believed that these men had indeed been their own ancestors. So the classical Greeks saw a complete and absolute continuity between the heroes who lived at the [time of the] Trojan War, as ancestors, and their own society; and they saw the war with Troy as one of the first episodes in an ongoing conflict between Europe, as represented by Greece, and Asia, as represented by, in the Trojan War, Troy, and in later generations especially by Persia.

The Romans, too, moving to the next great culture of the Mediterranean world, considered that the Trojan War was a matter of historical fact. The Romans traced their own ancestry back to the Trojans; they saw themselves as descendents of the other side, the descendents of the people who had been in conflict with the Greeks. The Romans traced their ancestry specifically back to the Trojan prince Aeneas, a member of a minor branch of the royal family who, we're told in the *Iliad*, is destined to survive the fall of Troy and flee with some survivors to found another country elsewhere. The Romans identified Aeneas as their own ancestor, and the other country he founded—as of course with the other culture he founded—as the beginnings of the Roman race and the Roman people. In fact, a very important Roman family, the Julii, whose most famous representative was Julius Caesar, traced their ancestry directly back to Aeneas through his son Iulus. So, like the Greeks, the Romans assumed without question that the Trojan War was a historical fact.

Now both Greek and Roman historians sometimes questioned what the motivations for the war had been. Some of them questioned whether in fact such a devastating war would have been fought over Helen, over an adulterous affair between Paris and Helen, and some of them came up with other explanations for why the war had been fought. But neither the war itself nor the existence of Troy were ever called into question in antiquity. The assumption that Troy had been an historical place, and that the Trojan War had actually happened, continued through the Middle Ages. But after the Renaissance, scholars began to question whether, in fact, there ever had been a Troy, or whether that Trojan War was purely a myth, something that had never, in any sense whatsoever, happened, rather than a mythologized memory of an actual historical event.

By the eighteenth century many, if not most, historians of antiquity believed that the Trojan War was in fact purely mythical. While others were still certain that there was some historical basis, some historical core, to the legend, at that point in the eighteenth century no-one was sure exactly where the city of Troy had stood, if indeed it ever had existed. Now, the general location of Troy, whether historical or mythical, was never in doubt; there was never any question that the general location referred to in the Homeric epics was the area called the Troad, that is, the northwestern corner of Turkey, near the Dardanelles or the Hellespont, as it was called in the ancient world. About 700 B.C., Greek colonists had settled in the Troad, and had built a settlement that they called Ilion—and of course, Ilion is another name for Troy. These Greek colonists had built a settlement that they called Ilion on a flat-topped hill in the Troad, in the Trojan plain, a hill that in modern Turkish is called Hisarlik. And Hisarlik is going to be very important throughout the rest of this lecture.

So in about 700 B.C., colonists from Greece went to the area where they thought Troy had been and built a town, a Greek-speaking town, a Greek colony, on this flat-topped hill called Hisarlik, and they named that colony Ilion, which seems to indicate that was where they thought Troy had stood. Later the Romans renovated Ilion, rebuilt it, built a city of their own there, which they called Ilium Novum; n Latin that means "New Ilion." So, both the Greeks and the Romans, fairly early on, had identified not just the Troad in general, but this hill called Hisarlik, as probably the site of the actual ancient city of Troy.

This area, Ilium Novum, Ilion, Hisarlik—whatever name you want to call it by—was a site of pilgrimage in the ancient world from very early on. Ancient visitors to the site included the Persian king Xerxes; on his way to invade Greece in the fifth century B.C., he stopped to pay homage to the great heroes who had fought at Troy. Alexander the Great visited in the late fourth century B.C., Alexander the Great who so identified himself with Achilles that supposedly he slept with a copy of the *Iliad* under his pillow. I am not sure which roll, which scroll, which books, of the *Iliad* he put under his pillow, but supposedly he considered himself the new Achilles. And in the first century, Julius Caesar visited the site that was identified with Troy, the site of Novum Ilium, to pay homage to his own ancestors, who he thought had originally come from there. This site, Hisarlik was continuously inhabited until the fourteenth century A.D., at which point it fell into disrepair, was abandoned, and by the eighteenth century even the site of Ilion, the Greek town, or Novum Ilium, the Roman town, had been forgotten.

Interest in finding the exact site again began in the eighteenth century, when scholars started to think, "Well, perhaps there had been a Troy; it would be interesting to go and look at the Troad and see what we can find, see if there are any traces of an ancient city there." This impulse, this desire to try to find the site of Troy really came into its own in the nineteenth century, when archeology began to develop as an actual science with a set methodology and set kind of goals. The burgeoning science of archaeology, the development of archaeology, made it feasible for the first time for scholars to study the possible sites of Troy and try to determine where, if anywhere, an ancient city had stood.

Now one problem, when archaeologists started examining the Troad in the eighteenth and nineteenth century—when archaeologists came into existence and started examining the Troad—was that there were visible traces of ancient cities there on Hisalik and in other places, but those visible traces were all Greco-Roman; that is, they were the traces of the settlements I have talked about just a couple of minutes ago, of Ilion and of Novum Ilium. And fairly quickly, this was figured out; that what you could see at the Troad, what you could see on Hisarlik and other areas in that site, was simply not old enough, could not be Homer's Troy. In 1822, an interested amateur named Charles McLaren suggested that Hisarlik in fact was the site not just of the Greek Ilion and the Roman Novum Ilium, but also had been the original site of Homer's Troy. But his suggestion, made in 1822, attracted very little attention from professionally-trained classicists. One problem was that Hisarlik seemed too small. It just didn't look large enough to have held the citadel described by Homer. Another problem was that there were all sorts of large flat-topped promontories dotted around the Troad, any one of which could have been the site of a great city. What marks Hisarlik out apart from any others?

So McLaren's suggestion, which turned out to have been somewhat prescient, lay dormant, more or less, until the 1860s, when another British subject, a man named Frank Calvert, whose family had actually lived in Turkey for generations and who, as it happened, owned part of Hisarlik, began preliminary excavations on the site. Calvert found several things when he began excavating the hill of Hislarlik, but again they were all much too late; they were all traces of late antiquity or at least from Roman times. None of them were nearly old enough to belong to the period about which Homer was writing. In 1870, perhaps—this is still controversial, we still aren't sure exactly how this happened, but perhaps at Frank Calvert's suggestion, Heinrich Schliemann, a self-taught German archaeologist, began his extensive excavations at Hisarlik. Heinrich Schliemann is widely recognized today as the discoverer of Troy, the excavator of Troy. Some people think that perhaps Frank Calvert should be given more credit than he has so far been given, but Schliemann is definitely the one who did the first major excavations at Hisarlik and who is currently still recognized as the discoverer of Troy.

Schliemann was controversial in his own day, and he is perhaps more controversial today; but there is little to no doubt that he correctly identified, at Hisarlik, the remains of the major prehistoric city of the area. Hisarlik was the site of a city that lasted not just from the time Homer writes about on, but from much earlier than that. The ruins that Schliemann found in Hisarlik actually date back to around 3000 B.C.; it was an extremely ancient site continuously occupied for many, many generations. Now, I said that Schliemann is controversial—was and is controversial. There are several reasons for that. It has, unfortunately, been demonstrated by modern scholars, pretty much beyond doubt, that Schliemann lied about several details of his own biography, and that he lied about some of the details of his excavations at Hisarlik. To give an example about how he lied concerning details of his own biography, in one of his books about his search for Troy he tells a very moving story about how when he was a little boy, I think eight or ten years old, he was looking at a book about the fall of

Troy with his father; and there was an engraving of Aeneas fleeing from the burning Troy, Aeneas carrying his father on his back and leading his little son by the hand. And little Heinrich said to his father, "The illustrator must have seen the ruins of Troy to draw so beautiful a picture of it," at which his father said, "No, no, my son; this is purely an imaginary picture. No one knows where Troy was, if there ever even was a Troy." And this fired young Heinrich with a desire to excavate Troy; and he says that he and his father decided, on the spot, that he would grow up to find Troy. It is a great story; a little boy inspired with a life-long ambition that he then grows up to fulfill. Unfortunately, evidence from Schliemann's own diaries, and more importantly, from letters to his father, seems to make it pretty clear that the first his father had ever heard of this defining moment of Schliemann's life was when the book was published containing this story. In other words, Schliemann made it up because it sounded really good.

That isn't really important, one might say, in the overall scheme of whether or not what he found at Hisarlik was or was not Troy. Slightly more disturbing is that he apparently lied about, embellished, falsified—however you want to put it—some of the details of his own excavations at Hisarlik. He postdated his journal, for instance; he wrote entries in his journal describing what he had found and when he had found these things after the fact, and then dated them as though he was keeping them contemporaneously. All right, maybe he just didn't have time to write up his journals in the field, and maybe he had a very good memory. But he also did things like claiming that his wife, Sophia, was present to witness the discovery of various great finds when contemporary records, such as letters and diaries, show that she was in Athens at the time; she wasn't even in Turkey.

So Schliemann did lie or, to put it a little more kindly, did embellish and embroider a great many details; obviously, to make this story seem more romantic, more enchanting, more appealing. In fact, Schliemann is rather eerily reminiscent of none other than Odysseus. He embellished his story to make it appeal to his audience, and appeal to his audience it most definitely did. This doesn't, by itself, mean that Schliemann lied about the overall content of his finds, but the fact that he is known to have been untruthful in these rather minor details has caused some scholars to question his truthfulness in the larger details. Some scholars have, in fact, even questioned the authenticity of some of his most spectacular finds. He has been accused of forging some of the artifacts that he found at Hisarlik and also at Mycenae in Greece. But the balance of scholarly opinion today seems to indicate that the objects Schliemann claimed to have found are, in fact, genuine. There are still some scholars who raise questions about the circumstances in which he says he found them, but the artifacts themselves are pretty widely now accepted as being genuine.

Schliemann has also been criticized for his method of excavation. There is no question that his method of excavation was highly destructive and would never be tolerated on a modern archaeological dig. For instance, he started at Hisarlik by digging a vast trench right through the middle of the hill, all the way down to ground level, thereby destroying a great deal; just plowing right through it to get down to the bottom level, where he did in fact find some very ancient walls, walls that were much more ancient than he thought, in fact. So his method of excavation was enough to give modern archaeologists screaming nightmares. However, Schliemann was one of the fathers of archaeology; archaeology was really just in the process of being invented when Schliemann worked, and he really, I think, cannot be faulted for not abiding by guidelines, protocols, methodologies that did not yet exist. Looking back at him, we can say he did very, very badly; but at the time, he did what everyone would have done, and no-one was doing any thing any different. There was no scientific guideline to follow at this point. And to give him credit, Schliemann was one of the first archaeologists to understand how important it was to work out some sort of sequencing of pottery shards, some sort of methodology by which you could tell which bits of pottery were older and which bits were younger, so that you could tell—by where they were in the levels that you excavated, you could have some sense of relative dating. He was one of the first archaeologists to recognize the importance of paying attention to such details as that.

He can, however, be faulted for unscrupulousness. If he can't be faulted for not abiding by a methodology that did not yet exist, he can be faulted for unscrupulousness in his dealings with the Turkish government, in particular. When Schliemann got the permission to excavate in Turkey, he promised that he would hand any artifacts he found over to the Turkish government. And yet, what he actually did was smuggle many of his most important finds out of the country into Germany. The most infamous of these smuggling jobs was his removal of what he called the "Treasure of Priam" out of Turkey, and his taking of it to Germany. The Treasure of Priam was a great hoard that Schliemann found in 1873, the last year of his first dig at Hisarlik. It consisted of a great many things, including copper cauldrons; bronze, silver, gold cups; copper lanceheads; lots and lots of golden jewelry—gold rings, bracelets, headbands, earrings, etc., most famously two magnificent diadems, one of which consisted of over sixteen thousand tiny pieces of gold threaded on gold wire. Schliemann had his wife, Sophia, photographed wearing that diadem, and said that she was wearing the jewels of Helen. Once again, his tendency to romanticize; this had to be the Treasure of Priam himself, and that diadem had to be the crown of Helen of Troy herself, and Sophia in it was Sophia dressed in the jewels of Helen. Actually, the Treasure of Priam was about a thousand years too old to belong to the period at which the Trojan War supposedly happened.

Schliemann smuggled this Treasure of Priam out of Turkey to Germany, and there—just to digress for a moment—it had an extremely interesting history. It was in a museum in Berlin until 1945, when, in another sack of a beleaguered city, it disappeared. The Treasure of Priam disappeared from Berlin in 1945, and until very recently it was believed lost. Even just a very few years ago, books talking about Schliemann would say that undoubtedly, the Treasure of Priam was melted down by some Russian soldiers, who used it to buy whatever. In 1993, however, long-standing rumors were confirmed, that the Treasure of Priam was in fact sitting in boxes in the basement of the Pushkin Museum in Moscow, and in 1996 the Treasure of Priam went on public display in Moscow. And now, even as we speak, there is an ongoing controversy about who do these artifacts belong to. Germany wants them back; they were stolen from Germany in the siege of Berlin, the sack of Berlin, in 1945 and taken to Russia. Russia says, more or less, "Possession is nine-tenths of the law; we have got them, we intend to keep them"; and meanwhile, on the sidelines, Turkey is saying, "Wait a minute; what about us? Schliemann stole them from us in the first place—we want them back." So Schliemann's unscrupulous dealing with the Turkish government 120-some years ago has repercussions now, as these three nations fight over who should have control of the Treasure of Priam.

Schliemann, without question, found the remains of a great and important civilization at Hisarlik. He was looking for Homer's Troy; both at Hisarlik and at Mycenae in Greece, he found the first evidence of prehistoric Bronze Age civilization. He interrupted his excavations at Hisarlik to go to Greece and excavate Agamemnon's citadel of Mycenae as well. At Hisarlik, he had uncovered a site that was constantly occupied from around 3000 B.C. to around 1100 B.C. and then again later. The traditional date of the Sack of Troy, of course, was 1184 B.C., so it seems at least quite possible that the site Schliemann discovered at Hisarlik was, in fact, destroyed by warfare at about the time Homer says it should have been. In Mycenae, Schliemann also uncovered the ruins of a great prehistoric civilization.

Now Mycenae was a little bit different of a situation from Hisarlik. The site of Mycenae had never been forgotten; it had never entirely disappeared. Remnants of its walls, the very tops of its walls and of its famous Lion-Gate, had been visible always; everyone knew where Mycenae was. What Schliemann did there was to excavate it, to uncover the traces of the city, and to discover just how wealthy, just how magnificent, it had been. There had never been any doubt in the Greek mind, in the ancient world, that the people who had lived at Mycenae were their own ancestors; Schliemann discovered just how great a civilization the civilization that centered around Mycenae and other contemporaneous cities had been. His most spectacular find there was the famous gold mask that he found on a buried skeleton, and, of course, again, with his usual flair for romanticism, Schliemann dubbed this the mask of Agamemnon, and said that he had excavated the grave of Agamemnon himself. Again, it is, in fact, too early—the mask of someone who predated any possible Agamemnon by several hundred years.

So Schliemann had found evidence of flourishing civilizations, both in Turkey about where Troy ought to be, and on Greece at about the time period when Agamemnon's civilization should have existed. But had he found Homer's Troy? Had he found a city that ever went to war with Greece? That is a much more difficult question, and opinion is still divided on that question. There is no doubt that the Mycenaeans were, as the Greeks believed they were, the actual ancestors of later Greeks. This was conclusively demonstrated in the 1950s, when the writing system used by the Mycenaeans was deciphered and was discovered to be an early form of Greek. There is no question that the people who lived in the palace Schliemann excavated at Mycenae, and in other palaces from the same time period on the Greek mainland—there is no question that those people were indeed the ancestors of the Greeks.

The association of Hisarlik with a Troy that the Mycenaeans could ever have interacted with is still more problematic. Schliemann found a city, as I already said, that had been inhabited for a great length of time. The successive settlements at Hisarlik have been numbered by archaeologists, Troy One through Troy Nine, starting at the bottom and working up. Schliemann thought that Troy Two was Homer's Troy; that was where he found the Treasure of Priam, that was the most magnificent of the cities that he saw as he excavated; and, unfortunately for Schliemann, Troy Two is actually about a thousand years too early to be Homer's Troy. So whoever the Treasure of Priam belonged to, it wasn't Priam. Schliemann's first successor, Wilhelm Dörpfeld, identified Troy Six, which had been destroyed around 1270 B.C., as the Homeric city. Dörpfeld believed it was destroyed by siege; later archaeologists thought it was more likely to have been destroyed by an earthquake. Dörpfeld was succeeded by Carl Blegen, who thought that Troy Seven-A—Troy Seven is divided into Troy Seven-A and Troy Seven-B—Blegen thought that Troy Seven-A, which was destroyed by fire around 1190 B.C., was the city of Priam.

When Blegen stopped excavating in 1938, Troy lay undisturbed; no one excavated at Hisarlik for another fifty years. But in 1988, new excavations were started under the auspices of the Universtiy of Tubingen and the University of Cincinnati in America. So, Hisarlik is being excavated once again, and attention is once again being paid to the possibility that Troy Six did in fact have interactions with Mycenaean culture. Apparently, how it was destroyed, how Troy Six was destroyed—whether by siege or by earthquake or by fire or by some combination of those—is not as clear as Carl Blegen thought it was, and archaeologists are once again directing their attention to Troy Six as the possible timeframe for Homer's Troy, as a possible candidate for Homer's Troy.

There is one other strand of absolutely fascinating but, as so often in archaeology, tantalizingly ambiguous evidence about whether or not the civilization Schliemann found at Hisarlik is the civilization that Homer called Troy. There are a number of thirteenth-century B.C.—that is, from the 1200s B.C.—documents from the Hittite empire, that contain references to two kingdoms, one of them called the kingdom of the Ahhiyawa and the one called the Wilusa, and these documents imply that the people of Ahhiyawa and the people of Wilusa went to war together. Now, some scholars think that, in the Hittite language, Ahhiyawa is an approximation of "Achaia," Homer's word for Greece; and that Wilusa is an approximation of "Ilios" or "Wilios" as it was at first pronounced, Homer's term for Troy. If this is correct, then when the Hittite documents say that the people of Ahhiyawa went to war with the people if Wilusa, we have independent confirmation that the people of Achaia and the people of Ilios went to war together. But other scholars, as always, reject this identification, say, "No, the Hittite terms do not match the Greek terms; the Hittite terms are not reflections of the Greek words that Homer uses; this is purely coincidental." So the relevance of the Hittite documents to the question of whether or not there was a Trojan War, and whether or not what Schliemann found at Hisarlik were the remains of Troy, the relevance of the Hittite documents remains uncertain. The jury is still out on that one.

Most modern scholars, I think, would agree that Schliemann found the city that gave rise to the legends of the Trojan War; that he found a great civilization, flourishing in the Troad, at about the right time, and that whether or not there ever was an actual war, it was the existence of that city that gave rise to the legends of the war. But controversy remains about whether there ever in fact was such a war—I don't think any one believes it was over Helen, by the way, if it actually was fought—but controversy remains about whether there ever was such a war at all. We may find out, as current excavations continue, there is always the possibility that they will find absolutely clenching evidence, a store of Trojan documents, for instance, recounting that the people of Achaia came from over the seas and attacked them. Seems unlikely; that probably would have been found by now if it existed, but is at least possible. On the other hand, current excavations may continue to tell us more and more about the successive cities that were built at Hisarlik, and more and more about the people who lived there, without ever clenching the question of whether Hisarlik ever was Homer's Troy or whether there ever was a Trojan War.

But fascinating as it would be to know the exact history of the interactions, if there ever were any, between the Mycenaeans of Greece and the people who lived at Hisarlik, our appreciation of Homer, thankfully, does not depend on this. Just as our appreciation of Mallory's tales of King Arthur does not depend on the historical validity of whether or not there ever was a Dark Age king named Arthur, so the *Iliad* and the *Odyssey* do not depend on whether or not Hisarlik is Troy and whether or not there ever was a war there. Homer's Troy and Homer's Greeks and Homer's Trojans are characters of myth, not figures of history; and like the best fictional characters of any and all cultures, they transcend the specific circumstances that gave them birth. That they do so transcend their specific circumstances, that they soar beyond the limitations of whether or not they are based in history, is at one and the same time Homer's achievement, his epics' glory, and our very great good fortune.

Timeline

c. 3000–c. 1000 B.C.	Successive cities occupy Hisarlik; one of them may have been "Homer's Troy."
c. 1600–c. 1100	Mycenaean civilization flourishes in Greece.
c. 1270	Destruction of Troy VI; Dörpfeld thought this was Homer's Troy.
c.1300–1200	Hittite documents mention Ahhiyawa and Wilusa, which may be references to Achaia and Ilion, and imply a war between the two.
c. 1190	Destruction of Troy VIIa; Blegen identified this as Homer's Troy.
1184	The most commonly accepted traditional date for the Fall of Troy.
c. 800?–780?	The alphabet introduced into Greece.
c. 750?–700	The *Iliad* and *Odyssey* are perhaps transcribed into writing.
c. 530	Peisistratos, tyrant of Athens, perhaps orders a "recension" or standardization of the Homeric epics.
334 B.C.	Alexander the Great visits the site of Troy, and offers sacrifices to Achilles.
c. 3rd–2nd c. B.C.	The Alexandrian scholars edit the epics, writing copious marginal notes or "scholia" on them. The epics are probably divided into their standard book-divisions at this time.
48 B.C.	Julius Caesar visits the site of Troy.
29?–19 B.C.	Virgil writes the *Aeneid*, modeled on the Homeric epics but taking the

viewpoint of the Trojans (whom the Romans considered their ancestors). Book II of the *Aeneid* gives the fullest extant account of the Sack of Troy. The *Aeneid* was left incomplete when Virgil died in 19 B.C..

A.D. 1054 .... Permanent break between Roman Catholic and Greek Orthodox churches leads to rapid loss of knowledge concerning Greek language and literature in the West.

c. 1170 .... *Le Roman de Troie* by Bevoit de Saint-Maure brings the Trojan War story into the troubadour tradition.

c. 1313–1321 .... Dante writes *The Divine Comedy*.

1396 .... Manuel Chrysoloras offers classes in Greek in Florence. This begins the revival of interest in Greek literature in Europe.

1450 .... The Vatican Library is founded: it had acquired nine copies of the *Iliad* and four of the *Odyssey* by 1475.

1453 .... The Sack of Constantinople by the Ottomans. At this point, a great many Greek scholars flee to Italy, bringing manuscripts with them. This is when the study of Greek becomes important in Europe.

1495 .... Aldus Manutius founds the Aldine Press in Venice and begins printing editions of Greek classics.

1498 .... Erasmus begins teaching Greek at Oxford. He becomes professor of Greek at Cambridge in 1511.

1508	Girolamo Aleandro begins courses in Greek in Paris.
1795	F. A. Wolf publishes *Prolegomena to Homer*.
1822	Charles McLaren suggests that Hisarlik is the site of Troy.
1865	Frank Calvert does trial excavations at Hisarlik.
1870–1873	Heinrich Schliemann conducts his first excavations at Hisarlik. He finds the "Treasure of Priam" in 1873.
1874–1878	Schliemann conducts excavations at Orchomenos, Mycenae, and Ithaka.
1878	Schliemann's second excavation at Troy.
1882–1883	Schliemann's third excavation at Troy.
1888–1890	Schliemann's final excavation at Troy, which ended with his death.
1928	Milman Parry publishes his "oral composition" theory of Homeric verse.
1945	The "Treasure of Priam" disappears from Berlin's Museum for Prehistory and Early History, and is presumed destroyed.
1988–present	Joint German-American excavations carried out at Troy.
1993	Official confirmation that the "Treasure of Priam" is in the Pushkin State Museum of Fine Arts in Moscow, as had been reported in 1991.
1996	The "Treasure of Priam" goes on exhibition in Moscow.

Glossary

ambrosia: The food of the gods. In the *Iliad* the gods anoint the dead bodies of Patroklos and Hektor with ambrosia to protect them from corruption. See also *nektar*.

Analysts (or Separatists): In Homeric studies, scholars who argue that the *Iliad* and the *Odyssey* are compilations of many separate, shorter poems.

aristeia: A "type scene" in which a particular hero fights with exceptional valor. An *aristeia* may be only a few lines long (for instance, Agamemnon's in *Il*. XII) or may extend for several books (for instance, Achilles' in *Il*. XIX–XXII).

athanatoi: "Deathless ones." A term used to refer to the gods, particularly as contrasted to mortals, or *thnêtoi*.

bard: The singer of epic poetry. In a preliterate culture, a bard recreates his song in each performance, using traditional formulas and type scenes as building blocks of his poetry.

dactylic hexameter: The meter of epic. It is constructed of six "feet," each consisting of *either* a dactyl (one long syllable followed by two short syllables) or a spondee (two long syllables). The resulting line is flexible and varied in Greek, though it tends to sound pedestrian in English.

Epic Cycle: A series of epics, no longer extant, which told the story of those episodes of the Trojan War not contained in the *Iliad* and the *Odyssey*.

epithet: An adjective or group of adjectives closely associated with a character's name. Examples include "Hektor *of the shining helmet*," "*swift-footed* Achilles," and so on.

formula: In Parry's definition, "a group of words which is regularly employed under the same metrical conditions to express a given essential idea."

geras: A "prize of honor"; a particularly valuable or esteemed token of distinction conferred on a warrior by his peers. Chryseis is Agamemnon's *geras*; Briseis is Achilles'.

guzlar: A South Slavic bard, such as those studied by Milman Parry and Albert Lord. The *guzlar* chants his songs to the accompaniment of a stringed instrument called a *guzle*.

Hisarlik or Hissarlik: The flat-topped hill in the Troad where Schliemann located the prehistoric ruins of Troy.

Hittites: Indo-European people whose kingdom flourished in Anatolia from c. 1650–c.1200 B.C. Some scholars believe that Hittite documents mention Greece (Achaia) and Troy (Ilion), and even imply a war between the two.

"The Homeric Question": The great scholarly question of whether the Homeric epics were written by a single author (or perhaps by two authors) or are compilations of various shorter, traditional poems. See also *Analysts* and *Unitarians*.

in medias res: "In the middle of the subject." This phrase describes the typical opening of an epic.

Indo-European: The prehistoric parent language of Greek, Latin, Sanskrit, most modern languages of Europe, and many modern languages of India. Indo-European was never written down, but scholars have made hypothetical reconstructions of some of its words and forms by comparative study of the languages which descended from it. The people who spoke this language are referred to as "Indo-Europeans."

Ithaka: Odysseus' home island.

kleos, **pl.** *klea*: Glory or fame; that which others say about one, particularly after one's death. *Kleos* is what epic conveys upon its heroes. The phrase *kleos aphthiton*, "imperishable glory," exactly parallels the Sanskrit *sravas aksitam* and may reflect an original Indo-European poetic phrase for imperishable glory.

mênis: Wrath; the first word of the *Iliad*, where it refers especially to Achilles' anger. Elsewhere in Homer, the word is used only in association with gods.

mêtis: Wisdom, skill, cunning, craftiness. Odysseus' most common epithet is *polumêtis*, "of much *mêtis*."

Mycenaean culture: The name given by archaeologists to the prehistoric Bronze Age culture discovered by 19th-century archaeologists.

Myrmidons: Soldiers under the command of Achilles.

nektar: The drink of the gods. See also *ambrosia*.

Nekuia: Odysseus' visit to the Underworld, *Od*. XI. The scene that opens *Od*. XXIV, which shows the souls of the suitors arriving in Hades, is often called "the second *Nekuia*."

nostos: Return or homecoming. Throughout the *Odyssey*, Odysseus strives for his own *nostos* and the *nostos* of his companions. Some scholars think that *nostos*-poetry was a whole subcategory of epic, to which the *Odyssey* belonged. One poem of the Epic Cycle was entitled *Nostoi*, or returns. The English word *nostalgia* literally means "longing for return/homecoming."

Ogygia: The island of the nymph Kalypso, where Odysseus was held captive for seven years.

polutropos: "Of many turns." This ambiguous epithet, used to identify Odysseus in the first line of the *Odyssey*, refers both to his wanderings and to his cleverness.

proem: The opening lines of an epic, which introduce the main theme of the poem.

psyche: Often translated as "soul," this word originally seems to have meant "breath." It is what leaves the body at death. Though it survives in some sense in Hades, its existence there is vague and shadowy.

Scheria: The island of the Phaiakians, where Odysseus is treated with marvelous *xenia*.

Telemachy: The first four books of the *Odyssey*, which concentrate on Odysseus' son Telemachos.

thnêtoi: "The dying ones." A term used to refer to human beings, particularly as contrasted to the immortal gods, or *athanatoi*.

thrift: In discussing Homeric verse, this refers to the fact that different phrases used to describe one character will occupy different metrical positions in the line. Sometimes also called "economy."

timê: Honor, especially the external, visible tokens of honor bestowed on a warrior by his peers. See also *geras*.

type scenes: Standardized scenes that are repeated with minimal variation in the epics. They include short, fixed descriptions of feasting, of setting sail, etc., as well as longer and more flexible accounts of battle. See also *aristeia*.

Unitarians: Scholars who believe that the Homeric epics were composed in their present form by one poet, not assembled from various much shorter poems.

xenia: "The guest/host relationship." Our term "hospitality" does not adequately convey the seriousness of the concept. *Xenia* was protected by Zeus, and covers the whole range of obligations that guests and hosts (*xenoi*, see next entry) have to one another. Violations of these obligations bring dire consequences: Paris' theft of Helen was, among other things, a violation of *xenia*, as are the suitors' actions throughout the *Odyssey*.

xenos: A guest, host, friend, stranger, or foreigner (cf. *xenophobia*). The range of this word's meanings reflects the essential nature of *xenia* (see previous entry), which does not depend upon prior acquaintance but operates between strangers. Once two men have entered into a relationship of *xenia* by one of them staying in the other's house, they are "guest-friends" and have obligations to one another.

Biographical Notes

I. Real People

Blegen, Carl (1887–1971). American archaeologist, who directed the University of Cincinnati's excavations at Troy (Hisarlik) from 1932 to 1938. He argued strongly that Troy VIIa, from c. 1250 B.C., should be identified as Homer's Troy.

Calvert, Frank (1928–1980). A British citizen who lived in the Troad (and worked as American consul). His family owned part of Hisarlik, and Calvert probably directed Schliemann's attention to it as the most likely site of Troy. Calvert had done some trial excavating in 1865, before Schliemann arrived in Turkey, and perhaps should be recognized as the actual discoverer of Troy.

Dörpfeld, Wilhelm (1853–1940). Schliemann's successor as excavator of Troy and Mycenae. He thought that Homer's Troy should be identified with Troy VI (c. 1300).

Homer (c. 700 B.C.E.?). The name traditionally given to the bard of the *Iliad* and the *Odyssey*. But there is little to no agreement about when or where such a person lived, or even if it is reasonable to refer to one bard for the epics at all.

Lord, Albert (1912–1991). A student and colleague of Milman Parry who carried on Parry's Yugoslavian fieldwork after Parry's tragically early death.

McLaren, Charles (1782–1866). Scottish journalist and editor of the 6th edition of the *Encyclopedia Britannica*. He suggested, in 1822, that the ruins of ancient Troy must be at Hisarlik.

Parry, Milman (1902–1935). An American scholar whose 1928 doctoral dissertation for the University of Paris was the first clear demonstration of the importance of formulas and oral compositional techniques in the Homeric epics. Just before his early death, he was engaged in fieldwork on oral poetics in Yugoslavia, where he traveled in 1933 and 1934–35.

Schliemann, Heinrich (1822–1890). German archaeologist; the "discoverer of Troy" and excavator of Mycenae. He began excavations at Hisarlik in 1871 and discovered the "Treasure of Priam" in 1873. From 1874–1876 he ran excavations in Greece, notably at Mycenae and

Orchomenos, and returned to Troy in April 1876. Though he did not understand the complexity or age of the ruins he excavated, misidentifying Troy II (c. 2200 B.C.) as Homer's Troy, Schliemann deserves great credit for his pioneering work.

Wolf, Friedrich August (1759–1824). Author of *Prolegomena to Homer* (1795), which gave rise to the 19th-century controversy over "the Homeric Question."

II. Epic Characters: Humans, Monsters, and Gods

(Note on transliteration of names: With one exception, I have followed the transliteration used in Richmond Lattimore's translations, since those are the versions I recommend that students buy. The one exception is the name *Achilles*. While *Achilleus* is certainly more correct, *Achilles* has become the standard English spelling to such a degree that I find it hard to adjust to any other.)

Achilles. Greatest Greek warrior. His withdrawal from battle because Agamemnon takes his concubine Briseis, and his subsequent return to avenge the death of his friend Patroklos, form the framework of the *Iliad*.

Agamemnon. Commander-in-chief of the Greek forces. Brother of Menelaos; husband of Klytaimestra. In the *Iliad*, his initial refusal to surrender his concubine Chryseis and subsequent appropriation of Achilles' concubine Briseis motivate Achilles' withdrawal from battle. In the *Odyssey*, the story of his murder by Aigisthos and Klytaimestra, and the vengeance taken by his son Orestes, is frequently cited as a parallel to Odysseus' family situation.

Aias the Greater. Son of Telamon; the greatest Greek warrior after Achilles. He figures prominently in the *Iliad*. According to the Epic Cycle, he committed suicide out of shame after the Greeks voted to ward the dead Achilles' armor to Odysseus rather than to him. His ghost is still angry over this slight when it appears in *Od.* XI and refuses to speak to Odysseus. (His name may be more familiar in the Latinized form Ajax.)

Aias the Lesser. Son of Oïleus. He raped Kassandra in Athena's temple during the Sack of Troy, thus bringing down Athena's anger on all the Greeks. Menelaos recounts how he was drowned by Poseidon (*Od.* IV).

Aigisthos. Cousin of Agamemnon and Menelaos, who seduces Klytaimestra while Agamemnon is away at war. He murders Agamemnon upon his return from Troy, and is himself killed by Agamemnon's son Orestes. This story is frequently cited in the *Odyssey* as a parallel to Odysseus' family situation.

Aiolos. The "king of the winds." He gives Odysseus a bag with all the contrary winds in it, but unfortunately the companions open the bag just before they reach Ithaka.

Alexandros. See Paris.

Alkinoos. King of the Phaiakians, husband of Arete, father of Nausikaa.

Andromache. Wife of Hektor, mother of Astyanax. She appears several times in the *Iliad*, most notably in her conversation with Hektor (*Il.* VI) and her lament over his corpse (*Il.* XXIV).

Antikleia. Odysseus' mother, whose ghost he sees in the *Nekuia*.

Antinoos. With Eurymachos, one of the two ringleaders of the suitors. The first suitor to be killed by Odysseus (*Od.* XXII).

Aphrodite. Daughter of Zeus and Dione; wife of Hephaistos (in the *Odyssey*, though not in the *Iliad*); mother (by the mortal Anchises) of the Trojan Aeneas; lover of Ares. Goddess of sexual passion. She motivates Paris' abduction of Helen. Favors the Trojans.

Apollo. Son of Zeus and Leto, twin brother of Artemis. In the *Iliad*, he appears mainly as the god of prophecy and as the bringer of plague and sudden death. Later authors would stress his association with reason, healing, and music. His identification with the sun is much later than Homer.

Ares. Son of Zeus and Hera; god of war; particularly associated with the physical, bloody, distressing aspects of war (cf. Athena).

Arete. Phaiakian queen, wife of Alkinoos, mother of Nausikaa (*Od.* VII–VIII).

Argos. 1) Agamemnon's city. 2) Odysseus' old dog, who dies upon seeing his master (*Od.* XVII).

Artemis. Daughter of Zeus and Leto; twin sister of Apollo. A virgin goddess. She is the patron of hunters, of wild animals, and girls before their marriage. She brings sudden death to women. Her identification with the moon is later than Homer.

Astyanax. Baby son of Hektor and Andromache; appears with his parents in *Il.* VI. During the Sack of Troy, he is thrown from the walls of the city and killed.

Athena. Daughter of Zeus, who sprang from his brow fully grown and wearing armor. She is the goddess of warfare in its nobler aspects (cf. Ares). A virgin goddess, she is associated with wisdom, cleverness, and weaving. In the *Odyssey*, she appears as Odysseus' special patron. Usually favors the Greeks, but becomes enraged with them during the Sack of Troy.

Briseis. Achilles' concubine and *geras*. Agamemnon's taking her motivates Achilles' withdrawal from battle in *Il.* I.

Charybdis. A very dangerous whirlpool, personified as a female entity. Odysseus has to sail between her and Skylla.

Chryses. An old priest of Apollo. Agamemnon's refusal to return his daughter Chryseis motivates the opening episode of the *Iliad*.

Chryseis. Daughter of Chryses; concubine and *geras* of Agamemnon. His refusal to return her to her father motivates the opening episode of the *Iliad*.

Circe (Kirke). Goddess, daughter of Helios the sun-god, enchantress. She turns half of Odysseus' companions into swine. Odysseus spends one year with her as her lover.

Demodokos. The bard of the Phaiakians, who sings three songs in *Od.* VIII.

Diomedes. A Greek warrior, who wounds Ares and Aphrodite during his *aristeia* in *Iliad* V. Exchanges armor as a token of *xenia* with Glaukos (*Il.* VI).

Eumaios. Odysseus' swineherd, who remains loyal to his master. The disguised Odysseus goes to his hut and receives *xenia* from him in *Od.* XIV. Eumaios fights with Odysseus and Telemachos to defeat the suitors.

Euryalos: A young Phaiakian, son of Alkinoos, who insults Odysseus by saying he does not look like an athlete.

Eurykleia. Odysseus' and Telemachos' old nurse. She recognizes Odysseus by the scar on his thigh (*Od.* XIX).

Eurylochos. Odysseus' second-in-command; often opposes or argues against Odysseus' commands. Encourages his companions to kill and eat Helios' cattle (*Od.* XII).

Eurymachos. With Antinoos, one of the two ringleaders of the suitors; his words to the seer Halitherses in *Od.* II illustrate the suitors' rejections of their society's most important mores.

Eurynome. Odysseus' and Penelope's housekeeper.

Glaukos. Trojan ally, close friend of Sarpedon. Exchanges armor with Diomedes as a token of *xenia* (*Il.* VI).

Hades. Brother of Zeus, husband of Persephone. Ruler of the Underworld (Tartaros), which comes to be called Hades after him.

Halitherses. Ithakan seer, who tries to reason with the suitors in *Od.* II.

Hekabe. Queen of Troy, wife of Priam, mother of Hektor, Paris, and Kassandra. (May be more familiar in the Latinized spelling of her name, "Hecuba.")

Hektor. Crown prince of Troy, son of Priam and Hekabe, husband of Andromache, father of Astyanax. He kills Patroklos and is killed by Achilles.

Helen. Daughter of Zeus and Leda, sister of Klytaimestra, wife of Menelaos; the most beautiful woman in the world. Her seduction (or kidnapping?) by Paris is the cause of the Trojan War.

Helios. The sun god. Father of Circe. Owner of the cattle on the island Thrinakia, which Odysseus' companions eat although they have been warned not to do so.

Hephaistos. Son of Zeus and Hera, or perhaps of Hera alone. In the *Iliad*, he is married to Charis; in the *Odyssey*, to Aphrodite. He is lame and ugly. The smith-god, who forges Achilles' new armor in *Iliad* XVIII and to some extent represents fire itself.

Hera. Wife and sister of Zeus, mother of Hephaistos and Ares. She is the patron goddess of marriage and married women. In the *Iliad*, hates the Trojans and favors the Greeks.

Herakles. Greatest Greek hero, son of Zeus and the mortal woman Alkmene. He lived (probably) two generations before the Trojan War. He is cited as a paradigm of the hero throughout both epics; Odysseus speaks to his spirit in the Underworld (*Od.* XI).

Kalchas. Seer/soothsayer for Agamemnon and the entire Greek army.

Kalypso. Nymph (or minor goddess) who keeps Odysseus captive on her island Ogygia for seven years.

Kassandra. Daughter of Priam and Hekabe; sister of Hektor and Paris. During the Sack of Troy, Aias the Lesser rapes her in the temple of Athena. This outrage motivates the goddess' anger at the Greeks.

Klytaimestra. Wife of Agamemnon, mother of Orestes, half-sister of Helen. She takes Aigisthos as her lover while Agamemnon is away at Troy, and assists Aigisthos in murdering him upon his return. This story is frequently cited in the *Odyssey* as a parallel to Odysseus' family situation.

Laertes. Father of Odysseus, father-in-law of Penelope, grandfather of Telemachos. Appears in *Od.* XXIV.

Laistrygones. Monstrous cannibals who destroy 11 of Odysseus' 12 ships (*Od.* X).

Leodes. Young suitor, the first to try to string Odysseus' bow.

Lykaon. Young son of Priam; half-brother of Paris and Hektor. He fruitlessly begs Achilles for mercy in *Il.* XXI.

Medon. Odysseus' herald, who served the suitors unwillingly. Odysseus spares his life at Telemachos' request.

Melanthios. Odysseus' goatherd, who is disloyal to his master; brother of Melantho. He brings armor and weapons to the suitors in *Od.* XXII.

Melantho. One of Odysseus' slavewomen, disloyal to her master; lover of Eurymachos; sister of Melanthios.

Menelaos. Brother of Agamemnon, husband of Helen. Prominent figure in the *Iliad*; appears briefly in *Od.* IV.

Nausikaa. Young Phaiakian princess who befriends Odysseus when he washes up on the shores of Scheria (*Od.* VI).

Nestor. Oldest and wisest of the Greeks; appears in both the *Iliad* and (briefly) in *Od.* III.

Odysseus. Husband of Penelope, father of Telemachos, son of Laertes and Antikleia. Cleverest and craftiest of the Greeks; an important character in the *Iliad*, where he takes part in the Embassy to Achilles (*Il*. IX). Main character of the *Odyssey*.

Orestes. Son of Agamemnon and Klytaimestra. He avenges his father's murder by killing Aigisthos and Klytaimestra. This story is frequently cited in the *Odyssey* as a parallel to Odysseus' family situation.

Outis: "Nobody," or "Noman," the name by which Odysseus identifies himself to the Cyclops Polyphemos.

Paris (also called Alexandros). Son of Priam and Hekabe, brother of Hektor; prince of Troy. His abduction or perhaps seduction of Helen from her husband Menelaos motivates the Trojan War.

Patroklos. Achilles' dearest friend, who goes into battle wearing Achilles' armor and is killed by Hektor.

Peleus. Achilles' father; husband of Thetis. He does not appear in the *Iliad*, but is alluded to very frequently.

Penelope. Wife of Odysseus, mother of Telemachos. One of the main themes of the *Odyssey* is her courting by 108 suitors and the difficulties this causes her. The question of whether or not she will remain faithful to Odysseus permeates the epic.

Persephone. Wife of Hades, queen of the Underworld.

Phemios. Odysseus' bard, who served the suitors unwillingly. Odysseus spares his life at Telemachos' request.

Philoitios. Odysseus' cowherd, who is loyal to his master. He fights with Odysseus and Telemachos to defeat the suitors in *Od*. XXII.

Philoktetes. The greatest Greek archer in the Trojan War. Odysseus says that he himself was "second only to Philoktetes" as an archer (*Od*. VIII).

Phoinix. Achilles' old "foster-father," takes part in the Embassy to Achilles in *Il*. IX.

Polyphemos. Cyclops, son of the god Poseidon (*Od*. IX). His curse of Odysseus, who blinded him, motivates most of Odysseus' troubles in the *Odyssey*.

Poseidon. Brother of Zeus, god of the sea. In the *Iliad* he favors the Greeks; in the *Odyssey* he hates Odysseus for blinding his son, the Cyclops Polyphemos.

Priam. King of Troy, father of Hektor and Paris, husband of Hekabe. He visits Achilles in *Il.* XXIV to ransom Hektor's body.

Sarpedon. Trojan ally from Lykia, son of Zeus. Close friend of Glaukos. He is killed by Patroklos in *Il.* XVI.

Skamandros. A river of Troy; personified, it battles Achilles in *Il.* XXI.

Skylla. A six-headed, human-devouring monster. Odysseus has to sail between her and Charybdis.

Teiresias. The great Theban seer whose spirit Odysseus consults in the Underworld (*Od.* IX).

Telemachos. Son of Odysseus and Penelope. The first four books of the *Odyssey* (the *Telemachy*) focus on him. In Books XVI–XXIV, he helps his father defeat the suitors.

Thetis. Sea-goddess; mother of Achilles; wife of Peleus.

Xanthos. 1) One of Achilles' immortal horses, who speaks to him in a human voice at the end of *Il.* XIX. 2) Another name for Skamandros.

Zeus. The ruler of the Olympian gods. Brother and husband of Hera; brother of Hades and Poseidon; father of Aphrodite, Apollo, Ares, Artemis, Athena, and perhaps Hephaistos. Originally a sky-god, he controls thunder and lightning. The patron of justice, suppliants, and *xenia*.

Bibliography

Essential Readings: A Selection of Translations of the Homeric Epics

Lattimore, Richmond, trans. *The Iliad of Homer*. Chicago and London: The University of Chicago Press, 1951; *The Odyssey of Homer*. New York: Harper Perennial, 1991. These are my preferred translations for several reasons. First, Lattimore translates the Greek line by line; thus, line references to the original make sense for this translation as well. This is very helpful to the student who is reading supplementary materials that include line references. Second, Lattimore preserves Homer's formulas in his translation; whenever Homer repeats precisely the same words, Lattimore repeats precisely the same words. This goes a long way toward preserving the "feel" of Homer in English. Third, Lattimore's language is somewhat archaic and difficult sounding. Again, this is truer to the original than a more idiomatic rendering would be, since the dialect of the epics is itself an artificial, poetic dialect. Fourth, Lattimore's meter consistently gives as adequate a sense of Homer's hexameters as can well be done in English, and at times is magnificent.

Acknowledgment: Quotes in these lectures from *The Odyssey of Homer*, translated by Richmond Lattimore, copyright 1965/1967 by Richmond Lattimore, were used with permission by arrangement with HarperCollins Publishers, Inc.

Fitzgerald, Robert. *The Iliad*. New York: Anchor Press, 1989; *The Odyssey*. New York: Vintage Books, 1990. Many people prefer these translations for their readability. They are very good modern English poetry; however, in my estimation they do not accurately convey the feeling of Homer's style. Fitzgerald's meter does not even attempt to convey the hexameter, and he does not preserve the formulas.

Fagles, Robert. *The Iliad*. New York: Penguin USA, 1998; *The Odyssey*. New York, Penguin USA, 1997. These new translations received a great deal of critical attention when they appeared, most of it very favorable. Although I prefer them to Fitzgerald's versions, in my view they are marred by excessive use of colloquial language (e.g., phrases such as "cramping my style"). Similarly, Fagles' meter does not capture the feeling of the Homeric hexameter.

Supplementary Readings

(Note: The amount of scholarly writing on Homer is staggering; hundreds of books have appeared in the past 10 years alone. In fact, it is a common lament among classicists that no one individual could possibly be familiar with everything that has been written about Homer. Faced with this vast amount of scholarship, I have tried to winnow out a representative selection of useful and interesting studies. I have avoided books that assume knowledge either of Greek or of complicated modern theoretical approaches. I have also included several works that disagree, at least to some extent, with my own view of some of the issues raised by the epics, so that students may gain some sense of the range of possible interpretations that the epics elicit. Finally, I have tried to pick works that have good bibliographies, to aid those students who wish to continue their journey through the thickets of Homeric scholarship.)

Allen, Susan Hueck. *Finding the Walls of Troy: Frank Calvert and Heinrich Schliemann at Hisarlik.* Berkeley and Los Angeles: The University of California Press, 1999. A fascinating, well-written, and meticulously documented account of the work and interactions of these two archaeologists, which argues that Calvert deserves credit as the actual discoverer of Troy.

Austin, Norman. *Archery at the Dark of the Moon: Poetic Problems in Homer's Odyssey.* Berkeley, Los Angeles, London: University of California Press, 1975. A well-written, detailed analysis of several key themes in the *Odyssey.* Particularly interesting discussion of Odysseus' and Penelope's interactions before and after the slaughter of the suitors.

———. *Helen of Troy and Her Shameless Phantom.* Ithaca and London: Cornell University Press, 1994. Discusses Helen's role in Homer and other Greek authors, including the version of her story that said only a phantom went to Troy. Explores Helen's fundamental dual nature as both woman and goddess.

Clay, Jenny Strauss. *The Wrath of Athena: Gods and Men in the Odyssey.* Princeton: Princeton University Press, 1983. A very well-written, clear discussion, focusing on Odysseus' relationship with Athena but covering many important critical issues.

Cohen, Beth, ed. *The Distaff Side: Representing the Female in Homer's Odyssey.* New York, Oxford: Oxford University Press, 1995. A collection of important essays spanning the disciplines of classics, history, and art history.

Doherty, Lillian Eileen. "Sirens, Muses, and Female Narrators in the *Odyssey*," in Cohen, *Distaff Side*, pp. 81–89. A thought-provoking examination of the importance of the Sirens in the epic.

Edwards, Mark W. *Homer: Poet of the Iliad*. Baltimore and London: The Johns Hopkins University Press, 1987. A well-written discussion of some of the major themes and issues of the *Iliad*. Includes detailed commentaries on several key books.

Fitton, J. Lesley. *The Discovery of the Greek Bronze Age*. Cambridge: Harvard University Press, 1996. A readable and entertaining account of the pioneering archaeologists who excavated the most important Bronze Age sites.

Gantz, Timothy. *Early Greek Myth: A Guide to Literary and Artistic Sources*. 2 vols. Baltimore, London: Johns Hopkins University Press, 1993. An extremely detailed survey of all the sources of traditional Greek myths. The materials on the Trojan War are in Vol. 2.

Griffin, Jasper. *Homer on Life and Death*. Oxford: Clarendon Press, 1980. An elegant, beautifully written discussion of Homer's presentation of mortality.

Hölscher, Uvo. "Penelope and the Suitors," in Schein, *Reading the Odyssey*, pp. 133–140. An examination of Penelope's motivations for coming down to see the suitors in *Odyssey* XVIII.

Kirk, Geoffrey. *The Songs of Homer*. Cambridge: Cambridge University Press, 1962. A discussion of the nature, genesis, and quality of the Homeric epics, which pays detailed attention to historical background and the Parry-Lord theory of oral composition. Clearly written and well worth reading, even if somewhat dated.

Lord, Albert Bates. *The Singer of Tales*. New York: Atheneum, 1978. Uses the fieldwork Lord and Parry did in the former Yugoslavia as a basis for theorizing about the formation of Homeric verse. Fascinating reading for anyone at all interested in oral poetry and how it works.

Lowenstam, Steven. *The Scepter and the Spear: Studies on Forms of Repetition in the Homeric Poems*. Lanham, MD: Rowman & Littlefield Publishers, Inc., 1993. A reassessment of the forms and significance of repetition in the Homeric epics, in light of the discoveries of Parry and Lord. Several intriguing interpretations, well-written, and all Greek quotations are translated.

Morrison, James V. *Homeric Misdirection: False Predictions in the Iliad.* Ann Arbor: University of Michigan Press, 1992. As the title indicates, this book examines false or misleading predictions in the *Iliad* and argues that they are a method for building suspense among an audience that already knows the basic outlines of the traditional story.

Murnaghan, Sheila. "The Plan of Athena," in Cohen, *The Distaff Side*, pp. 61–80. Examines Athena's role throughout the *Odyssey*, with special attention to Book XIII.

Nagler, Michael N. "Dread Goddess Revisited." In Schein, *Reading the Odyssey*, pp. 141–161. An interesting analysis of Circe, Kalypso, and Penelope, with detailed discussion of the import of Odysseus and Penelope's bed.

Nagy, Gregory. *The Best of the Achaeans: Concepts of the Hero in Archaic Greek Poetry.* Baltimore, London: Johns Hopkins University Press, 1979. Very densely written, technical examination of several key words in Homer, focusing especially on *kleos*. Recommended for those with an interest in the workings of the Greek language (all Greek is transliterated).

————.*Greek Mythology and Poetics.* Ithaca and London: Cornell University Press, 1990. A collection of essays on a wide range of subjects, which examines Greek poetry and mythology in its wider Indo-European context, particularly through comparison with Indic mythology and poetics. Chapters 2 (Formula and Meter) and 4 (Patroklos, Concepts of Afterlife, and the Indic Triple Fire) are particularly relevant for this course.

Olson, S. Douglas. *Blood and Iron: Stories and Storytelling in Homer's Odyssey.* Leiden, New York, Köln: E. J. Brill, 1995. A well-written and thought-provoking discussion of several of the major critical issues in the *Odyssey*. Interesting reading.

The Oxford Classical Dictionary. 3rd ed. Eds. Simon Hornblower and Anthony Spawforth. Oxford and New York: Oxford University Press, 1996. The standard one-volume reference work on Greek and Roman antiquity.

Parry, Milman. *The Making of Homeric Verse: The Collected Papers of Milman Parry.* Ed. Adam Parry. Oxford: The Clarendon Press, 1971. All of Parry's published and unpublished writings on Homer, collected by his son. Parry's arguments are highly detailed and assume knowledge of Greek, but will make fascinating reading for any student who wants to learn more about Parry's insights on the epics' composition.

Powell, Barry. *Homer and the Origin of the Greek Alphabet*. Cambridge: Cambridge University Press, 1991. A highly controversial work, which argues that the alphabet's adaptation for the Greek language was motivated by the desire to record the Homeric epics. This argument has not found wide acceptance among scholars, but the book is thought-provoking and lucidly written. It also provides a great deal of information about early non-alphabetic writing systems.

Schein, Seth L. *The Mortal Hero: An Introduction to Homer's Iliad*. Berkeley, Los Angeles, London: University of California Press, 1984. An excellent, lucid, informative introduction to several of the major themes of the *Iliad*. This book had a profound influence on my own understanding of the *Iliad*, though I have come to disagree with Schein on several points.

————, ed. *Reading the Odyssey: Selected Interpretative Essays*. Princeton: Princeton University Press, 1996. Collects several important essays on specific aspects of the *Odyssey*.

Seaford, Richard. *Reciprocity and Ritual: Homer and Tragedy in the Developing City-State*. Oxford: Clarendon Press, 1994. As the title indicates, Homer is only part of this book's subject matter. However, there are several chapters on the Homeric epics that are thought-provoking and useful.

Segal, Charles. *The Theme of the Mutilation of the Corpse in the Iliad*. Mnemosyne Suppl. 17. Leiden: E. J. Brill, 1971. Traces the theme of mistreated corpses throughout the *Iliad*, with special discussion of Achilles' treatment of Hektor. Clearly written, readable, and interesting; unfortunately, Greek quotations are usually not translated.

Shapiro, H. A. "Coming of Age in Phaiakia: The Meeting of Odysseus and Nausikaa," in Cohen, *Distaff Side*, pp. 155–164. Compares Homer's description of the Odysseus-Nausikaa scene with its representations in Athenian art of the 5th century B.C.E., and concludes that an implicit threat of rape was very much part of the 5th-century audience's understanding of the scene.

Shay, Jonathan. *Achilles in Vietnam: Combat Trauma and the Undoing of Character*. New York: Athenaeum, 1994. A fascinating and deeply disturbing book. Dr. Shay, a psychiatrist who treats Vietnam veterans suffering from post-traumatic stress disorder, reads the *Iliad* against the background of those veterans' experiences. The book contains a great deal of profanity (in quotations of veterans' statements to Dr. Shay) and some extremely graphic descriptions of combat violence, and so may not be appropriate for all students. But those who can stomach its uncompromising portrait of the reality of war will find it intensely thought-provoking.

Slatkin, Laura M. "Composition by Theme and the Mêtis of the *Odyssey*," in Schein, *Reading the Odyssey*, pp. 223–237. Discusses the importance of the concept of *mêtis* for the narrative and thematic structure of the *Odyssey*.

———. *The Power of Thetis: Allusion and Interpretation in the Iliad.* Berkeley: University of California Press, 1992. An elegant little (122 pp.) book which examines Thetis' role in the *Iliad* and the poet's use and adaptation of myths not recounted within the epic itself.

Vernant, Jean-Pierre. "Death with Two Faces," in Schein, *Reading the Odyssey*, pp. 55–61. A discussion of Homer's depiction of death, with close attention to Achilles' words to Odysseus in *Odyssey* XI.

———. "The Refusal of Odysseus," in Schein, *Reading the Odyssey*, pp. 185–189. A detailed discussion of Odysseus' refusal to become immortal and stay with Kalypso.

Wolf, F. A. *Prolegomena to Homer: 1795.* Trans. Anthony Grafton, Glenn W. Most, and James E. G. Zetzel. Princeton: Princeton University Press, 1985. A clear, readable translation of this groundbreaking work, with detailed and helpful notes.

Wood, Michael. *In Search of the Trojan War.* A fascinating, well-written, and well-documented examination of the evidence for the historicity of the Trojan War. Includes many illustrations, maps, etc.

Woodford, Susan. *The Trojan War in Ancient Art.* Ithaca: Cornell University Press, 1993. A useful summary of the mythical background to the Trojan War, with illustrations from ancient art.

Zeitlin, Froma I. "Figuring Fidelity in Homer's *Odyssey*," in Cohen, *Distaff Side*, pp. 117–152. An extremely detailed examination of the depiction of female fidelity in the *Odyssey*, focusing primarily on Odysseus' and Penelope's bed and its connections with the rest of the epic.

Notes

Notes

Notes

Notes